GOODS FOR SALE

By the same author
The Great Workshop: Boston's Victorian Age

GOODS FOR SALE

Products and Advertising in the Massachusetts Industrial Age

Chaim M. Rosenberg

University of Massachusetts Press   *Amherst and Boston*

Copyright © 2007 by Chaim M. Rosenberg
All rights reserved
Printed in China

LC 2006028856
ISBN 1-55849-579-7 (library cloth); 1-55849-580-0 (paper)
ISBN 13: 978-1-55849-579-1 (library cloth); 978-1-55849-580-7 (paper)

Designed by Sally Nichols
Set in Goudy Old Style and Goudy Handtooled
Printed and bound by C&C Offset Printing Company Ltd.

Library of Congress Cataloging-in-Publication Data

Rosenberg, Chaim M.
  Goods for sale : products and advertising in the Massachusetts industrial age /
    Chaim M. Rosenberg.
        p. cm.
  Includes bibliographical references and index.
  ISBN-13: 978-1-55849-580-7 (pbk. : alk. paper)
  ISBN-13: 978-1-55849-579-1 (library cloth ed. : alk. paper)
  ISBN-10: 1-55849-580-0 (pbk. : alk. paper)
  ISBN-10: 1-55849-579-7 (library cloth ed. : alk. paper)
  1. Manufacturing industries—Massachusetts—History—19th century. I. Title.
  HD9727.M4R67 2007
  381.09744'09034—dc22
                                                    2006028856

British Library Cataloguing in Publication data are available.

Contents

Foreword

The places in Dr. Rosenberg's history are familiar enough: Fitchburg, Lawrence, Lynn, Worcester, Springfield, and most every mill town and city in Massachusetts. The ways of work and living, however, are far from anything we now know or remember.

His period, primarily the century from 1820 to 1920, was dominated by long hours of human labor devoted to tending machines and perfecting their output. Very few machines functioned then in ways that could be called automatic. Most needed material to be fed into them: cloth to the sewing machine, paper to the press, boards to the box maker, iron bars to the forge, coal to the furnace and stove. All these machines had to be fussed over frequently, and their products, whether bicycles, locomotives, or cotton sheets, had to be filed, adjusted, bolted and screwed, hand sewn and finished up by hand. Few labored on anything that could be called an assembly line. Shoes moved from bench to bench, stoves were assembled on the factory floor, while the cotton was sorted at the top of the mill, only to pass stage by stage, floor below floor, through rooms filled with lines of identical machines for carding, spinning, weaving, and repairing.

A small mill might have a dozen machines and two dozen hands, a large textile factory demanded an army of thousands. Whether Massachusetts mill village or factory town, the machines had to be tended by thousands of men, women, and children, Americans and immigrants both.

At the core of all this energy and work, and at the core of Dr. Rosenberg's history, stood the capitalist who financed the enterprises and the inventors who designed the products. In some cases one man filled both roles. But capital for machines and the ingenuity to realize ideas and put them to work created this unique century.

As the narrative progresses, the reader will undoubtedly find important contrast with which to judge the present. What might all those piano and organ factories mean? Americans used to sing; they had not yet been silenced by radio, records, and CDs. They made music everywhere: at home, in church, in union halls, at picnics and parties. And what of the brightly colored trade cards that illustrate this history? Recall a time of dark suits, black and brown dresses, ill-lit rooms, horse manure, coal smoke, dust and dirt everywhere. People hungered for color, so that the trade cards joined the larger movement for colorful lithographs that appeared in every home.

There is a delight in recalling the old products and their names. Together they form a yardstick by which we can measure our own nano-tech, biotech, corporate Massachusetts. The inventors that Dr. Rosenberg so ably chronicles enhanced the needs and processes of ordinary life. They made things locally, and most of what they made could be understood and repaired by their users. It was a machine age that blossomed with tools for living.

Sam Bass Warner, Jr.

Preface

I was born in South Africa but left that sad country in 1960 after completing medical school. I continued my medical training in Israel, England, and Australia before having the good fortune to come to Boston in 1968 to start a career in psychiatry. I well remember my first tour of the Back Bay with its elegant townhouses built in the French style during the second half of the nineteenth century. I enjoyed riding the trolley to Park Street station and walking up the hill toward the gold-domed Massachusetts State House, designed by Charles Bulfinch and completed in 1798. From the State House my walk took me through Beacon Hill, with its eighteenth-century Regency-style homes, on my way to Cambridge Street. The Federal-style Harrison Gray Otis House, also designed by Bulfinch and completed in 1796, sits at 141 Cambridge Street. From there I walked toward the Ether Dome of the Massachusetts General Hospital. Yet another Bulfinch masterpiece, the Ether Dome was completed in 1823. Old as they are, these buildings are a lot younger than nearby Faneuil Hall, completed in 1743, and Boston's oldest public building, the Old State House, completed in 1713.

I knew that Boston was an old city, approaching its four hundredth birthday in 2030. But I was not prepared for what I saw outside Boston proper. Cambridge, across the Charles River, is famed for Harvard University and the Massachusetts Institute of Technology, but East Cambridge was filled with workers' housing and abandoned factory buildings. Huge redbrick mills sat empty along the Merrimack River in Lowell, Lawrence, and Haverhill. The picture was similar in the former whaling port of New Bedford and in Fall River, as well as in the shoe manufacturing towns of Lynn, Malden, and Brockton. Traveling west to Maynard, Worcester, Springfield, and North Adams, I saw more abandoned mills and empty downtowns. These vacant mill buildings were the ghosts of the Massachusetts Industrial Age.

Nineteenth-century Massachusetts became heavily industrialized. Textiles and footwear were the dominant industries, but most everything consumers wanted was made in Massachusetts. The state had an extensive transportation system linking the outlying factories with the port of Boston. The city of Boston had seven railroad terminals. During that century, Massachusetts was transformed from an agrarian economy into an urbanized manufacturing powerhouse. By the end of the 1920s, the Massachusetts redbrick industries had run their course and were in decline. The cities and towns mirrored the fall of their industries. The central shopping districts that hummed with activity when the factories were busy fell quiet, and the homes around the factories were left to decay.

Much of my career was spent working in these old factory towns. For years those great mills that once employed thousands of workers intrigued me. Who built the industries and what was their motivation? Why were the factories located where they were? What was their source of power? What did they make, and how were the products sold? Who were Elias Howe Jr., Jonas Chickering, William Madison Wood Jr., Lydia Pinkham, Eben Marsh, Walter Baker, and the twin brothers Freelan and Francis Stanley, who left their names in the pages of history? Who were Mr. Lowell and Mr. Lawrence after whom great textile cities were named? I wanted to learn how people lived during the time when heavy industry dominated the economy of Massachusetts. I also wanted to know why these great industries failed. When I finally gave up my medical practice, I set out to find the answers to my questions.

Highways and urban sprawl now bypass much of what remains of nineteenth-century industrial Massachusetts. But the evidence of the past can readily be found along the rivers, in the old town centers, and in the records of the historical societies and libraries. Over the years I have visited and studied many of the old industrial towns around the state. Also, I have collected trade cards once issued by Massachusetts companies to advertise their goods. These colorful cards were popular from 1870 until the start of the twentieth century, when advertising began to shift to the newspapers and magazines. The trade cards reflect the aspirations and values of their times. This book describes the products made and sold in Massachusetts during the height of its Industrial Age. The text is mainly illustrated with the finer examples of trade cards and photographs from my collection.

Chaim M. Rosenberg
Needham, Massachusetts

Acknowledgments

There are many stories to tell about Massachusetts from the beginning of European settlement to the present day. I have chosen to examine the period when water and then steampower turned the machines, and when thousands upon thousands of immigrants found work in the factories. Over the years historians and literary folk have observed the transition from the farm to the city, from the crafts to mass production, and from travel by horseback to the comfort of a seat in a railroad car. The historical societies and the great libraries throughout Masssachusetts have carefully preserved their writings to the benefit of modern-day scholars. I am especially grateful to the staffs of the historical societies of Lowell and Taunton, the archives of the Commonwealth of Massachusetts, the Boston Public Library, the Newton Free Library, and the Wellesley College and the Harvard Business School libraries. They helped me find obscure yet fascinating texts related to the industrial growth of Massachusetts during the nineteenth and early twentieth centuries.

I would like to thank the two readers (whose identities are not known to me) who plodded through the early draft of this book and made helpful suggestions to give form to a jumble of ideas. I am delighted that my Ode to Massachusetts has found a Massachusetts publisher. Bruce Wilcox, director, and Carol Betsch, managing editor, of the University of Massachusetts Press transformed the solitude and drudgery of research and writing into a pleasure. Amanda Heller edited the manuscript with a masterly yet delicate touch. The great scholar Sam Bass Warner Jr. honored me by reading the text and writing the Foreword.

I have used company trade cards to illustrate the book. Nearly all of them are more than a century old. Their charm and vibrancy are a tribute to the commercial artists and the lithographic techniques of a former age. These particular trade cards show the products made in Massachusetts and offered for sale during the second half of the nineteenth century.

The cards also show the values of the times, the early advertising methods, and the evolution of the consumer society. I looked at thousands of trade cards before selecting the more than one hundred thirty here to illustrate the story of the gilded age of Massachusetts industry. I rummaged through antique dealers' stacks, and reviewed the collections at the Boston Public Library and the American Antiquarian Society in Worcester. During the late nineteenth century, trade cards were avidly collected by children and adults alike and pasted into scrapbooks. These forgotten scrapbooks rested quietly in attics for most of the twentieth century. Now rediscovered, American trade cards have entered the marketplace and are enthusiatically bought and sold. Most of the cards in my collection were found through the miracle in the Internet linking collectors to dealers across the nation. The trade cards I gathered together were handled with respect by the sellers and came to my address carefully packed. The U.S. Postal Service and our local mail carrier, Paul Ross, delivered every one of them safely to our home. The preservation of these small and fragile cards over the past century or more shows that people valued them as a part of the American story. I hope that my book will add to the importance of trade cards in depicting American life and commerce during a bygone age.

My wife Dawn, above all others, helped me to complete this book. She applauded my ideas, encouraged the research, accompanied me to museums, visited the factories, suffered my silences, admired the pictures, and corrected the drafts of the text. She supported me during the low moments by gently assuring me of the value of my task. We have been together a long time, and life with her is still an adventure. *Goods for Sale* is as much her book as it is mine.

C. M. R.

GOODS FOR SALE

ᵛ Introduction

British colonists settled in Massachusetts nearly two hundred years before the start of the American Industrial Revolution. The small party on the *Mayflower* landed at Plymouth in 1620. They were followed three years later by a group that settled near Cape Ann and established the coastal towns of Gloucester and Salem. A third party, under the leadership of John Winthrop, arrived in 1630 on eleven ships. A number from this group established the towns of Boston and Cambridge. The early settlers came mostly from Suffolk, Norfolk, and Essex in southeast England. Over the next ten years, twenty thousand more Englishmen followed, and the Massachusetts Bay Colony was solidly established. The settlers named their new communities after their old towns in England. Most clung to the coastline, but a few venturesome souls explored the interior. One party, led by William Pynchon, traveled west in 1636 into the wilderness to trap animals for their furs. They settled along the banks of the Connecticut River and named their settlement Springfield after the town in Essex, England, where Pynchon was born.

Most of the early settlers were Puritans who arrived in family groups. In England they had been largely self-sufficient as farmers or fishermen, or they followed trades such as shoemaking, cloth making, and carpentry. There were few aristocrats among them. Few were either very rich or very poor. The settlers who came to Massachusetts closely resembled in age, sex ratio, occupation, and family structure the English population they had left behind. Many of the families even brought one or two indentured servants with them to the New World (Anderson 1991). These twenty thousand or so early settlers were the seed stock for the American Yankees who spread throughout Massachusetts and the other New England states, to New York, and to points beyond. By 1700 there were 100,000 descendants, and by 1800 over 1 million (Fischer 1989).

In Massachusetts many started small family farms, planting crops and raising animals. Others looked to the ocean for their livelihood. The

❧

waters around Massachusetts Bay Colony were teeming with fish. The settlers cut the abundant trees and floated the logs down the rivers to the shipyards. They built small ships to bring in the ocean's bounty. By 1660, shipbuilding had become a major Massachusetts industry (Morison 1961). The colonists learned to dry and salt the fish so it would keep longer, and they were soon producing more from their farms than they needed for themselves. Now they were ready to trade.

Much of the dried fish was sent from Massachusetts to markets in Europe. But the colonists' closest trading partners were the small British settlements in Virginia and the larger settlements along the eastern fringes of the Caribbean. The British arrived in Barbados and the Leeward Islands of St. Kitts, Nevis, Montserrat, and Antigua at about the same time their fellow countrymen settled in Massachusetts. They were linked by culture, language, and family ties. Sugarcane grew abundantly on these small Caribbean islands, and soon all the available land was given over to its cultivation. The British in the Caribbean became dependent on their New England cousins for their food and fuel. After the British occupied Jamaica in 1655, Massachusetts extended its trade to that sugar island as well.

Ships from Boston, Newburyport, Salem, and other Massachusetts ports regularly called on the British sugar islands. The ships carried wood for fuel and horses to turn the grinding wheels in the sugar mills. The Massachusetts ships also brought salted fish and farm products to feed the planters, their white indentured servants, and the tens of thousands of African slaves working in the tropical sun on the sugar plantations. The ships returned with indigo, cotton, tobacco, and especially raw sugar and molasses. Boston built a thriving industry fermenting molasses and distilling it into rum. By 1717, Massachusetts had sixty-six distilleries, and rum had replaced cider and beer as the most popular alcoholic beverage in the American colonies. It became the coin of commerce for Massachusetts. Barrels of rum were carried to Britain, but much of it went to the west coast of Africa to be bartered for slaves, who were sold in the Caribbean and in the American South. The Massachusetts ship owners and their captains made a profit on every leg of their journeys.

By the early eighteenth century, Massachusetts extended its overseas trade to the French sugar islands of Guadeloupe, Martinique, and St. Domingue. Here sugar and molasses could be had at lower prices. This shift in trade caused great consternation among the growers in the British sugar islands. To protect their interests, they petitioned the British government to impose the Molasses Tax of 1733 and followed it with the Sugar Act of 1764. These placed prohibitive taxes on American trade with foreign ports. To reinforce the acts, British ships patrolled the seas and British customs officers checked the cargoes coming into Massachusetts ports. The British were determined to control their colonies from London and to block Yankee entrepreneurship.

Colonial Massachusetts also had a well-established craft cottage industry. Benjamin Willard began making clocks in 1764 in his workshop in the village of Grafton. Small-scale shoe shops started up in Lynn and Haverhill and spread to other towns. A number of cabinetmakers tried their hand at making copies of the pianos and organs imported from Europe. Using local bog iron, John Ames of Easton figured he could build

J. E. Tyler, commission merchant, of 44 Long Wharf, Boston, circa 1805. Commission merchants imported and sold goods. After 1813 several of these merchants invested in the local mills and acted as sales agents, charging a commission of 1.5 to 2 percent.

(COURTESY THE AMERICAN ANTIQUARIAN SOCIETY, WORCESTER, MASS.)

a better and cheaper shovel than the ones coming from England. Skilled craftsmen all over Massachusetts used hand tools to weave cloth, build a clock, cobble a pair of shoes, or make a chair or a piano from start to finish and one at a time. Boston, Salem, Newburyport, and other towns gave employment to saddlers, wheelwrights, blacksmiths, coopers, ships' chandlers, and tailors.

Yankee farmers, traders, and craftsmen became increasingly angry over "taxation without representation" and were emboldened to fight for their independence. Rebellion against British rule was in the very air of Boston. The Revolutionary War severed the long-established trade links between Britain and its sugar islands on the one side and the independent United States on the other. Cotton no longer reached the textile factories of Manchester, and American lumber, fish, and farm products were no

T. Smallwood,
CABINET MAKER & UPHOLSTERER
BOSTON.

MICHAEL ANGELO

LEVI L. CUSHING,
CARVER,
No 79, Broad Street, opposite Custom House Street,
BOSTON.

Orders for carved work of any description will be attended to with fidelity and despatch.

L. L. Cushing continues the above business in Poplar Street, as usual, where orders will meet with prompt attention. ☞N. B....Models of any kind executed at the shortest notice.

Engraved and Printed by N. Dearborn, 20, State Street.

Before the Industrial Revolution gathered speed, master craftsmen hired apprentices and journey-men for small factories to weave cloth, cobble shoes, or make furniture, using hand tools. Thomas Smallwood, cabinetmaker and upholsterer of Boston, advertised a line of furniture including chairs, sofas, beds, writing desks, and display cabinets. Levi L. Cushing at 79 Broad Street, Boston, specialized in carved woodwork for sailing vessels. These illustrations date from the early nineteenth century.

(COURTESY THE AMERICAN ANTIQUARIAN SOCIETY, WORCESTER, MASS.)

longer sold to Barbados and Jamaica. Britain stopped sending its textiles and other manufactured goods to America, and the British islands stopped sending their coffee, sugar, and molasses.

Despite the war with Britain, the Yankees continued to trade with the French and the Far East. Ships from Salem and Boston traveled to South America, rounded Cape Horn, and sailed up thousands of miles to the northwest coast of North America. Here they took on furs and otter skins, which they carried to Canton. In Canton, they traded their furs for silk textiles and fine China crockery before returning to their homeports. The entire journey on their small sailing ships took two to three years to complete. The men from Massachusetts found a ready market back home for these luxury goods.

Industrial Period

The peace accord signed after the Revolutionary War found the United States still dependent on Europe for its manufactured goods and fine textiles. Either of two opposing models for America lay ahead. Thomas Jefferson, aware of the degradation surrounding the English factories, uttered his famous pronouncement, "While we have land to labor then let us never wish to see our citizens occupied at a work-bench. For the general operations of manufacture, let our work-shops remain in Europe." Alexander Hamilton, who favored the growth of American manufacturing, voiced the opposite view, writing, "Not only the wealth but the independence and security of a country appear to be materially connected with the prosperity of manufacturers" (Prude 1999).

Britain was determined to maintain its manufacturing lead by preventing the export of tools and machinery and even skilled workmen who could assist in creating an American textile industry. In 1789, Hamilton aided the establishment of the New York Manufacturing Society and became a charter subscriber of a woolen factory to be established in lower Manhattan. Hamilton posted spies in England to learn the secrets of its textile technology, especially the workings of Richard Arkwright's waterwheel (Chernow 2004). While Alexander Hamilton as secretary of the treasury was focusing on the industrial development in New York and New Jersey, a more significant event was taking place to the north in Rhode Island. In 1790, the twenty-two-year-old Englishman Samuel

Slater landed in New York and made his way to Pawtucket, a village near Providence, where Moses Brown had started a small textile mill.

Samuel Slater—called the Father of the American Industrial Revolution—was born in 1768 in Belper, Derbyshire, in England. The son of a yeoman farmer, Samuel was apprenticed at age fifteen to Jedediah Strutt, who owned a textile mill in nearby Milford. Strutt, a former partner to Richard Arkwright, used a waterwheel to power his mill. During the six years of his apprenticeship, young Slater learned all about the latest technology in textiles. He considered that the textile industry in England had passed its prime. The young and ambitious Slater committed to memory his knowledge of British textile machinery and decided to seek his fortune in America.

Moses Brown, one of the wealthiest men in Providence, had built a small factory (two stories high and measuring only twenty-six by forty feet) in Pawtucket, where handloom weavers made corduroy, denim, and other fabrics. Brown, who was eager to mechanize his mill, invited Slater to join him. The mechanically gifted Slater built a copy of Arkwright's machinery, to be powered by the waters of the Blackstone River. The shift from handloom to machine was a serious threat to the traditional craftspeople, but Slater assured them that there would be jobs aplenty in the mill tending the equipment. The Brown-Slater enterprise was soon selling its yarn locally and to stores in Providence and Boston. Over the next twenty years, Slater established a number of small textile mills in Rhode Island and southern Massachusetts, proving that textiles could be competitively made in the United States even after British goods were again coming in (Prude 1999).

The peace between the United States, Britain, and France did not last. The Embargo Act of 1807 and the war with Britain of 1812–15 again disrupted trade links and exposed the vulnerability of the young nation. The time had come, the wealthy Boston merchants agreed, for America to move from an agrarian society to manufacturing and to break its dependence on Europe for factory-made goods. The Boston mercantile community, which had become rich on cod and trade, was now ready to invest its money in the new industries at home.

Massachusetts lacked most of the ingredients needed for industrial growth. Its earth yielded no gold or silver and little iron, coal, or fossil fuel. Taking their cue from their distant cousins in Britain, the Yankees of Massachusetts ingeniously created their own industries, using their rivers for power and their ships to bring in the raw materials. Boston and the other port towns lacked sufficient waterpower to drive industry. Instead, the Massachusetts Industrial Revolution had its start on the Charles River in Waltham, some ten miles west of Boston. At this site in 1814 the Boston Manufacturing Company built its first textile mill. Yankee manufacturing and the region's long-established tradition of trade would prove a formidable combination.

The driving force behind the Boston Manufacturing Company was Francis Cabot Lowell. He was born in 1775 into a prominent family from the town of Newburyport. His father, Judge John Lowell, was a lawyer who had made his fortune disposing of captured British ships during the War of Independence. His mother, Susanna, came from nearby Salem, where her father had made his fortune as a shipping merchant. Now a family of means, the Lowells moved to Boston, and Francis attended Harvard College. After graduating in 1793, Francis Cabot Lowell became a leading merchant; he owned one of the largest warehouses on India Wharf near Boston Harbor. By his thirties he was already a wealthy man, but his health was precarious. In 1810, Lowell with his family left for England to recuperate. During his two years away from Boston, he toured the textile mills in Lancashire and saw firsthand the great advances in manufacture that had propelled the British to the forefront of the Industrial Age.

Francis Cabot Lowell hatched a plan to establish a textile industry in Massachusetts. On his return to Boston, he shared his vision with his brother-in-law Patrick Tracy Jackson, his cousin Benjamin Gorham, his business partner Uriah Cotting, and a fellow man of business, Nathan Appleton. They would establish a corporation to raise the needed $400,000 (a veritable fortune at that time). They chose Waltham as the site for their first factory. Here, the Charles River opens into a lake before it narrows to a ten-foot fall in water level, thus generating the power to turn the waterwheel and drive the machinery. With the help of Paul Moody, a skilled engineer, Lowell designed a factory to complete the manufacturing process from raw cotton to finished cloth in one facility.

Determined to avoid the squalor and human degradation he had witnessed around the English mills, Lowell decided to employ young, single New England farm girls to work in his factory. They would be housed, fed, and supervised by the company in return for twelve hours a day, six days a week of work. The raw cotton for the Waltham enterprise came on Boston-based sailing ships from the American South. The Waltham mill produced durable cloth mainly for the farming community. Three mills were built at Waltham, and the Boston Manufacturing Company—America's first large-scale industrial enterprise—became a success.

Francis Cabot Lowell died in 1817, but his partners took his vision forward. By now, more Boston merchants wanted a share of the textile business. They funded America's first planned industrial town at East Chelmsford, later renamed Lowell in memory of Francis Cabot Lowell. The town of Lowell was built on a site along the Pawtucket Falls of the Merrimack River. In the space of one mile the river drops thirty-two feet, creating abundant waterpower. This power was mobilized to turn the large waterwheels of the mills. A system of rotating gears and shafts carried the power to the machinery inside the buildings. After 1828 a more efficient system of leather belts and pulleys was used to transmit the power from the main shaft along branch lines and on to the machinery. This system of belts and pulleys became the standard for other mills across the state. The group of founders, later known as the Boston Associates, also built textile mills along powerful rivers at Chicopee and Lawrence in Massachusetts, Manchester in New Hampshire, and Saco in Maine.

When peace between the United States and Britain was concluded in 1815, the flood of cheap British textiles threatened the budding textile industry of New England. In 1816 the United States imposed protective tariffs of 20 percent to aid the local industry. In 1824 protective tariffs on imported textiles were increased to 30 percent, and in 1828 the tariff (known as the Tariff of Abominations) went even higher. In the 1840s, American textiles were again threatened by low-cost British imports. In 1842 yet another round of tariffs on imports was imposed. With the help from these protective tariffs, the textile mills of New England were able to compete with imports and to establish the industry firmly on American soil.

FROM WATERPOWER TO STEAMPOWER

The next great technological advance was the steam engine. In 1835, Boston was joined to Lowell by the steam-powered railroad. Now the raw cotton arriving by ship at the port of Boston was sent rapidly by rail to the textile factories. In return, the finished textiles were dispatched to Boston

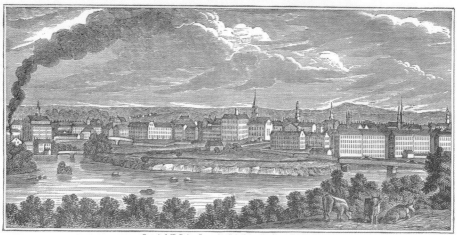

Drawn by J. W. Barber—Engraved by E. L. Barber, New Haven, Conn.

EAST VIEW OF LOWELL, MASS.

The above is an eastern view of the central part of Lowell as seen from the elevated ground on the Dracut or northern side of Merrimac
river.   The entrance of Concord river into the Merrimac is seen on the left.

*Lowell, 1841, America's first planned industrial city. Built along the Merrimack River
to harness the waterpower. Note the mills along the riverbank. The smokestack (far left)
marks the beginning of the age of steam power.*

for shipment to ports to the south and abroad. By the 1850s, the steam
engine freed the factories from their dependence on waterpower. Anthra-
cite coal was shipped from Pennsylvania mainly to the port of Boston but
also to Portsmouth, New Hampshire. From there the coal was hauled on
freight cars to the textile mills and burned to generate steam power for
the machinery. The use of steam power led to larger factories in Lowell
and Lawrence, some employing thousands of workers apiece. Fall River,
New Bedford, Haverhill, and other New England towns also built large
cotton and woolen textile factories that used steam power. Tall smoke-
stacks were built alongside the mills to carry the acrid smoke high into
the air. By 1870, nearly two out of every three textile mills in the United
States were located in New England. Massachusetts alone accounted for
over one-third of the nation's textile production. The mills were producing a wide range of products, including printed cotton, flannels for blankets, and worsted wools for finer clothing. The textile industry became
the largest industry in Massachusetts. In 1880 over eighty thousand workers were employed in the Massachusetts textile factories.

The vast redbrick textile mills were built with Massachusetts money. The Crompton & Knowles Loom Works of Worcester, together with the nearby Whitin Machine Works and the Draper Company, built the machinery for the textile industry. As new technologies came along, these factories converted from steam power to fossil fuel and electricity. (The Lowell mills had started to use hydroelectricity by 1910.) The factories were aided by the expansion of the transportation network. In 1850 the nation's railroads built around the steam engine were confined largely to the Northeast. Thirty years later, railroads had spread to Chicago and farther west and to the south. Goods made in Massachusetts could be sent by rail to inland markets or on steam-powered ships leaving from Boston.

The textile industries showed that unskilled workers could rapidly learn to use powered tools to make product parts, which were assembled at the end of the production line. The method of mass production of textiles was applied to the other Massachusetts industries. By the time the shoe, piano, sewing machine, and other industries were ready for large-scale production, however, waterpower was already giving way to steam power. The new factories no longer needed to be built alongside rivers. Now they were built close to the railroads needed to bring in the coal. Using steam power, the shoe industry of Brockton, Haverhill, and Lynn developed near the center of the towns. The textile and shoe industries of Massachusetts helped outfit the Union Army during the Civil War. After the war, Massachusetts, already highly urbanized and industrialized, entered its Gilded Age, producing the tools to make all manner of goods.

During the period from 1860 to 1920, Massachusetts had over two hundred separate textile factories and several hundred shoe factories. While these were the dominant industries, all kinds of goods were made in Massachusetts. By 1880 the system for large-scale manufacturing in the state was well established. Local banks and insurance companies provided the funds to build the factories. The flood of impoverished immigrants yielded an ample supply of cheap labor. An integrated transportation system brought raw cotton, wool, leather, iron, and coal to the factories, while a street trolley system transported the workers to and from their jobs. The factory owners joined their manufacturing skills to Massachusetts's long-established experience in trade. Immigration and the spread of population to the West and the South created new markets for the products that Massachusetts made.

The textile town of Lowell was doubly famous as a major center for patent medicinals, and the shoe town of Lynn was also the home of Lydia Pinkham's Vegetable Compound. In an age before antibiotics and effective public health, patent medicines were big business in Massachusetts. Home remedies, often containing alcohol or opiates, were extensively advertised and sold in stores across the nation. Their wide acceptance, despite any proof of efficacy, illustrates the vulnerabilities of those times. Massachusetts was also known for its watches and railroad clocks made in Waltham. Wooden furniture was produced in Gardner. Boston was a major center for organ and piano production, publishing, and advertising as well as a leader in prepared foodstuffs. Worcester became a major industrial center focused on textile machinery, steel, wire, farm equipment, firearms, and corsets. Springfield was a center for precision tools, firearms, lawn mowers, and soaps. The sewing machine had its start in Massachusetts. Taunton and Chelsea became major centers for the manufacture of kitchen ranges and parlor stoves. Manufacturing reached into every corner of the Commonwealth. At the close of the nineteenth century, Massachusetts was a manufacturer of horse buggies, freight cars, bicycles, motorcycles, and even automobiles.

Nevertheless, some types of manufacturing were underrepresented in Massachusetts. Compared with the Midwest, the state played a decidedly small role in beer manufacture. By 1895, over two thousand breweries were operating in the United States, but few of them were in Massachusetts. The Massachusetts rum industry, so lucrative in the eighteenth century, was in decline a century later. The immigrants arriving from central and southern Europe preferred their familiar wine over Yankee rum. Nor was Massachusetts known for cigarettes, cigars, or chewing tobacco.

As the goods traveled farther from the factories, new methods of marketing developed. Boston became the center for commission houses (wholesale merchants) which sold the products of the Massachusetts mills to retail outlets across the nation and all over the world. Large quantities of textiles reached the sweatshops of New York. The Massachusetts companies appointed selling agents in the major American cities. Industrial-

OPPOSITE: *J. M. Marston & Co., 226–230 Ruggles Street, Boston, made hand and foot powered precision machinery. This illustration shows their 1893 circular saw with an attachment for boring. The machine weighed 405 lbs. (with borer) and cost $72, delivered in Boston. Most of the Massachusetts tool companies were outside Boston.*

No. 1.

Hand and Foot Power Circular Saw,

WITH ATTACHMENT FOR BORING.

These machines are now made with our improved iron top, and with boring attachment and patent groovers are the most desirable of any on the market, and are indispensable to wood-workers.

They are made in two numbers, the only difference being in the weight of the balance wheels; No. 1 has a 40 lb. balance wheel; No. 2 has a 70 lb. balance wheel. The same boring attachment goes on to either machine. The cut below represents the machine with boring attachment and side treadle in place.

The machines are put up with two 7-inch saws, one cross-cut and one rip, set and filed ready for use; two cutting-off gauges, one ripping gauge, two crank handles and wrench. They are sent out all ready to run when taken out of the crate.

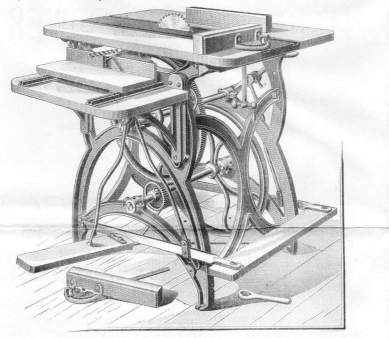

The frames of these machines are made entirely of iron, and are of sufficient weight and strength to make fastening to the floor unnecessary. In construction we use nothing but the very best iron and steel, and all parts are designed with reference to the work they are to perform. The treadles are made of wrought iron, and the cranks have extension handles that can be adjusted to different length of stroke. Our *Improved Adjustable Top* with iron centre 10 inches wide, running the whole length of the table, is a great improvement, and enables us to run the gauges with great accuracy. Send for descriptive catalogue.

Price, No. 1, $60.00, with Borer, $67.00 ; Weight, 330 lbs., with Borer, 367 lbs.

Price, No. 2, $65.00, with Borer, $72.00 ; Weight, 362 lbs., with Borer, 405 lbs.

ization came to Massachusetts well before it reached most of the nation. In 1860 the United States had 35,000 miles of railroad track. During the next thirty years another 100,000 miles of track were added. The steam-powered railroads crossed the nation from the East to the West Coast and from north to south. In 1870 the U.S. population was slightly under 40 million; it was nearly double that thirty years later. The per capita income of the urban population began to rise toward the end of the nineteenth century, giving working folk more disposable income.

ADVERTISING AND TRADE CARDS

The first advertisement in an American newspaper appeared in the April 24, 1704, issue of the *Boston News-Letter*. This simple advertisement offered a reward for the return of two anvils "stolen from Mr. Shippen's wharf." The *Boston News-Letter* was the first newspaper in the American colonies, and it continued publication until 1776. The *News-Letter* covered events in London and Europe and also listed the arrival and departure times of ships, death notices, and church events. Over its seventy-two-year history the newspaper carried advertisements for locally made products.

James Norris (1990) has shown how advertising helped transform the country after the Civil War. Advertising created brand awareness and enticed people to buy the products. Catalog companies such as Montgomery Ward & Co., Spiegel, Stern, and Sears, Roebuck brought a wide range of manufactured goods to the American home. Sewing machine companies and patent medicine companies were among the first to advertise nationwide. So were Walter Baker's Cocoa and the biscuit companies. Advertisements for organs and pianos and for jewelry were aimed at the affluent market. Ads for Mason & Hamlin and Chickering pianos appeared regularly in quality magazines such as *Harper's Weekly*. Clocks and watches made in Waltham were also advertised nationwide. These advertisements regularly made extravagant claims for the efficacy and uniqueness of the products.

Albert Pope of Boston popularized bicycle riding through extensive advertising, as well as by financing *Bicycling World* magazine and sponsor-

OPPOSITE: *Advertising trade card for Chase & Sanborn, selling coffee, chocolate, cocoa, and tea. These cards (3 x 5 inches on average) were handed out at stores or at fairs to advertise the products for sale. Card designed by the William Forbes Company, Boston, circa 1888.*

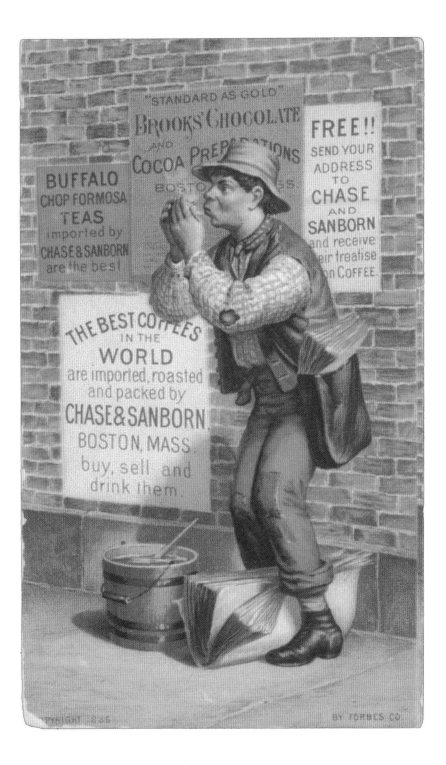

GILT EDGE.

949

GILT EDGE
(IN LARGE BOTTLES) Is the ONLY Gloss Dressing for Ladies Shoes that contains OIL to SOFTEN
the Leather and make it wear LONGER.   237 239 241 ALBANY STREET,
SOLE MANUFACTURERS
Whittemore Bros. & Co., BOSTON, Mass.

BRIGGS PIANOS
BOSTON.

Compliments of
IVERS & POND.
PIANO CO.
BOSTON, MASS.

W. W. STALL,
509 Tremont Street,   Boston.
SAFETY BICYCLES.

QUINCY MARKET AND FANEUIL HALL, BOSTON, MASS.

Faneuil Hall (built 1743) and Quincy Market (built 1826) were long the center of trade in Boston. Farmers delivered their products by horse cart. These markets lost their importance as the city's commercial center moved to Washington Street and Tremont Street in the early twentieth century.

Custom Department.

BOSTON, JULY, 1888.

IN ACCORDANCE WITH OUR USUAL CUSTOM EACH MID-SUMMER, WE WILL FOR A TIME, IN ORDER TO KEEP OUR CUSTOM FORCE EMPLOYED IN OUR WORKSHOPS, TAKE MEASURES AND MAKE TO ORDER, PANTALOONS WHICH WE HAVE HERETOFORE MADE AT $8, $9 AND $10,

AT · THE · REDUCED · PRICES · OF · $6 · AND · $7.

OUR ASSORTMENT OF PATTERNS INCLUDES THE FINEST GRADES AND MAKES OF BOTH FOREIGN AND DOMESTIC FABRICS IN THE LATEST STYLES.

A. SHUMAN & CO.,

Washington and Summer Streets.

THIRD FLOOR.— ELEVATOR.

This illustration (1888) shows A. Shuman & Co., one of Boston's early department stores. Note the horse-drawn trolley on Washington Street.

OPPOSITE: *Some of Bufford's children, circa 1885–1890. John Henry Bufford's company was a leading Boston lithographer. His blond, blue-eyed children with pursed lips graced trade cards for various companies.*

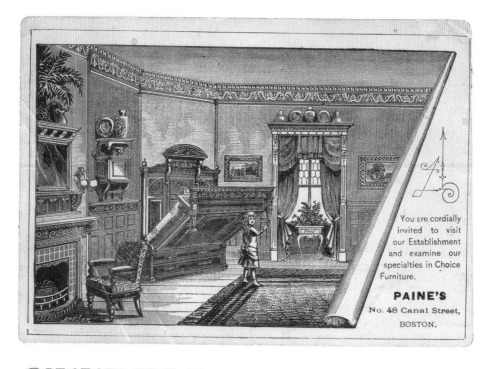

Paine's Furniture Manufactory made and sold furniture from its large establishment at 48 Canal Street, near the busy terminal of the Boston & Maine Railroad. Horse cars took customers to and from the store.

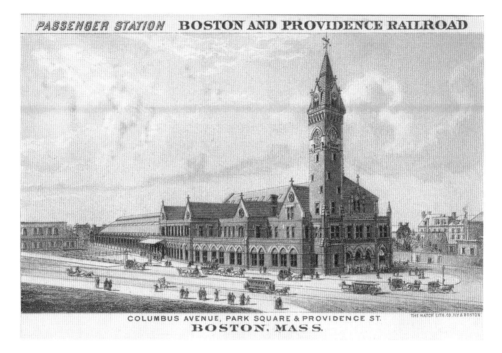

PASSENGER STATION **BOSTON AND PROVIDENCE RAILROAD**

COLUMBUS AVENUE, PARK SQUARE & PROVIDENCE ST.
BOSTON, MASS.

THE HATCH LITH. CO. N.Y. & BOSTON

The terminal of the Boston and Providence Railroad on Columbus Avenue. Seven railroad lines converged on Boston after 1835, linking it with the surrounding towns, the other New England states, and beyond. The Boston and Providence terminal was designed (1872) by the Boston architectural firm founded by Robert Swain Peabody (1845–1917) and John Goddard Stearns Jr. (1843–1917). Peabody & Stearns also designed the Breakers and other Newport mansions as well as the imposing Machinery Hall of the 1893 World's Columbian Exposition in Chicago. Another famed Boston-based architect was H. H. Richardson (1838–1886). During his short life Richardson designed Trinity Church in Boston as well as the Ames Free Library of North Easton and the Converse Memorial Library of Malden, Massachusetts.

The Boston & Hingham Steamboat Company, 1881. By the close of the nineteenth century, Boston was connected to the outside world by an elaborate system of street trolleys, ferry boats, railroads, and steamships. The department stores, banks, offices, businesses, restaurants, and theaters in downtown Boston attracted tens of thousands of visitors each day.

ing bicycle races. The bicycle craze expanded into specialty clothing and bicycle supplies. By 1893 there were 1 million bicycles in the United States. The industry peaked in 1899, when over a million bicycles were sold in a single year. Pope's Columbia bicycle was the most popular, but it had competition from hundreds of other bicycle factories across America. After 1900 the bicycle market cooled despite heavy advertising. In 1910 only 160,000 American-made bicycles were sold.

Massachusetts was the home of major non-alcoholic beverage companies. Ayer's and Hood's sarsaparilla and Moxie were made in Lowell. Cliquot Club, flavored with ginger, came from Millis, Massachusetts. Thanks to advertising all these drinks enjoyed nationwide popularity, at least until Coca-Cola came along.

Advertising took a great leap forward with the introduction of lithography. A book published by the Boston Athenaeum (Pierce & Slautterback 1991) lists over one hundred large and small lithographic companies active in Boston during the period 1825–1880. Springfield was the home of the Milton Bradley Lithographic Company, and other towns had their own lithographic companies. The many advertising firms give testimony to the commercial opportunities then available in Massachusetts. The lithographers met the needs of their clients for portraiture, drawings of homes, businesses, and factories, views of towns, book covers, and for product advertisements, including trade cards. The lithographic companies produced stock trade cards with blank spaces for the business to print its particular message. A smaller number of the cards were designed specifically for one enterprise.

The trade cards were multicolored and aimed to catch the eye. Some were elaborate minor works of art. Many feature the innocence of young children, a common Victorian theme also seen in the photographs of the Liddell sisters by Charles Lutwidge Dodgson, better known as Lewis Carroll, the author of *Alice in Wonderland*. Some of the trade card illustrations were crude caricatures showing black and Asian people as servants and objects of ridicule. Among the artists drawing the trade cards was Boston-born Winslow Homer, who served his apprenticeship at L. Prang & Co. of 159 Washington Street. The young Childe Hassam, whose later Expressionist-style paintings captured the mood of late-nineteenth-century Boston, also learned his craft at one of the Boston lithography shops.

Among the best-known Boston lithographers was John Henry Bufford, born in 1810 in Portsmouth, New Hampshire, the son of an ornamental sign maker. Bufford served his apprenticeship with William and John Pendleton of Boston, who started America's first lithography company. One of his fellow trainees was Nathaniel Currier, born in Roxbury, Massachusetts. Currier left Boston for New York, where he started what was to become the country's greatest lithography company, Currier & Ives. In 1835, Bufford went to New York to work for Currier. Five years later he returned to Boston and started his own firm on Washington Street. In 1865 his sons Frank and John Jr. were made partners, and the firm became known as J. H. Bufford & Sons. Bufford remained the most prominent lithographic printer in Boston until his death in 1870. His sons continued the business as Bufford Sons Lithographic Company. It was this company that produced many of the trade cards for Massachusetts-based businesses from 1870 to 1900, including Lydia Pinkham Vegetable Compound, New Home Sewing Machines, Gilt Edge Shoe-Gloss, and Ivers & Pond Pianos.

William H. Forbes started his business in 1862 in two rooms on Washington Street. Fifteen years later his company employed nearly five hundred workers, producing billheads, tickets, labels, theater posters and playbills, as well as engravings of famous paintings. Forbes manufactured the trade cards for many Massachusetts companies, including Chase's Liquid Glue, Chase & Sanborn Coffee, and the Boston & Hingham Steamboat Company. In 1884 the Forbes Lithographic Manufacturing Company moved to Chelsea, where it occupied eighteen buildings. The company continued to grow, opening offices in other American cities as well as in London. Forbes did well during the first half of the twentieth century, even producing banknotes for the Free French government during World War II. The company was sold in the 1960s, however, and closed its Chelsea plant.

Armstrong & Co., founded in Boston in 1871, specialized in color plates for illustrated books published by the Riverside Press and Scribner's. Armstrong also made the trade cards for Kennedy Biscuits and Mellin's Food. The Beacon Lithographic Company designed cards for Walter Baker's Chocolates, Slade's Spices, and some of the Boston piano companies. By now manufacturers were reaching beyond their home base. Many of the trade cards for Massachusetts-based companies were designed in New York, and local lithographic companies were working with clients in other states.

This book is illustrated with the trade cards issued by companies that had their start in Massachusetts. Cards were usually three by five inches in size, smaller than postcards. Known as Victorian Trade Cards, they were given out by merchants as cheap and colorful souvenirs of advertised products. Vast numbers of trade cards were distributed at the great expositions, including the Philadelphia Centennial Exposition of 1876, the Chicago Columbian Exposition of 1893, the Buffalo Pan-American Exposition of 1901, and the St. Louis World's Fair of 1904. These expositions helped build national markets for Massachusetts-made goods.

These trade cards displayed the full range of available goods and services. Youngsters and adults across the nation avidly collected them. The cards were pasted into scrapbook albums, some of which were found many years later in attics. The individual cards were removed from the pages, leaving glue marks on the back. Many of the cards carry a date. Some show babies, young children, or attractive young women. Other cards show products such as musical instruments, sewing machines, stoves, or pianos. The trade cards tell us a great deal about the location of the companies, the products they made, and the prices they charged. Much like advertisements of today, these nineteenth-century trade cards convey concerns about health, appearance, envy, prestige, and social status.

Many trade cards carry the name and address of a retail store, showing how far the goods traveled from their place of manufacture. By 1900, Massachusetts-made textiles and shoes, pianos, patent medicines, bicycles, machinery, and precision tools were offered for sale in large and small towns across the nation.

RETAILING

From its beginning until the 1740s, Boston was the largest settlement in British North America. The town's population was hemmed in between the port and the Boston Common. Its mercantile life was concentrated around the port. In 1743, Peter Faneuil built his famous hall to replace the outdoor marketplace near Long Wharf. Within the walls of Faneuil Hall, farmers sold their produce to the townsfolk living nearby. Boston suffered a loss of population during the Revolutionary War along with the decline of its West Indies trade. At war's end the town began to grow again. The population in 1800 was 25,000; by 1825 it had reached 60,000.

In 1826 the north and south buildings of Quincy Market opened on either side of Faneuil Hall to accommodate the growing trade in the town. Foodstuffs were sold in Fanueil Hall, while sailmakers, tobacconists, dry goods stores, agricultural suppliers, and importers occupied the shops in the Quincy Market buildings. The buildings, situated near Boston Harbor, also accommodated the growing trade between the United States and foreign markets. Warehouses were filled with raw cotton and wool bound for the textile mills and leather for the shoe factories. The products made in the outlying factories were sent to the commission houses (wholesale dealers) in Boston to be shipped abroad. Long Wharf, the largest on Boston Harbor, led up to State Street and toward the Old State House. Banks and insurance companies began to build their homes along State Street.

By the middle of the eighteenth century, the bustling commercial life of Boston could no longer be contained in the small area around Faneuil Hall and Quincy Market. The retail trade moved to Washington Street and Tremont Street with extensions into Summer Street and Winter Street and around Scollay, Adams, and Haymarket squares. Efforts to expand the retail shopping area into the Boston Common were thwarted by the Boston elite, who saw the Common as their private domain (Domosh 1996).

The world's first department store, Bon Marché, opened in Paris in 1838. The store offered a wide range of goods under one roof, sold at fixed prices, with a money-back guarantee. The store also contained a restaurant. This model of shopping proved attractive and soon spread to major cities around the world. Department stores became the anchors of the downtown urban districts. In 1858, Rowland Hussey Macy, a former Nantucket whaler, opened his famous department store on Sixth Avenue in Manhattan.

In Boston, Eben Jordan and Benjamin Marsh founded the Jordan Marsh department store, which settled on the corner of Washington and Winter streets. In 1865, R. H. White & Co. opened its store at 32 Winter Street. A few years later, White & Co. moved to Washington Street, followed by R. H. Stearns, Raymond's, and William Filene's department store. The offices of most of Boston's daily newspapers were also located along Washington Street. The street was also lined with many specialty stores. Oil stoves and lamps were sold at 43–45 Washington Street. Barry, Beale & Co. stationers were at 108–110, the men's outfitter Leonard Morse

& Co. at 131–137, Wilmot's clothing store at 261–263. Hats and bonnets were sold at 478, Blake's Great Piano Palace was at 612, the Waldorf Lunchroom at 702, and Grant & Brown stationers at 873 Washington Street. Washington Street also attracted many theaters. The Boston Music Hall, the Museum of Fine Arts, and the Horticultural Society were close by.

The network of horse-drawn street trolleys as well as seven railroad terminals brought thousands of people from the suburbs and surrounding towns each day to shop and work in downtown Boston. The side of Tremont Street along the Boston Common was the favorite promenade for the well-off and the well-dressed. Tremont Street itself was clogged with horse-drawn traffic moving in both directions. The southern part of the street was lined with the better shops catering to the carriage trade. The volume of traffic into this narrow retail area intensified after 1890 when the electric streetcar shortened the travel time into Boston. In 1898 a tunnel under Tremont Street was completed to relieve the congestion. The subway—America's first—was served by four stations, with Park Station opening at Winter Street in the heart of Boston's retail district. The section of Tremont Street at Boylston Street, close to the elite Back Bay, was the retail outlet for Boston's piano companies and became known as Piano Row. Smith Piano & Organ had its showrooms on Tremont Street, with Mason & Hamlin at 154, Ivers & Pond at 183, Vose & Sons at 170, and McPhail Pianos at 167 Tremont Street.

Boston's wholesale and retail shoe trade was concentrated around Tremont Row at the intersection of Tremont and Hanover streets. Kitchen ranges and parlor stoves were sold on Union Street, close to Fanueil Hall. These and many other goods made in Massachusetts were marketed by commission houses, which in turn sold the products to the Boston retail stores along Washington and Tremont streets.

The period from 1860 to 1920 can be described as the Gilded Age of Massachusetts industry. The Commonwealth was a major producer of textiles and footwear as well as an array of products from biscuits to bicycles and pianos to patent medicines. The extensive transportation system brought the raw materials to the factories and distributed the manufactured goods across the nation and around the world. These enterprises were financed with local money. The head offices were in Boston, Worcester, or Spring-field. Extensive advertising boosted sales, especially the use of trade cards. All the cities and towns across the Commonwealth benefited from the industrial expansion. Main Street was the center of commercial life in Worcester and in Springfield. The textile city of Lowell centered its retail life on Merrimack Street, Lawrence on Essex Street, Lynn on Market Street, Fall River on South Main Street, and New Bedford on Purchase Street. But it was Boston that remained the mercantile and cultural heart of the Commonwealth of Massachusetts.

This book describes the goods made in Massachusetts and marketed around the United States of America and the world during its Gilded Age.

1

❧ TEXTILES

"He's not running any museums." This remark was attributed to the company director on the closing in 1963 of the unprofitable Stevens Mill in North Andover, Massachusetts, established in 1813. The rise and fall of the textile industry in Massachusetts had taken a century and a half to complete. The Merrimack Company's first mill in Lowell began to produce cotton textiles in September 1823. Soon, more mills were built along the Merrimack River and the nearby canals. Streets were laid out and houses, shops, schools, and churches were constructed. By the close of 1845, thirty-one cotton mills had been built along the waterways of Lowell. The great Boott Millyard, with six linked mills between the Merrimack and the eastern canal, gave employment to hundreds of workers. At first these were young women who came from the farms of New Hampshire and Maine, much like the "mill girls" of Waltham. The impoverished Irish, French Canadian, and other immigrants arriving in Massachusetts to seek work in its new factories soon replaced them. Textiles became the dominant industry of Lowell, which grew from a village in 1821 to a city of 34,000 in 1850, second only to Boston as the most populous town in the state. In 1835 the Boston & Lowell Railroad commenced service.

Founded in 1845, the second great textile city of Lawrence (named for Abbott Lawrence) was built at Bowdell's Falls down the Merrimack River from Lowell. Many of the directors of the Lawrence enterprise were the same people who had built Lowell. The first Lawrence mill, called the Bay State, entered production in 1847, making shawls and flannel. The Arlington Mill made mohair goods, and the huge Pacific Mills produced cotton textiles. The development of Lawrence was followed by the construction of textile mills in the southern Massachusetts towns of Fall River and New Bedford, which were desperate for a new industry after

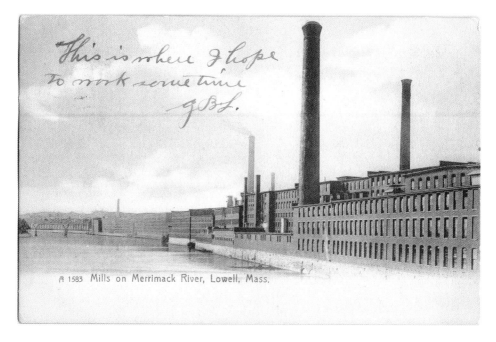

A 1583 Mills on Merrimack River, Lowell, Mass.

Large textile mills lined the Merrimack River and the canal system at Lowell. The early mills had waterwheels turning in the water, and the power was carried by a system of pulleys and belting to the machinery inside. Later steam plants, powered by coal, replaced the water-wheel. Pennsylvania coal came by ship to the ports of Boston and Portsmouth and then by rail to the mills. Tall chimney stacks spewing out pollutants became the symbol of the age of steam power. The illustration dates to circa 1900.

Pennsylvania petroleum eliminated the demand for whale oil. The early mills were built close to the riverbanks and were equipped with water-wheels to generate waterpower. Cotton was purchased from the American South. Later, with the coming of steam power, huge quantities of coal were brought in.

Unlike in Lowell and Lawrence, the textile industry of southern Massachusetts was not supported by Boston money. With whaling in decline, the ship owners of New Bedford and Fall River moved their money into textiles. In 1848, Joseph Grinnell opened the Wamsutta Mill, soon to be followed by the Potomska, Grinnell, Achushnet, and Oneka mills. In 1899, New Bedford opened the Textile School to train its children for work in the mills. The city grew rapidly as a textile center. By

1920, the forty mills in New Bedford employed some 30,000 workers, and the total population exceeded 120,000.

THE SELLING OF TEXTILES, 1815–1880

The Massachusetts textile mills, some of which employed three thousand or more workers, were enormously expensive to build. Large sums of borrowed money were used to construct the dams and canals. Banks charged interest of up to 15 percent. The investors expected a 10 percent return each year, and in tough times, workers' salaries were cut. The hundreds of textile mills across Massachusetts appointed agents to sell their goods and to generate the money to pay their own costs. Between the factory and the retail customer stood the counting houses, commission dealers, wholesalers, shippers, bankers, and insurance companies, all of which took their share. By the time the goods were sold to the retail customer, the price of the goods had doubled.

Many of the men involved in marketing the textiles were also investors in the mills. For a representative example, it is useful to examine the life of Nathan Appleton (1779–1861), one of the pioneers of the Massachusetts textile industry (Gregory 1975). The Appletons were a Puritan family originally from Great Waldingfield, Suffolk, in England, where they owned two hundred acres and a manor house. Samuel Appleton and his family arrived in Boston in 1635 hoping for a freer life in the New World. He settled in the town of Ipswich, where he received two hundred acres and began to farm. A century later Appleton's descendants, together with other village folk, left Massachusetts and moved a few dozen miles north to New Hampshire, where they established the town of New Ipswich.

Nathan was the ninth of twelve children of Deacon Isaac Appleton and his wife, Mary. The boy attended the local school, where he excelled in spelling and mathematics as well as in English and Latin. He hoped for an academic career, but the family could not afford to send him to college. Instead, at age fifteen, Nathan Appleton was sent to Boston to work in the store owned by his older brother Samuel. The store attracted some of Boston's leading families. Samuel got the idea of widening its appeal by importing quality goods from England. He established a counting house (offices used to transact business) and mercantile warehouse on Washington Street. In 1800, when Nathan came of age, he was made a full partner,

This advertisement for the Continental Clothing House, 744–750 Washington Street, Boston, circa 1880, demonstrates the benefits of dressing well. Fitz Herbert in his stylish Continental suit is simply irresistible to the young women of Boston.

and the enterprise was renamed the S. & N. Appleton Company. By now the Appletons were no longer shopkeepers but went by the more prestigious title of merchants.

Early in the nineteenth century, Samuel traveled to England to establish contacts and to buy inventory for his growing enterprise. He purchased quality dry goods, lace, fans, watches, and other items that would find a ready market in Boston. The goods were shipped from Liverpool and arrived in Boston ten to twelve weeks later. It was Nathan's task to prepare the goods for sale soon after the ship docked. The Appletons expanded their activities by traveling to the Carolinas to buy cotton and rice for shipment to England This in turn gave them the money to buy manufactured English goods. Nathan was already developing a reputation as a shrewd but honest merchant with a vast knowledge of textiles.

Jefferson's embargo and the war of 1812–15 severely reduced trade between Massachusetts and Britain. Nathan's career changed after a meeting in 1810 with fellow American Francis Cabot Lowell. The men agreed that overseas trade was precarious and that manufacturing textiles at home offered greater opportunities. In 1813, Appleton was among the twelve men of business to buy shares in the Boston Manufacturing Company. The directors of the company decided to concentrate on cotton textiles. The first product produced in their Waltham mill was coarse, heavy cloth to replace the fabrics imported from India.

With his considerable experience in merchandising, Nathan Appleton was selected to sell the cloth. Appleton formed Benjamin C. Ward & Co. as the sole selling agents for the Waltham textiles, working on a commission of 1 to 1.5 percent. Sales rose briskly. In its first year (1815) Ward & Co. had sales of $2,574. Four years later, sales of Waltham cloth had increased to over $121,000. Appleton was also heavily involved in the Merrimack Manufacturing Company, which built the textile town of Lowell, and in the Essex Company, which developed the textile town of Lawrence. A shareholder in over thirty mills in Massachusetts, New Hampshire, and Maine, he served as president of the board of several of the mills and was a director of twenty of them. He was selected to sell the products of several of these mills and established James W. Paige & Co. as their commission agents. Nathan Appleton and his commission houses shifted entirely from importing goods to the task of marketing textiles made in

New England. Bales of textiles from the various mills were sent to Boston by rail and stored in Appleton's warehouses until they were sold.

Even before the Civil War, the New England states were no longer the main customers for the textiles coming from their factories. Selling agents such as Appleton sold their wares in New York, Pennsylvania, and as far south as Mobile and New Orleans. Railroads carried Massachusetts-made cloth into the interior and returned with farm produce from the Ohio Valley. Appleton's companies sent textiles to South America, Canada, and Europe. Markets were even established in Russia, India, and China.

Much of the dynamism of the Appleton companies depended on the man himself. As Appleton aged and was distracted from business by politics (in 1830 he was elected to the U.S. House of Representatives), his enterprises began to suffer. The Depression of 1837 and the reduction of tariffs after 1857 also affected the sales of Massachusetts cloth. Furthermore, New York was fast eclipsing Boston as the nation's textile center. James W. Paige & Co., A. & A. Lawrence, and other textile sales agencies moved their head offices from Boston to New York.

By the start of the Civil War, the original Massachusetts mill owners were either retired or dead. Appleton's favorite child, Fanny, married Henry Wadsworth Longfellow, the beloved American poet. Fanny suffered a terrible death in July 1861 when her clothing caught fire. Nathan Appleton died the day after her funeral and is buried in Mount Auburn Cemetery alongside her.

Another Boston merchant who became a pioneer in textile manufacturing and selling was Abbott Lawrence (1792–1856). The Lawrence family settled in Massachusetts in 1635. Abbott's father had a farm in Groton, where the boy attended local schools. He was later apprenticed to his older brother Amos, who had moved to Boston, where he specialized in imports from China and Britain. The two formed the partnership of A. & A. Lawrence & Co. Abbott Lawrence was one of the prime movers in the founding of Lowell and also of Lawrence, the second textile city on the Merrimack River, which was named for him. A. & A. Lawrence was one of Boston's major commission houses and sold the textiles of several of the larger mills. Abbott Lawrence served two terms in the U.S. Congress (1835–37 and 1839–40, when he resigned). In 1848 he became an unsuccessful candidate on the Whig ticket for the office of vice president of the United States. He went on to serve as United States ambassador to Great Britain (1849–52), but during his absence, his Boston business began to suffer.

His nephew, Amos Adams Lawrence (1814–1886), grew up with the advantages of wealth. Amos attended Harvard College and decided to become a merchant, but "not a plodding, narrow-minded one pent up in the city, with my mind always in my counting-room. . . . I would be at the same time a literary man in some measure and a farmer" (Lawrence 1888). In preparation for his career, Amos spent time touring the mills in Lowell and traveling around the South and to Ohio. He took up a position with Almy, Patterson & Co., a Boston dry goods commission house, and then joined the family firm of A. & A. Lawrence & Co. Determined to succeed on his own merits, Amos opened his own counting room in the Phillips Building near Liberty Square. His firm was selected as selling agents to the Cocheco Mills and the Salmon Falls Company. In 1860 he bought a mill in Ipswich to make hosiery. In 1870 his firm was selected as sole selling agents for the Arlington Mills in Lawrence, and he became very wealthy as both the owner of textile mills and a selling agent. Amos Lawrence was appointed a director of the Suffolk Bank and the Provident Institution for Savings. He was active in establishing a steamship line between Boston and New Orleans.. In a union of prominent families, he married Sarah Elizabeth Appleton, daughter of William Appleton. Their business empire would spread throughout the country. Lawrence, Kansas, is named for Amos Lawrence and Appleton, Wisconsin, for his wife's family (Lawrence 1888).

By 1880 there were 11,246 tailors in Boston, many of whom worked in the garment industry (Handlin 1972). But the greatest market for Massachusetts textiles was the readymade garment industry in New York City. The industry started to develop during the Civil War. After the war, it expanded with the massive influx of immigrants into the city. The invention of the Singer industrial sewing machine facilitated the growth of the garment industry. Early on, seamstresses and tailors worked long hours at home. After 1880, apartments were turned into sweatshops that doubled as living quarters. These sweatshops, employing mainly Italian and Jewish immigrants, grew into large clothing firms. The larger sweatshops employed hundreds of workers, bent over sewing machines twelve hours a day for a wage of six dollars a week. The exploitive system came tragically to the attention of the public on March 25, 1911, when a fire broke out on

CHAPTER 1

Clothes for Outdoor Life

Clothes that stand the racket of fishing, tramping, hunting, and look well through it all — they must have good stuff in them.

Forestry Cloth is made by the American Woolen Company especially for this purpose. It is pure wool, protects the body, guards against chill.

It is closely woven, turns wind and showers. Soft gray green, blending with rocks and foliage. All weights. The registered trade mark name

FORESTRY CLOTH

IS STAMPED ON THE BACK OF THE CLOTH

Forestry Cloth is used by the U. S. Government for its Forestry Service.

For riding, motoring and golfing suits, the American Woolen Company makes a pure wool fabric, Olivauto Cloth — that has style on top of wearing quality. Fashionable olive brown. Closely woven. Doesn't show dust or grease spots.

Samples of Forestry and Olivauto Cloth sent on request. If your tailor cannot obtain them we will supply you through regular channels as we do not sell at retail. Send check or money order for quantity desired (3½ yards for man's suit). Olivauto Cloth, $3.50 per yard; Forestry Cloth, $2.75 for medium weight.

American Woolen Company

Selling Agency   *Wm. M. Wood, President.*

AMERICAN WOOLEN COMPANY OF NEW YORK

American Woolen Bldg., 4th Ave., 18th to 19th Sts.

the eighth floor of the Asch Building in lower Manhattan. Five hundred workers, mainly young women employed by the Triangle Shirtwaist Company, were caught in the fire. Most managed to escape, but the blaze consumed 146 lives. The Triangle Shirtwaist fire led to significant changes in labor laws as well as improvements in building safety and in the operations of the fire department.

THE AMERICAN WOOLEN COMPANY

Textiles were a precarious business. Up-and-down economic cycles, worker unrest, and cutthroat competition led to frequent mill closings and bankruptcies. In June 1893 the stock market crashed, and numerous banks, railroads, and mills across the country were driven into receivership. After tariffs on imported cotton and wool textiles were reduced, the American mills faced ruin under the onslaught of goods imported from Europe. The answer seemed to lie in consolidation, resulting in many mergers in the banking, railroad, and steel industries as well as textile mills.

Despite his name, William Madison Wood Jr. (1858–1926) was no Yankee blueblood. In fact, he was the son of humble Portuguese immigrants from the Azores, who settled on Martha's Vineyard only a few years before his birth. His mother was of mixed Portuguese-English birth; her father, Charles Madison, was born in London. Young William's father worked on the whaling ships, first on Martha's Vineyard and later in New Bedford. The Woods had ten children, of whom four died before reaching adulthood. The father died of tuberculosis when William was only twelve years old, and the boy was forced to leave school to support his mother and his siblings. He found work as an office boy at the Wamsutta Cotton Mills in New Bedford. William was self-educated and early on showed a flair for finance and organization. In 1886, twenty-eight-year-old William Wood moved to Lawrence to work for Frederick Ayer, the owner of the failing Washington Mills. Frederick was the younger brother of James

OPPOSITE: *In 1909, the American Woolen Company moved its headquarters from Boston to New York City. The company did very well during World War I making cloth for millions of uniforms and blankets, but many of its mills shut down during the Great Depression. In 1950, American Woolen merged with Textron, which closed the remaining Massachusetts mills. This advertisement dates from 1912.*

Cook Ayer, who had made his fortune in patent medicines. Three years later Wood was put in charge of the factory. In 1899, William Madison Wood Jr. became the guiding force in consolidating eight mills (seven in New England and one in New York) to form the American Woolen Company. He married Ellen Ayer and became Frederick Ayer's son-in-law (Roddy 1982).

From his office at 245 State Street in Boston, Wood controlled his growing empire. He bought the raw wool from producers across the United States, Australia, and South America. In 1905 he built the world's largest worsted mill. Named the Wood Worsted Mill, the factory in Lawrence had nearly a quarter of a million spindles and 1,500 looms and employed seven thousand workers. Nearby, Wood built the smaller Ayer Mill.

American Woolen began as a Massachusetts-based company, but in 1909 it built its office building, standing three hundred feet tall, at Park Street South and East Eighteenth Street in New York City. American Woolen did spectacular business during World War I. By 1921 the company controlled fifty-eight mills, mainly in New England, with over forty thousand workers (fifteen thousand in Lawrence alone) filling one-fifth of the nation's textile needs. American Woolen had contracts with the government to provide cloth for uniforms for the army and navy.

The growth of the woolen textiles industry in Lawrence and other New England towns benefited Boston. With half of America's woolen mills concentrated in this small area, Boston became one of the world's leading wool markets. Huge wool warehouses were constructed alongside the harbor and down Summer Street. Wool merchants became an important segment of Boston's moneyed classes. Among the directors of the American Woolen Company was Augustus D. Juilliard of New York. He left a large endowment to the New York Institute of Musical Art. In gratitude, the institute was renamed the Juilliard School.

Starting in the mid-1920s, American Woolen experienced significant deficits. The new management responded by closing down plants and putting workers out on the street. The closed mills were sold off at pennies on the dollar. The diminished company struggled on during the 1930s but benefited greatly from government contracts during World War II. After the war, the decline commenced anew, and what remained of the once mighty American Woolen Company was sold off to Textron, Inc., of Providence, Rhode Island.

WILLIAM CARTER OF NEEDHAM

In 1680 the citizens of Dedham, Massachusetts, paid ten English pounds to buy a large tract of Indian-owned land. Lying largely within a U-shaped bend of the Charles River, this land was incorporated in 1711 as the village of Needham, named after the English town of Needham Market. The community remained largely agricultural until the close of the eighteenth century, when paper and corn mills were built to take advantage of the waterpower at the upper and lower falls along the course of the Charles River.

In 1852 the Boston & Woonsocket commenced service and ran through the town of Needham. The growing town attracted English textile workers, who set up knitwear factories. First, Jonathan Avery started a knit-goods factory in the town. Then James and Thomas Beles arrived in Needham in 1852 from Leicestershire and set up a small factory making stockings and jackets. The most successful of these English newcomers was William Carter, formerly of Derbyshire, who specialized in children's clothing. Carter built a large knitwear factory close by the railroad station at Needham Highlands and another factory overlooking Rosemary Pond, employing hundreds of people. Carter's baby wear soon became a fast favorite of mothers all over Boston and New England. The company remained in Needham for over one hundred years, until it was sold and moved to Atlanta.

THE STEVENS FAMILY OF ANDOVER

The Massachusetts textile firm with the longest history is linked with the Stevens family of Andover, Massachusetts. John Stevens came from England in 1638 as part of the Puritan migration. He landed at Newburyport but made his way ten miles inland with the promise of a large acreage of arable land. The Stevenses together with generations of Andover farmers settled into a life as self-sufficient farmers, raising their animals and tilling their fields. With their wool and flax, the women engaged in the time-consuming task of making cloth sufficient for the needs of the family.

Nathaniel Stevens (1786-1865), came of age at a time when men from Massachusetts were reaching beyond family farming to start businesses.

Nathaniel was educated at the Phillips Academy in Andover before serving as an apprentice to a local farmer, John Carlton. He had too adventurous a spirit for farming, and set off to the port town of Salem to become a sailor. When the time came to settle down, he returned to Andover and married. With the help of his father-in-law, Nathaniel in 1813 set up a woolen mill alongside Cochichewick Brook, where it enters the Merrimack River. At that time, American wool milling was still in its infancy. Before Stevens began, there were fewer than a hundred small wood-built wool mills in the whole of the United States, most of them in New England (Ferguson 1970). These wool mills predated the redbrick cotton mills built in Waltham in 1814 by the Boston Manufacturing Company. The success of these mills was helped by the importation to New England of merino sheep from Spain. The merino wool was much finer than the wool previously available.

Nathaniel Stevens knew little about wool milling. He relied on the Scholfield brothers, recently arrived from England, who had the necessary experience and technical ability. Rather than compete against finer imports, Stevens specialized in coarse flannel used to make underwear. In 1821 he reached beyond the local market, selling to Boston, New York, and Philadelphia commission houses. Eventually, Nathaniel Stevens became a wealthy man with investments in banks, mills, railroads, and insurance companies.

After the death of Nathaniel Stevens, his textile businesses came under the control of his sons. One son, Horace, died of scarlet fever and another, George, from typhoid fever, leaving only Moses T. Stevens in charge. The wool mills benefited mightily during the Civil War. After the war, however, fierce competition and cheap imports led to many bankruptcies. The marketplace was becoming more sophisticated, and the Stevens company responded by adding silk, cotton cloth, and worsted goods among its products. The commission house of Faulkner, Kimball & Co., located at 48–50 Franklin Street in Boston, was selected as the sole selling agent for the Stevens mills.

In 1883, John Peters Stevens (known as J. P.), the eldest son of the deceased Horace, went to work for Faulkner, Kimball & Co. as a clerk in its Boston offices. The wool trade now entered a period of turmoil. The growth of the American Woolen Company posed a grave threat to the Stevens company. In response J. P. Stevens, together with his uncle and his cousins, set up their own commission house to market the family's products. Thus began the era of J. P. Stevens & Co. of Boston, which became one of the largest of the American textile manufacturing and marketing companies (Minchin 2005).

≈

New England maintained its dominance in textile manufacture well into the nineteenth century. By 1860, 80 percent of the capital invested in cotton textiles was in New England (Massachusetts accounted for 34 percent, New Hampshire 23 percent, Maine 6 percent, Connecticut 7 percent, Rhode Island 10 percent, and Vermont 1 percent of the national total). At the close of the century, Massachusetts alone had over 100,000 textile workers, with many thousands more working in mills in the other New England states. But with textile production increasing in the South, competition for markets was becoming intense.

2

SEWING MACHINES ❧

Elias Howe Jr. was born in 1819 in the farming community of Spencer, lying some thirty miles to the west of Boston. He was educated in the village school and then joined his father working on the family farm. At age nineteen, Elias left to seek his fortune in one of the factories in Boston. He found work in a machine shop, where he overheard the comment, "Invent a sewing machine, and it will ensure you an independent fortune." The idea became indelibly imprinted on his mind. By age twenty-four he was married with three children and living on nine dollars a week. Extreme poverty and concern for the future of his family encouraged him to concentrate on the idea of inventing a sewing machine.

After a number of false starts, Howe hit upon the idea of using a threaded needle with an eye near the point, interacting with a shuttle carrying a second thread, moving back and forth. He built a prototype in 1845 and received a patent for his invention on September 10, 1846. But his friends were unimpressed, and the local tailors refused to try the new machine, despite its superiority to hand stitching. Howe despaired of ever selling his machine in the United States. In 1846 he sent his brother to England to try to sell the machine there. William Thomas in London agreed to buy the rights to the invention for the sum of £250, and so guaranteed himself a vast fortune. Thomas asked that Elias Howe come to England to perfect the machines there. Howe sailed to England in 1847, but hard times followed him. In 1849 he returned to the United States, an embittered and poor man. He found work as a humble journeyman mechanic to support his family.

During the years when he was away in England, other innovative men had built thriving sewing machine companies using Howe's design. The most famous of these men was Isaac Merritt Singer. When Howe was still in Boston busy refining his sewing machine, Singer, an obscure mechanic, was working nearby. Singer improved on Howe's design and built his own sewing machine. In time, the Singer Company became the largest sewing machine maker in the world. Howe discovered that other companies, too, had copied his patented design. He sought damages, but it took ten years of legal battles before a Massachusetts judge ruled in Howe's favor, finally settling the case. From 1854 until his patent expired in 1867, Elias Howe received royalties on every sewing machine made in the United States, including those made by the Singer Sewing Machine Company. Howe became a very wealthy man. In 1865 he opened his own sewing machine factory in New York. Two years later, Howe was dead at age forty-eight.

Between 1850 and 1900 there were 250 companies in the United States that made sewing and stitching machines. Forty-five of them had their start in Massachusetts. New York State was the home of some forty sewing machine companies, Pennsylvania sixteen, Illinois seventeen, and Ohio twenty-two. Willox & Gibbs opened its workshop in Providence, Rhode Island. The Weed Sewing Machine Company was founded in Hartford, Connecticut, and the Shaw and Clark Sewing Machine Company was established in Biddeford, Maine. Samuel Baker and Thomas White opened their factory in Brattleboro, Vermont, and the Franklin Sewing Machine Company was established in Mason Village, New Hampshire.

Grover, Baker & Co. began the manufacture of sewing machines in 1851, working out of a five-story factory facing Haymarket Square in the heart of Boston. Its machines, according to its advertising, were used for "sewing leather, and all kinds of cloth." William Emerson Baker, born in Roxbury in 1828, joined forces with a Boston tailor named William Grover. Baker sold his company and retired a very rich man at age forty. The company moved to New York City and sold its machines in its store at 403 Broadway. In 1868, Baker bought an eight hundred–acre property in Needham, Massachusetts, where he built America's first amusement park. The Puritan Manufacturing Company at 210 South Street, Boston, manufactured stitching machines used in the shoe industry. The Reece Button-Hole Machine Company (founded 1881) at 500–514 Harrison Avenue, Boston, used an ingenious machine that cut and sewed buttonholes on suits and overcoats. A single worker could make eight thousand buttonholes a day.

The commercial sewing machine was a boon to the ready-to-wear clothing industry. The Boston Sewing Machine Company and the American Sewing Machine Company were also located in Boston. S. A. Davis invented a rotary shuttle sewing machine and opened a factory in Foxboro. The business failed but reemerged in 1880 as the Foxboro Company, with capital of $150,000. The sewing machine was exhibited in 1881 at the fair of the Massachusetts Charitable Association in Boston, where it was awarded the gold medal. Despite their numbers, very few of the sewing machine companies had any endurance, and most closed down after a few years. Some of the entrepreneurs tried their hand more than once at various combinations of partnerships, usually without lasting success.

A more enduring Massachusetts sewing machine company was started in 1858 in the small town of Orange by Thomas H. White (then aged twenty-two) and William L. Grout. They began as chair makers but switched to sewing machines as the new industry started to grow. White and Grout pooled their savings, bought a lathe and a drill press, and opened a small machine shop in nearby East Templeton to build their hand-operated, single-thread sewing machines, which they labeled the New England. White built the machines and Grout, with his horse and cart, took to the road to sell them. After a year the partnership ended, and Grout went off to Winchendon, Massachusetts, to start his own company. White moved his company to Orange, Massachusetts, into a bigger factory close by the railroad. By 1862 he employed over thirty men in his factory, building the New England sewing machine.

In 1866, Thomas White decided that the country was moving to the booming West. He closed his Massachusetts plant and moved to Cleveland, Ohio, to be near his major markets. Still he built the New England sewing machine, priced at ten dollars each. The Cleveland-based White Sewing Machine Company became a major producer and made machines for Sears, Roebuck & Co., among other distributors. The White Company, still in Cleveland, continues in business as a sewing machine company.

Meanwhile, the men of Orange, Massachusetts, went on building sewing machines. Stephen French, John Wilson Wheeler, and A. J. Clark—who had all previously worked with Thomas White—built the

The New Home was the most successful of the Massachusetts sewing machine companies. The company began in business in 1858 in Orange, where it built sewing machines until 1928. One of the original founders was Thomas H. White, who moved to Cleveland, Ohio, where he established the White Sewing Machine Company.

Home Sewing Machine and, after 1877, an improved model, which they called the New Home. This was the most successful of all the Massachusetts-built sewing machines. The growing company founded a large factory on the banks of the Millers River employing the skills of 750 workers. The assembly line produced five hundred sewing machines a day. Over 7 million New Home sewing machines were sold between 1877 and 1930. In Boston, New Home machines were sold in the company's store at 409 Washington Street. The company advertised extensively and opened sales offices across the nation. For over fifty years it dominated the small town of Orange, providing housing for the workers and schools for the children, as well as a company store, a community center, and a post office. In 1928, New Home was taken over by the Free Sewing Machine Company of Rockford, Illinois. Two years later the production of machinery, patterns, and dies was moved to Illinois, and sewing machine manufacturing in Massachusetts came to an end.

OPPOSITE: *Another New Home advertisement. This delightful trade card was given out at the company's booths at the World's Columbian Exposition in Chicago in 1893. At that time the New World sewing machine was sold in stores from Boston west to San Francisco and south to Atlanta.*

Nineteenth-Century Sewing Machine Companies in Massachusetts

Source: COOPER 1977.

SEWING MACHINE	COMPANY	TOWN	FIRST MADE	LAST MADE
Aetna	Planar, Braunsdorf	Boston	1867	1869
Bartlett	Goodspeed & Wyman	Winchendon	1866	1870
Blodgett & Lerow	Phelps	Boston	1849	1849
Goddard & Rice	Blodgett & Rice	Worcester	1849	1850
Boston	J. F. Paul	Boston	1880	
New Boston	Boston Sewing	Boston	1881	
Bosworth	Charles Bosworth	Petersham		
Bradford & Barber	Bradford & Barber	Boston	1860	1861
Chamberlain	Woolridge, Keene	Lynn	1853	1854
Chicopee	Chicopee Sewing	Chicopee Falls	1868	1869
Common Sense	Clark & Barke	Orange		
Florence	Florence Sewing	Florence	1860	1868
Crown	Florence Sewing	Florence	1879	1888
Dorcas	American	Boston	1853	1856
Empire	Empire	Boston	1860	1870
Finkle	M. Finkle	Boston	1856	1859
Finkle & Lyon	Finkle & Lyon	Boston	1859	1861
Folsom	J. G. Folsom	Winchendon	1865	1872
Foxboro	Foxboro	Foxboro		
Globe	J. G. Folsom	Winchendon	1865	1869
Goodyear & McKay	Goodyear & McKay	Boston		
Gold Medal	Gold Medal	Orange	1869	1876
Grover & Baker	Grover & Baker	Boston	1851	1875
Home	Johnson, Clarke	Boston	1869	1876
New Home	Johnson, Clark	Orange	1882	1930
National	Johnson, Clark	Orange	1874	1879
Howe's Improved	Nichols & Bliss	Boston	1852	1853
Leavitt	Nichols & Leavitt	Boston	1854	1856
Hunt	N. Hunt	Boston	1853	1854
Hunt & Webster	Hunt & Webster	Boston	1854	1857
Johnson	Emery, Johnson	Boston	1856	1865
Ladd & Webster	Ladd, Webster	Boston	1858	1866
Leader	Leader	Springfield	1862	1888
Leavitt	Nichols, Leavitt	Boston	1855	1876
Morey & Johnson	Safford & Williams	Boston	1849	1851
New England	Grout & White	Orange	1862	1863
New England	Clark & Barker	Orange	1863	1865
Folsom	J. G. Folsom	Orange	1865	1865
New Priscilla	Priscilla	Boston		
Novelty	C. A. French	Boston	1869	
Post Combination	Post Combination	Chicopee	1885	1888
Robinson	F. R. Robinson	Boston	1853	1855
Rotary Shuttle	Rotary Shuttle	Foxboro	1881	1884
Foxboro	Foxboro	Foxboro	1885	1887
Shaw & Clark	Shaw & Clark	Chicopee Falls	1867	1868
Springfield	Springfield	Springfield	1880	1882
Union	Johnson, Clark	Orange	1876	
Wesson	D. B. Wesson	Springfield	1880	
Wickersham	Buytterfield & Stevens	Boston	1853	
Williams & Orvis	Williams & Orvis	Boston	1859	1860

3

~ FOOTWEAR

The English settlers sent to America by the Massachusetts Bay Company were selected for their ability to be self-sufficient in the New World. Among the principal skills required was the ability to work with leather and to make footwear. During the earliest years of the settlement, tanneries were established and the General Court of the Massachusetts Bay Colony regulated shoemakers, furriers, and glove makers. It is little wonder that manufacturing shoes and boots became a large industry in Massachusetts.

During the long cold nights of winter, a farmer would fashion the leather to make footwear for his family. Early in the eighteenth century, cottage industries for the manufacture of footwear sprang up in Lynn, Haverhill, and other Massachusetts towns. In small rooms, often attached to the home, the master shoemaker working with his journeymen cobbled shoes for sale in the village store. Following the Revolutionary War, goods could move freely across the nation. Opportunities for American industry were limited, however, by the flow of cheap imports from England. In the 1780s, Ebenezer Breed and Steven Collins—two shoemakers from Lynn, Massachusetts—petitioned the Congress to impose tariffs on foreign-made footwear. In 1789, Congress imposed a protective tariff of 50 percent, giving the early American companies a chance to grow. In 1791 over 8 million pairs of shoes were made in the United States, while fewer than 75,000 pairs were imported (McDermott 1918).

Massachusetts became the center of the American shoe industry. Small shoe shops opened in many of the towns in the state. Elegant shoes were made for the local market, but cheap shoes were exported for the slaves working in the cotton fields of the American South and the sugar plantations of the Caribbean. Lynn became a center for ladies' shoes. By 1829 the town had a population of five thousand, many working in the shoe shops. Within thirty years the factory system was well established. In 1860, Lynn's shoe and boot manufacturers employed 5,767 men and 2,862 women.

The Mammoth Douglas Factory. Brockton, Mass.

The mammoth William Douglas shoe factory, founded in Brockton in 1876, sold men's shoes at $3.50 a pair. At that time Massachusetts was the center of the American shoe industry.

Starting in the 1840s, industrialization led to the explosive growth of the shoe and boot industry. Mass-production methods replaced the cobbler's craft. Large steam-powered factories were built to hold hundreds of workers, each specializing in a given task. New machinery to cut and stitch leather greatly speeded up the rate of manufacture. Mass immigration provided workers for the factories and a market for the products, but soon the factories were producing much more than the local market could absorb. Improvements in transportation and communication allowed the shoe manufacturers of Massachusetts to find markets in other states and abroad.

In 1860, 100,000 people were working in the American shoe shops (70 percent of them men and 30 percent women). Two-thirds of these workers and two-thirds of all shoes and boots made in America came from Massachusetts. The Civil War provided abundant work for the Massachusetts shoe factories. The hundreds of shoe companies large and small in turn created opportunities for the commission houses and wholesale firms, which found customers for the enormous numbers of shoes made in Massachusetts factories. Although most of these shoe factories were outside Boston, some were in the city. Thomas G. Plant started as a shoemaker in Bath, Maine. Opportunity took him to Lynn, where he built a shoe factory. In 1897 he moved his factory to Jamaica Plain in Boston. The Plant Company grew to be the largest producer of ladies' shoes in the world. The company eventually occupied eight buildings with sixteen acres of floor space. At the start of the twentieth century, the Plant Company employed five thousand workers making seventeen thousand pairs of shoes a day.

The Massachusetts shoe and boot industry remained much more fragmented than the textiles industry. Very large shoe factories were built in Boston, Brockton, and Malden, but Lynn and Haverhill were home to many smaller firms. At the time of the World's Columbian Exposition in Chicago (1893), Lynn had over three hundred shoe companies and Haverhill over two hundred. Annual wages paid at that time to the workers in the factories varied from a low of $287 to $686, with an average of $442 (Quinn 1892).

Various industries allied to shoe manufacture sprang up in Massachusetts. The shipping firm of Bryant & Sturgis, located on Long Wharf in Boston, sent its ships to California to take on cargoes of hides. In the days before the Panama Canal, these sailing ships took eighteen months or more to complete their journey. The firm of Tyler, Rice & Co. sent its ships to Argentina in search of hides. One of the largest leather companies was the Howes Brothers Company at 321 Summer Street, Boston. It had distribution warehouses in New York, St. Louis, and Chicago and in England, and a leather purchasing office in Buenos Aires. In 1870 raw leather sold for twelve and a half cents a pound in Boston.

The Hub Gore Company of Boston boasted that it made the finest elastic for use in the manufacture of shoes. The company's heart-shape trademark was its guarantee against shrinking, fading, or bagging. M. S. Camil of 81–83 South Street, Boston, produced Alma brand shoe polish (patented in 1884). Made especially for ladies' shoes, it pledged to soften and preserve the leather. "Try it once and you will never use any other," its ads promised, warning, "Beware of imitations." The dust and grime of city streets were a boon to the shoe polish (called blacking) industry. In Boston, the George H. Wood & Co. trade card advertising ladies' shoe polish shows a dance class held in an elegant room. A row of pretty women, dressed in the European style of the early eighteenth century, curtsey with their left feet pointing forward, showing off their shiny black shoes. The bewigged male dance instructor, right foot forward, looks delighted. Whittemore Bros. & Co. of 174–180 Lincoln Street was another Boston company making polish for ladies' shoes. Its Gilt Edge brand claimed to be the "only gloss dressing for Ladies shoes that contains oil to soften the leather and make it wear longer."[*]

The port of Boston became a world leader in the importation of raw and tanned leather and the exporting of shoes and boots. In warehouses in the leather district, which developed near the port, leather was sorted and graded for sale to the shoe factories. Here were also the wholesale leather brokers and the commission houses that sold the finished shoes and boots. The Great Fire of 1872 severely disrupted the shoe industry in Boston. The blaze broke out at the corner of Summer and Kingston streets, in the heart of the leather district. It burned down 229 wholesale shoe dealers and 189 leather concerns, as well as 100 kindred businesses. Losses exceeded $10 million—a fortune at the time. The Great Fire consumed nearly all the finished leather needed for the factories in the eastern states, leaving them without supplies. In the wake of the fire, a new leather district was built on South Street and Lincoln Street, close by South Station. At this point Boston was home to one-third of the nation's wholesale leather businesses.

The indigenous peoples of South and Central America had long been familiar with a substance that oozed from certain trees in the forest. They called this substance *caoutchouc* (from the word meaning "weeping tree"). This material, known as India rubber, was first imported into the ports of Salem and Boston during the 1830s and led to much speculation as to its possible uses. Natural rubber did not take well to the New England climate. In the heat of the summer it became sticky and smelled bad, and in the winter it turned rock hard. Charles Goodyear (born in New Haven in 1800) became obsessed with rubber and was determined to find its commercial uses. Lacking training in chemistry, he spent years conducting random experiments with this natural substance, in the process impoverishing himself and his family. In 1838, Goodyear moved to Massachusetts to continue his experiments at the Eagle India Rubber Company in the town of Woburn. After more years of work he finally came up with a formula to keep rubber pliable even at extremes of weather. The rubber was combined with sulfur, spirits of turpentine, and lead and then heated to a temperature of 270 degrees Fahrenheit. This process was called vulcanization, derived from Vulcan, the Roman god of fire.

---

[*]History buffs will recall that in 1824 the twelve-year-old Charles Dickens was sent to work at Warren's Blacking, a shoe polish maker near the Thames River in London. Here he worked for six or seven shillings a week, while his father sat in the Debtors' Prison. The humiliating and lonely experience was later depicted in his novels *Oliver Twist* and *Hard Times*.

BOSTON
RUBBER SHOE
Co.

State House, Boston.

BOSTON
RUBBER SHOE CO.
BOSTON
U.S.A.
TRADE MARK

SEPTEMBER				
Sun	5	12	19	26
Mon	6	13	20	27
Tue	7	14	21	28
Wed 1	8	15	22	29
Thu 2	9	16	23	30
Fri 3	10	17	24	
Sat 4	11	18	25	

OCTOBER				
Sun	3	10	17	31
Mon	4	11	18	25
Tue	5	12	19	26
Wed	6	13	20	27
Thu	7	14	21	28
Fri 1	8	15	22	29
Sat 2	9	16	23	30

The Boston Rubber Shoe Company of Malden was established by Elisha Slade Converse. This scene of Boston drawn for the company's calendar for the year 1897 shows the Massachusetts State House and a corner of the Boston Common.

BOSTON RUBBER SHOE CO.

NOVEMBER

Sun	Mon	Tue	Wed	Thu	Fri	Sat
	1	2	3	4	5	6
7	8	9	10	11	12	13
14	15	16	17	18	19	20
21	22	23	24	25	26	27
28	29	30				

DECEMBER

Sun	Mon	Tue	Wed	Thu	Fri	Sat
			1	2	3	4
5	6	7	8	9	10	11
12	13	14	15	16	17	18
19	20	21	22	23	24	25
26	27	28	29	30	31	

Trinity Church,
Boston.

BOSTON RUBBER SHOE CO. BOSTON U.S.A.
TRADE MARK

The Boston Rubber Shoe Company. This picture from its calendar for 1897 shows Trinity Church in Copley Square after a snowstorm. Rubber overshoes are part of the attire of the well-dressed man and woman.

ABOVE AND OPPOSITE: *G. H. Wood, Whittemore Brothers, and M. S. Cahill were some of the Boston shoe polish companies, especially for ladies' shoes, circa 1885.*

Boston's retail shoe trade was centered along Winter Street, Tremont Row, and Hanover Street. The wholesale leather district burned in the Great Fire of 1872 but was rebuilt on South Street and Lincoln Street, near South Station.

Vulcanized rubber found many commercial uses, not least in the footwear industry. In 1853, Elisha Slade Converse and his older brother James formed the Boston Rubber Shoe Company in the village of Malden, a few miles north of Boston. The company made rubber shoes and rubber overshoes for the winter slush. It grew to 3,500 workers and became the largest employer in the town. In 1882, Elisha Converse was elected the first mayor of Malden. His generosity to the town is seen in the First Baptist Church and the Converse Public Library, which he funded. In 1908, Malden became the home of a second rubber shoe company. It was founded by Marquis Mills, who took his mother's last name, Converse, and called his company the Converse Rubber Shoe Company, no doubt to capitalize on the famous name. Converse Rubber Shoe grew with the expanding interest in sports. The Converse Rubber line of sports shoes included the Chuck Taylor All Star basketball sneaker. Both the Boston Rubber Shoe and the Converse Rubber Shoe companies were later bought out by larger firms, and shoemaking finally left Malden in the 1930s.

The market for Massachusetts-made shoes greatly expanded during the First World War. Millions of pairs of shoes were shipped to the battle-fields of Europe at a time when foreign competition was restricted. In 1915, Massachusetts accounted for half of all the shoe workers in America, and its factories produced half of the nation's shoes. In 1916, Brockton alone shipped out nearly 800,000 pairs of shoes. The leather importers, shoe factories, wholesale houses, and retail stores created an enormous business in Massachusetts.

The Boston retail shoe market centered on Winter and Summer streets, Tremont Row, and Washington Street. Massachusetts men spread across the nation establishing retail outlets. The L. C. Bliss Company of Whitman, Massachusetts, sold its Regal custom bench-made shoes out of its store at 109 Summer Street at a cost of $3.50 a pair. The company kept branch stores on Broadway in New York, Dearborn Street in Chicago, Chestnut Street in Philadelphia, Pennsylvania Street in Washington, D.C., and other cities. The mammoth Douglas shoe factory of Brockton claimed to make twenty thousand pairs of shoes a day for sale in its sixty-three stores and three thousand dealers across the nation.

The leaders of the shoe industry were important men in Massachusetts. William Claflin, governor of the Commonwealth from 1869 to 1872, owned a shoe company in Milford. William Lewis Douglas started as a shoemaker's apprentice but later built the great W. L. Douglas Shoe Company in Brockton. He served as mayor of Brockton and from 1905 to 1906 as governor of Massachusetts. A group of Lynn shoe executives under the leadership of Charles A. Coffin decided late in the nineteenth century that their city needed another major industry. The chose the new field of electricity and hired Elihu Thomson, an inventive genius, to move to Lynn to set up the new enterprise. Coffin and Thomson bought a building in West Lynn to manufacture electric lighting equipment. With Coffin's business savvy and Thomson's inventiveness, the company expanded and soon replaced shoes as Lynn's primary industry. Coffin and Thomson named their enterprise General Electric, which subsequently became one of the world's largest companies.

The dominance of Massachusetts in leather and rubber footwear was due largely to its early evolution from craftsmanship to mass production. Massachusetts men designed the tools that made it possible for new immigrants to learn quickly the skills needed to make the components for the shoe. In 1858, Lyman R. Blake from Whitman, Massachusetts, modified a Singer sewing machine to attach leather soles to uppers. The rights to this crude machine were sold to Gordon McKay, who refined it. By 1870 the McKay Shoe Machine Company was selling thousands of machines. Each McKay machine did the work of ten skilled workers using hand tools. In 1871, Charles Goodyear Jr. patented a stitching machine to make welt shoes. Next came the humble immigrant Jan Ernst Matzelinger, working in a Lynn shoe factory, the inventor of the hand lasting machine. These three machines revolutionized the shoe industry. Sidney W. Winslow Jr. brought these three innovations together in the United Shoe Machinery Corporation. Known affectionately as "The Shoe," the corporation became the world's premier shoe machinery company.

The United Shoe Machinery Corporation occupied an enormous factory in the town of Beverly, Massachusetts. By 1910 the factory housed 4,500 workers. The corporation leased rather than sold its equipment, and shoe factories throughout the United States and abroad paid the corporation royalties on every pair of shoes made using its machines. The company's technicians were sent far and wide to repair or replace the shoe machinery. The dominance of "The Shoe" and its leasing practices led to antitrust battles dating as far back as 1911. Its stock was long regarded as one of the bluest of the blue-chip investments until 1968, when the Supreme Court interpreted the Sherman Act to find that the United Shoe Machinery Corporation was engaged in monopolistic practices. The dominance of Massachusetts shoemaking and the shoe machinery industry was over.

4

❧ PIANOS AND ORGANS

Opening shop in 1791, Benjamin Crehore of Massachusetts was among the first piano makers in America. His ancestors arrived during the first years of the Massachusetts Bay Colony and settled in the town of Milton, to the south of Boston. Before his time, pianos were imported from Europe or made of European components. A number of gifted craftsmen, such as John Osborn and the brothers Alpheus and Lewis Babcock, worked in Crehore's piano shop. In 1825, Alpheus Babcock patented a single-piece iron frame for the piano. This innovation allowed pianos to be made larger, with longer and tighter strings that produced a bigger tone and prevented changes to the sound due to humidity and dampness. Small-scale piano shops opened in and around Boston, where cabinetmakers crafted each piano from start to finish before going on to make the next instrument. Eventually the factory methods of production in textiles and shoes were applied to piano making. The piano companies were built around a central steam power plant in which power was transmitted along pulleys and leather belts to the workbench. Now, each workman specialized in making a single component, using power tools, before assembly of the completed piano.

Jonas Chickering, who was to become America's first renowned piano maker, was born in Mason Village, New Hampshire, in 1798. His father was a blacksmith, but Jonas chose the trade of a cabinetmaker. While still a boy, he repaired a London-made piano in the town of New Ipswich. At age twenty he moved to Boston to work for John Osborn, serving his apprenticeship as a cabinetmaker and joiner. In 1823, Chickering and James Stewart set up the firm of Stewart & Chickering to build pianos out of a small shop on Tremont Street. Stewart soon gave up the business, leaving Chickering as the sole owner. In 1830, Chickering formed a new partnership to make uprights, this time with John Mackay, a sea captain who imported rosewood and

The Hallet & Davis Piano Company was established in 1839. Its factory was built around the steam power plant. A system of overhead pulleys and leather belting carried the power to each workbench in the six-story factory.

mahogany for the pianoforte cases. A few years later, Mackay was lost at sea together with a cargo of rare South American woods destined for Chickering factory. In 1843, Chickering received a patent for his improved one-piece iron frame and began building grand pianos with eighty-five keys instead of the sixty previously used in smaller instruments. These modifications improved the stability and tone of his pianos. Chickering also devised a method for over-stringing the square piano by setting the strings in two rows rather than one. This method not only saved space but also improved the sound by placing the bass strings over the more resonant section of the sounding board.

The excellence of his workmanship and the growing affluence of Bostonians greatly increased the demand for Chickering's pianos. Jonas Chickering was active in Boston's musical life and served for many years as the president of the revered Handel and Haydn Society. The Chickering piano won a prize in 1851 at the World's Fair at the Crystal Palace in London.

In 1837, Chickering built a piano factory at 300 Washington Street in Boston. When the factory burned down in 1852, he quickly set about building an even larger factory at 791 Tremont Street, on the new landfill of Boston's South End. This enormous piano factory was five stories in height and 262 feet in length. It was said to be the largest building in America, save for the Capitol in Washington. At the center of the building was a large steam engine that powered the sawing and planing machines for the whole factory. The Chickering factory supported its own arts department, where special designs were made to suit different-sized rooms and differing tastes. An ornate Louis XIV–style piano was a favorite model. In 1867 a full iron-frame Chickering grand piano caused a sensation and won a gold medal at the World Exposition in Paris. Jonas Chickering is credited with making piano manufacture a major American business. Abraham Lincoln kept the Chickering Grand model 5070 while he occupied the White House. Presidents Franklin Pierce and James Buchanan as well as the nation's twenty-sixth president, Theodore Roosevelt, also used Chickering pianos while in the White House.

Jonas Chickering died in December 1853, before the new building was completed. After his death, the business was taken over by his three Boston-born sons, Thomas, Charles, and George. Renamed Chickering & Sons, it was one of the largest piano manufacturers in the nation. Soon after the Civil War, Chickering was producing over two thousand pianos a year. Chickering Hall, seating two thousand people, opened on Fifth Avenue in New York in 1875 with the eminent pianist Hans von Bulow as the soloist. Boston had its own Chickering Hall, near the new Symphony Hall on Huntington Avenue. The virtuoso pianists of the day played at these concert halls. Following the death of the last of the Chickering brothers, the company began to have financial problems and joined with other piano makers to form the American Piano Company.

The early success of Chickering in Boston was part of a nationwide phenomenon. The rapid urbanization of America fostered the growth of concert halls, theaters, and dance halls. This exposure to music encouraged upwardly mobile families to purchase a piano for entertainment in the home. Keeping house and playing the piano were among the accomplishments expected of the well-off women of the period. Piano teachers were in demand to pass on musical skills to the next generation of well-to-do ladies.

Piano companies were established in New York, Philadelphia, Chicago, and other American cities. Stores selling organs, pianos, and sheet music opened in small and large towns across the country. The major piano companies established sales offices in other states, as well as selling their pianos abroad. In the Boston area, piano and organ factories were hard at work producing thousands of instruments each year. At first, most of these factories were located on Washington Street; they then moved to larger factories in the South End, with salesrooms in town on Tremont and Boylston streets.

The piano pioneer Benjamin Crehore had received financial help for his venture from the Vose family, who were prominent in business in Milton. James Whiting Vose (born 1818) learned the trade of cabinetmaking and worked in various Boston piano shops before opening his own factory in 1851. Later, he was joined in the business by his three sons. The three-story factory was soon too small, and Vose & Sons Piano Company moved to a much larger building in Watertown, where it manufactured over 100,000 pianos, both uprights and grands. The pianos were offered for sale in the company's Boston showrooms at 170 Tremont Street. Vose & Sons remained a family business for many years until the company was sold to the American Piano Company.

Hallet & Davis Company, established in 1839, built pianos out of its workshop on Washington Street. Some fifty years later the company expanded into a larger factory in Dorchester. While in the White House, President James A. Garfield kept a Hallet & Davis piano. Another Boston piano maker, the Everett Piano Company, was located in the South End at the corner of Harrison Avenue and Waltham Street and maintained its showrooms at 159 Tremont Street. The "sweet-toned" Everett pianos became especially popular for use in homes. The company was founded by Frank A. Lee, who sold it to the John Church Company of Cincinnati. The McPhail Piano Company was located at 1337–1359 Washington Street, with showrooms at 167 Tremont Street. Its founder, A. M. McPhail, was born in New Brunswick and moved to Boston, where he established his piano company.

The Emerson Piano Company had its start in Boston in 1849. Its founder, William P. Emerson, specialized at first in low-priced instru-

TOP: *This trade card was issued by the Ivers & Pond Piano Company of Boston, which maintained its showrooms at 217 Tremont Street. John F. Kennedy installed his Ivers & Pond piano in the White House during his presidency.*

BOTTOM: *Vose & Sons started making pianos in 1851. Their showrooms were on Piano Row at 170 Tremont Street, Boston.*

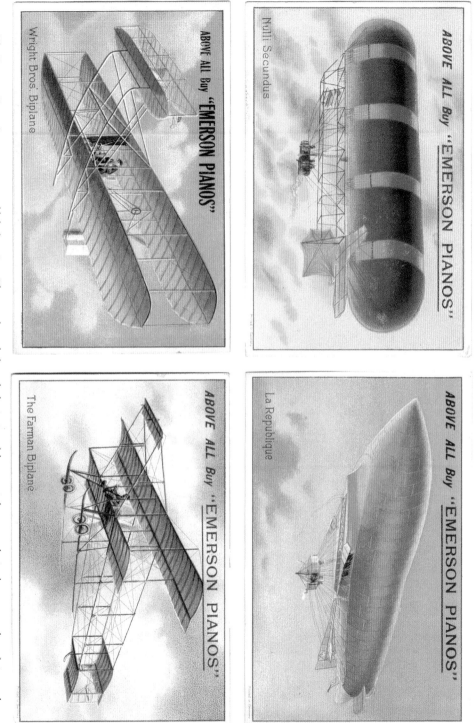

ABOVE ALL Buy "EMERSON PIANOS"

Nulli Secundus

ABOVE ALL Buy "EMERSON PIANOS"

Wright Bros. Biplane

ABOVE ALL Buy "EMERSON PIANOS"

La Republique

ABOVE ALL Buy "EMERSON PIANOS"

The Farman Biplane

The Emerson Piano Company was established in 1849. These trade cards from the beginning of the twentieth century depict the new wonders of air travel, including the Wright Brothers' biplane.

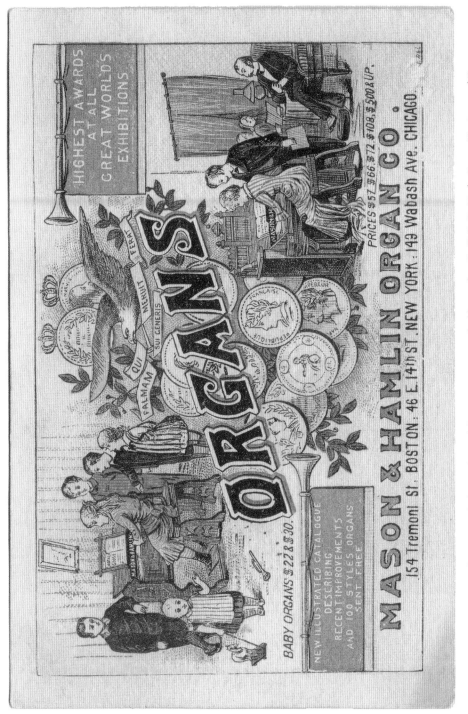

ABOVE AND FOLLOWING PAGE: *Boston was the home of several illustrious pipe organs builders such as E. & G. G. Hook, George Hastings, and Ernest Skinner. Reed organs for use in the home were built by Mason & Hamlin among others. Reed organs were relatively cheap, costing from $22 to $108 (1885 prices). The city of Worcester had several organ companies. Home organs lost popularity after 1890 as they yielded to the piano.*

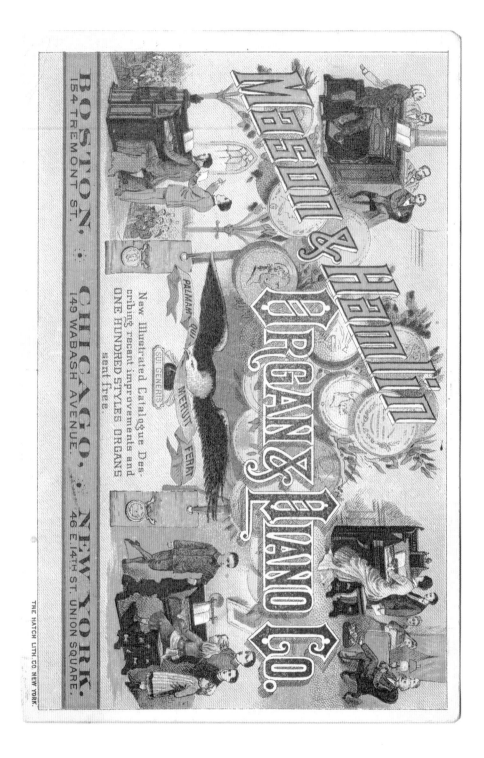

ments. In 1854 he hired C. C. Briggs to build a higher-quality piano. Briggs, an expert piano maker, improved the quality of the Emerson product. Later, at 1125 Washington Street, Briggs built pianos carrying his own name. W. H. Ivers began building pianos in Dedham in 1876. Four years later he took on a partner, and the Ivers & Pond Piano Company moved to Boston, then across the Charles River to Albany Street in Cambridgeport. When operating at full capacity, the plant employed 175 men and made three thousand pianos a year. The Ivers & Pond showrooms were on "Piano Row" at 183 Tremont Street. Ivers & Pond supplied pianos to the New England Conservatory of Music, then one of the largest music schools in the world. President John F. Kennedy had his Ivers & Pond piano installed at the White House.

The Guild Piano Company, established in 1861, maintained its Boston showrooms at 217 Tremont Street. The company prided itself on the "pure and sympathetic tone" of its pianos. These instruments were sold throughout the United States as well as in Europe, Cuba, South America, and India. The Smith American Piano and Organ Company, founded in 1834, was located at 531 Tremont Street. Smith American offered the assurance that its pianos were the best available, with their "full, rich, pure singing tone; finely regulated, delicate touch; perfectly even, well-balanced scale and their excellent finish." Both Kramer Pianos and Lexington Pianos were built in Boston. The New England Organ Company had its start in 1871 on Purchase Street in New Bedford. The company later expanded its operations to pianos and moved to 1397–1399 Washington Street in Boston. New England Organ & Piano later joined with Merrill Piano Manufacturing Company (established 1885), remaining in business until 1926. In 1892, William W. Poole started the Poole Piano Company on Appleton Street in Boston. Years later, the company moved to larger quarters on Albany Street.

George Steck, born in Cassel, Germany, where he learned the piano trade, came to Boston in 1857 and started his own piano company. George Steck & Company achieved international fame after his piano won first prize at the 1873 Vienna Exposition. The Steck piano factory was built along the Neponset River, where a large dock connected the plant to Boston Harbor. The company's storage yard had room for 1.5 million feet of lumber used to build the pianos. Four hundred workers were employed at the Neponset site. Later the Steck company expanded abroad, with factories in England, France, Germany, and Australia. At Steck Hall, opened on Clinton Place, New York City, in 1865, famous pianists would showcase the Steck piano.

Henry F. Miller was born in Providence, Rhode Island. He was trained as a musician before he decided to serve an apprenticeship at a Boston piano factory. Miller worked for several Boston piano companies until 1863, when he set out on his own. He was one of the pioneers of the American square grand piano, which he made in his workshop at 611 Washington Street. His three sons—all graduates of the Massachusetts Institute of Technology—joined the company. The Henry F. Miller & Sons piano factory moved in 1880 to a large red-brick facility in Wakefield, where the company built its Colonial brand piano and its Lyric baby grand. Miller & Sons had its Boston showrooms at 156 Tremont Street and warehouses in Philadelphia and Cincinnati. Its pianos were sold by dealers throughout America. Early in the twentieth century, the company expanded into the Chicago market and produced a line of furniture to match its pianos.

The story of Morris Steinert began in Bavaria in 1831. He had an ear for music, and early in his life he learned to play the violin and the piano. Young Morris came to New York as a nineteen-year-old and earned his keep selling eyeglasses door-to-door while trying to make a career as a music teacher. In 1857 he married, moved with his wife to the South, and opened a music store in Athens, Georgia. He found early success preparing the daughters of the well-to-do for their place in southern society. The Civil War forced the Steinerts to close their store and to return to the North. New York, however, was not hospitable, and the family moved on to New Haven, where Morris Steinert taught Yale students and established an orchestra, which later became the New Haven Symphony. He opened a music shop in the town and was selected as the local agent for the Steinway piano. His seven sons all joined the business, and M. Steinert & Sons opened stores in other New England towns. Their success in New England encouraged the Steinerts in 1883 to move their headquarters from New York to Boston. In 1896, Steinert Hall opened at 162 Boylston Street, overlooking the Boston Common, adjacent to the company's showrooms. Some of the world's greatest pianists performed in this concert hall.

In 1901, Steinert & Sons introduced its own line of pianos. First was the Steinertone piano, using Morris's own design for the actions. Two years later the company bought the Woodbury and Jewett piano works, situated in the town of Leominster, Massachusetts. To these lines the Steinerts added the Curtis and Hume piano models. The Curtis was named for the Curtis Hotel in the Berkshires, where Morris spent the summers. The Hume was named for the company's general manager, Archibald Hume. Steinert & Sons still carried the illustrious Steinway piano, but the Steinway Company threatened to withdraw its agency unless Morris Steinert ceased using his similar-sounding name on his pianos. The Steinert and Steinertone pianos henceforth became Hume pianos. The stock market crash of 1929 forced the closing of the Steinert-owned piano factories. Only three of the retail stores survived.

≈

Thomas Appleton (1785–1872) was a renowned Boston cabinetmaker. While still in his twenties he trained with the leading organ and piano makers of the town, including Alpheus Babcock. In 1820, Appleton opened his own shop, making organs in the eighteenth-century English style. Several Appleton organs have survived, including a splendid 1830 pipe organ now in the musical instrument collection of the Metropolitan Museum in New York. Early in the nineteenth century, Boston took the lead along with New York as one of the main organ-building centers in the United States. The market for pipe organs expanded massively with immigration, urbanization, and the building of grand churches, music academies, universities, music houses, and symphony halls. These organ companies also built the choral organs for smaller congregations. Massachusetts was the home of many dozens of pipe and reed organ companies. Their success endured from the early nineteenth century until the Great Depression.

Among the founding fathers of the better-known companies were Elias and George Greenleaf Hook, sons of a cabinetmaker from Salem, Massachusetts. The brothers adapted their craft to organ making and in 1827 formed their own company in Salem before moving it to Boston. E. & G. G. Hook & Co. grew into one of the leading pipe organ builders in America, making several dozen instruments each year. In 1864 the Hook brothers built the thunderous 52-stop, 3,504-pipe instrument that holds center stage at Mechanics Hall in Worcester,

Massachusetts. In 1872, Francis H. Hastings joined the partnership, which became Hook & Hastings. Several of its workers went on to establish their own organ companies. One of these workers was George Sherburne Hutchings, who started as a cabinetmaker but rose to become superintendent of the Hook factory. Later he established the Hutchings Organ Company, which remained in business until 1917. James E. Treat of Methuen and Joseph W. Steere of Springfield also had success building pipe organs.

Ernest M. Skinner (1866–1960) was born in Clarion, Pennsylvania, the son of a traveling tenor from Lowell, Massachusetts, and his soprano wife, from Houlton, Maine. They eventually settled in the manufacturing town of Taunton, Massachusetts, where the elder Skinners formed a light opera company, specializing in Gilbert and Sullivan. Ernest became fascinated with pipe organs while still a boy. In his early twenties Ernest moved to Boston and worked as a tuner for several small-scale organ builders before going to work for the Hutchings Organ Company. In 1898 he traveled to Europe to study the great organs, especially the organ at St. George's Hall in Liverpool. On his return to Boston, Ernest Skinner supervised the installation of many of the Hutchings organs, including one at Boston's Symphony Hall (Whitney 2003).

Skinner left Hutchings to set up his own organ company at 387 East Eighth Street in South Boston, the site of a former rubber works. From 1901 to 1931 the Skinner Organ Company built hundreds of pipe organs for cathedrals, concert halls, and colleges and became the most renowned name in American organs. To accommodate the increased work during the roaring 1920s, Skinner moved his company to a large four-story building on Sydney Street in Boston's Dorchester section, where he employed 250 craftspeople (Holden 1987). The company maintained a sales office at 677 Fifth Avenue in New York City. Skinner built the organs for the New England Conservatory of Music, the Eastman School of Music, and the universities of Boston, Chicago, and Michigan as well as for Yale and Princeton. A Skinner organ graces the National Cathedral in Washington, D.C., and Severance Hall, the home of the Cleveland Orchestra.

Ernest Skinner left the company at the start of the Great Depression. Renamed Aeolian-Skinner, under the leadership of Arthur H. Marks and G. Donald Harrison the company continued to build organs, including in 1949 the organ still at Symphony Hall in Boston. This organ incorporated parts of the hall's original organ, built fifty years earlier by George Hutchings and Ernest Skinner. The enlarged organ with fifty-nine voices and over 4,500 pipes was inaugurated on October 7, 1949, when the famed organist E. Power Biggs and the Boston Symphony Orchestra played Handel's Organ Concerto in D minor, op. 7, no. 4, under the baton of the conductor Charles Munch.

Aeolian-Skinner also built the replacement for the famed organ of the Mormon Tabernacle in Salt Lake City. In addition to organs for large institutions, the Aeolian-Skinner Company also made money building pipe organs for the homes of the wealthy. Changing tastes and the Great Depression put an end to this niche market. The great age of the Boston organ building was drawing to a close. The Aeolian-Skinner Organ Company remained in the Boston area until its demise in the 1970s.

Massachusetts was also a major center for the mass production of reed organs, built for use in the home. Lowell Mason served as head of the Boston Academy of Music. Mason introduced music into the curriculum of the Boston public schools. He was also active in the area of church music and is credited with writing the music to over four hundred hymns. His son Henry, also a gifted pianist, studied in Germany. In 1854, Henry Mason formed a partnership with Emmons Hamlin, an expert on the mechanics of sound. The Mason & Hamlin Company built reed organs in its steam-powered plant on Harrison Avenue in Boston's South End. The factory grew to become one of the largest reed organ producers in the world, turning out two hundred parlor organs each week. The organs ranged in price from $50 to $500 and were sold throughout the United States as well as in markets abroad. After 1882, when the demand for home organs began to decline, the company shifted to piano manufacture. Mason & Hamlin patented its improved method of stringing in 1883. According to the company's advertisements this was "the greatest improvement in pianos in half a century." Mason & Hamlin became one of the great brand names in American-built pianos, with factories in Boston, New York, Chicago, and Kansas City.

The Commonwealth's innovative second city, Worcester, was a major center of production of musical instruments. Jeremiah Carthart and Elias Needham began building their Melodeon organ in Worces-

ter in 1846 but moved their company to New York City in 1850. The
Loring & Blake Organ Company, established in 1868, boasted that its
Palace organs were "The Best in the World," having won numerous
prizes, including the highest honors at the World's Exhibition at Mel-
bourne, Australia, in 1889. Loring & Blake later moved its works to
Toledo, Ohio. The Worcester Organ Company and the Mason &
Risch Vocalion Company also began in Worcester. In the small Massachusetts town of Bridgewater, the brothers Isaac and Edmund Packard built organs. The company later moved to Fort Wayne, Indiana,
and was renamed the Fort Wayne Organ Company.

During the first quarter of the twentieth century, Massachusetts-
based organ companies tried to enter the vast theater organ market for
vaudeville halls and the silent movies. But the Wurlitzer Company of
Cincinnati and the Bartola Musical Instrument Company of Oshkosh,
Wisconsin, dominated this market. The coming of the talking movies
put an end to the theater organ.

≈

The great expansion in pianos for the home led to a demand for sheet
music. The Oliver Ditson Company of Boston, the first musical publishing house in America, met this need. Young Oliver began his career as an
apprentice printer. At age twenty-four he opened his own printing shop at
107 Washington Street. Here he combined his knowledge of printing
with his skills as organist at the Bulfinch Street Church. In 1836, Ditson
copyrighted his first musical printing. His store claimed to stock over
twenty thousand pieces of sheet music, from Europe and the United
States, for all instruments as well as for the voice. Pianos and other musical instruments were offered for sale or rent at Ditson's store. Ditson
moved to larger premises at 115 Washington Street and took on partners
to help with the fast-growing sheet music business. The company expanded
to New York, Philadelphia, and Chicago. Oliver Ditson died in 1888, but
the company carrying his name continued to expand. It established the
Monthly Musical Record, which became in 1898 the *Musical Record and
Review.* The need for even more space prompted the company to move its
printing works down the street to a ten-story building at 451 Washington
Street. The company headquarters were located along Piano Row, first at
150 Tremont Street and later at 178 Tremont Street.

As Boston's piano and organ companies opened branches elsewhere, the skills learned in Boston spread across the country. A branch of the Chickering company opened in Chicago, where the Acousti-grande piano was made. Moses W. Brown of Hampton, New Hampshire, came to Boston in 1886 to learn the piano trade. Ten years later he returned to his hometown to start a piano shop behind his house at 394 Winnacunnet Street. M. W. Brown Piano Manufacturers made pianos to order, for $175 and up. The cases of the pianos were made from walnut, mahogany, rosewood, or oak.

During the nineteenth century there were dozens of organ and piano companies operating in Boston. The Boston companies generally followed the English school of piano making, while the New York makers were more influenced by the German school. Boston-built pianos were sold across America and abroad, and other Massachusetts companies supplied the keys, strings, frames, hammers, and felts and the actions needed to make a piano. For instance, the Washburn & Moen Company of Worcester, Massachusetts, specialized in piano wire.

Organ and piano production constituted an important segment of the economy of nineteenth-century Boston. The piano factories together employed many hundreds of workers (in its prime, the Chickering factory alone had over six hundred workers). Clustered on Piano Row—actually a few blocks on Tremont and Boylston streets and a section of Washington Street—were some twenty piano showrooms. The piano companies used their showrooms to display their brands. There were also piano emporiums, selling brands made by companies outside Boston. Among these were the Blake's Great Piano Palace at 612 Washington Street and W. H. Berry at 592 Washington Street, which specialized in Kranich & Bach and William Schaeffer pianos. The companies offered convenient methods of payment, with terms up to three years.

Pianos were extensively advertised in the local and national press and in magazines. Trade cards were given out at the stores and were a popular method of advertising. Several of the piano companies used the talents of local lithographers such as Bufford & Sons and the Beacon Lithographic Company. Advertising was focused on the women of the household. Many of the trade cards show cherubs, adorable young girls, or pretty young women. The backs of the trade cards related the virtues of the pianos and described the terms of purchase. Emerson

The Simplex, built on May Street, Worcester, was but one of a thousand player pianos offered by American companies. A pneumatic or electric-powered mechanism inside the instrument read the piano rolls, making "musicians of us all." The gradual shift from the organ to the piano, the player piano, and then the gramophone undermined musicianship as a necessary component of cultivated life. Advertisement from 1903.

Pianos were pitched to the emerging middle class, while the costly grand pianos made by Chickering and Henry Miller were destined for the elegant music rooms of the Proper Bostonians.

The player piano (also called the pianola) gained popularity early in the twentieth century. By using punched piano rolls, the player could sit at the piano and produce wondrous sounds without actually depressing the keys or the pedals. Many companies, including several in Massachusetts, installed pneumatic or electric-powered mechanisms inside their pianos to read the piano rolls. One of the largest was the Simplex Piano Player Company of Worcester. In Pittsfield, the Tel-Electic Company made mechanisms to read piano rolls that could be installed in any type of upright or grand piano.

At the peak of the industry, Massachusetts was producing one-quarter of the nation's organs and pianos. Chickering looked to become the great American piano company, making one out of every ten pianos built in the United States. But the company lost its creative and commercial edge after the deaths of John Mackay and Jonas Chickering. In time, Chicago and New York became far larger piano centers than Boston. The New York firm of Steinway & Sons especially rose to prominence. Twenty-five thousand pianos were sold in the United States in 1869. By 1910, half of the pianos made in America came from western factories, especially in Cincinnati and Chicago. The total value of pianos made in America during 1910 alone was around $100 million. These pianos were sold by mail order, in department stores, and in company-owned outlets.

American production reached its peak that year with 350,000 pianos, half the world's total production (Germany produced 170,000, England 75,000, and France was a distant fourth at 25,000).

Jones, Ball & Poor, Silversmiths and Jewelers, 226 Washington Street, Boston, circa 1850.
Quality handcrafted silverware was sold to Boston's elite at this store. A half-century earlier
Paul Revere sold silver cutlery, tankards, and tea and coffee urns out of his store nearby at
50 Cornhill.

5

❧ THE DECORATIVE ARTS
Clocks, Watches, Silverware, Jewelry, Pottery, and Glassware

The British introduced the tall clock with a pendulum and weights late in the seventeenth century. The craft of clock making was carried across the ocean and taken up by craftsmen such as Benjamin Willard, Joseph Mulliken, and Daniel Munroe of Massachusetts, Seth Thomas and Eli Terry of Connecticut, and David Rittenhouse of Pennsylvania. The War of Independence and the embargo of 1807–9 slowed the importation of components and clocks from Europe and encouraged the home-grown industry. Elaborate clocks were made for the wealthy, but local clockmakers were interested in developing a wider market. The mass-production methods already used for textiles, shoes, and tools were now applied to clocks. In particular, Bristol, Connecticut, became the center of clock making. Novel designs such as the beehive and the banjo clock caught the public eye. Also popular were clocks that not only told the time but also gave the day and the month and even the phases of the moon and the signs of the zodiac.

Europeans first settled in the village of Grafton, Massachusetts, in 1671, when the English missionary John Eliot came to preach to the Nipmuck Indians. Situated between Boston and Worcester, the area attracted farming families. The town of Grafton was established in 1735, named for the duke of Grafton, grandson to Charles I. Among the town's earliest settlers was the Willard family. Benjamin Willard (1743–1803) left the town as a youth to apprentice with a clockmaker in Hartford, Connecticut. On his return to Grafton in 1764 he set about making clocks in his workshop using English-made tools. While still in his twenties, Benjamin moved his clock-making business to Roxbury to be closer to the Boston market. His younger brothers Aaron, Simon, and Ephraim later joined him there. In turn, some of their sons and grandsons continued in the craft of the Willard clockmakers.

The Waltham Watch Company took pride in the accuracy of its timepieces. Once the world's largest watchmaker, the Waltham factory closed in 1957.

Waltham (Octagon) Opera Watch

A gentlemen's time-piece
Extremely thin without sacrificing accuracy
$95.00 and up

The Willards are regarded as America's first family of clockmakers. Among them all, they built a variety of beautiful clocks, including the grandfather lyre, the regulator, the steeple, and their famous banjo wall clocks. Simon Willard made the clock for the Capitol building in Washington, D.C. His handmade mahogany grandfather clock stood over nine feet tall. Its face featured a rotating moon and a calendar. The movements were weight-driven, and the clock struck the half-hour and the hour. Simon Willard advertised that his chime clocks played six tunes; they were priced at the princely sum of $120. Simon believed in making his clocks available to people of more modest wealth as well. His smaller clocks sold for as little as $10 apiece. His brother Aaron moved beyond single clock manufacture, adopting mass-production methods to build dozens of clocks at the same time. Simon Jr. built the astronomical clock for the observatory at Harvard College. The few Willard clocks that have come down to the present day are prized as among the most valued of American timepieces. The Willard Home at 11 Willard Street, North Grafton, is preserved as a clock museum.

Among the most inventive of the Massachusetts clockmakers was Joseph Henry Eastman. He was born in 1843 in Georgetown. Even as a young boy he showed mechanical ability and was apprenticed to the Edward Howard Watch Company in Roxbury. He became well known in Boston and in 1880 joined the Harvard Clock Company. Four years later, Harvard Clock changed its name to the Boston Clock Company. It was this company that produced patented clocks with two sections, one to hold the time movement and the other for the striking mechanism. The Boston Clock Company was eventually sold to the Ansonia Watch Company of New York.

In 1894, Joseph Eastman gained the support of the town of Chelsea, Massachusetts, to set up his watch company there. The company soon failed. Eastman moved from one clock factory to another but was never quite able to capitalize on his creative abilities. He built elegant banjo and regulator clocks and worked on electric and magnetic clocks, but he ended up virtually destitute. The Chelsea Clock Company emerged from the failed Eastman Company and continues to this day as a maker of elegant marine clocks and barometers.

The largest Massachusetts maker of clocks and watches was the Waltham Watch Company, which had its start in 1853 when David Marsh, Edward Howard, and Aaron Dennison moved their watch company from Boston to Waltham. Their revolutionary plan was to build precision watches and clocks using interchangeable parts. A five-story redbrick building one thousand feet long was built to accommodate 2,500 craftspeople (60 percent male and 40 percent female) in what would become the world's largest watch company. Before the arrival of electricity, five boilers were used to generate over 300 horsepower. The engine room drove the five thousand pulleys and eight miles of belting, bringing power to every workbench in the immense factory.

The growth of population across the nation created a vast market. Waltham chronometers were used extensively by the railroad companies and helped to ensure that the trains ran on time. During the one hundred years of its existence, the company produced over 40 million watches, as well as marine and railroad clocks and compasses. The firm began to decline after World War II in the face of competition from Switzerland and Japan. The American company went out of business in 1957 and was replaced by Waltham International SA of Switzerland. Waltham watches are now made in Neuchâtel, Switzerland, largely for the Japanese market.

The Moulton family, originally from the county of Norfolk in England, settled in Newburyport in 1637 and established themselves as silversmiths. The Moulton clan carried their craft for generations. The fourth William Moulton formed a partnership with his talented apprentice Anthony Towle, who, in 1857, took over the firm, which became Towle Silversmiths, one of the most esteemed names in American silversmithing. The wealthy merchants of Newburyport and Salem purchased the individually crafted cutlery and ornamental silver made by Towle.

The craft of the silversmith was established in Boston long before the Revolutionary War. Boston's outstanding silversmith of the early colonial period was John Coney (1655–1722), who made silver pieces for the leading citizens of the town as well as ornamental silver for the churches and for Harvard College. In his store on Pudding Lane, Jacob Hurd (1702–1758) crafted silver tea services and flatware as elegant as any imported from England. Hurd passed down his skills to his sons, who also created museum-quality silver pieces. In the nineteenth century, Obadiah Rich, James Davis, William Hunneman, and the firm of Churchill & Treadwell, all of Boston, made silver objects for the home and for the church.

The best known of the Boston silversmiths was Paul Revere (1734–1816). He learned his trade from his father and namesake (who trained under John Coney) and inherited his shop. Revere employed several apprentices and built a thriving business among Boston's merchant class. He is of course best remembered for his midnight ride on April 18, 1775, from Boston to Lexington to warn the Patriots that British troops were on the march. After the war, Revere continued his trade. On June 6, 1787, he placed a notice in the *Massachusetts Centinel* stating that he had moved his business from Dock Square to 50 Cornhill. Revere informed his customers that he continued to produce for sale his silver tea and coffee urns, tankards, mustard pots, tureens, knives, forks, and spoons "made in the newest taste [and] done equal to any imported." Revere's neoclassical pieces are among the finest in the history of American silverwork.

Anticipating the decline of the handwork crafts, Paul Revere became one of the earliest American industrialists. In 1788 he opened a foundry to make bolts and nails for the shipyards and bells for the local churches. In 1801 he and his son Joseph opened a copper rolling mill in the town of Canton, Massachusetts. The Revere Copper & Brass Company mass-produced the copper-bottomed pots and pans that became known as Revereware.

Starting in the 1830s, Reed & Barton made sterling silver, silver plate, and pewter goods for the home. The company is still based in Taunton, Massachusetts, a center for metalwork including iron kitchen ranges and parlor stoves. The illustration dates to 1896.

The American silver, silver plate, and pewter trades grew with the Industrial Revolution and the use of mass-production methods. Jewelry making arrived in Attleboro, Massachusetts, in 1810 and replaced textiles as the town's primary industry. Attleboro specialized in low-cost jewelry using gold and silver plate. In 1867 the town had twenty-five jewelry establishments, and seventy-five by 1880. These included the Attleboro Chain Company, Quaker Silver, the Watson Company, and the Frank. W. Whiting Company. The Cobb, Gould Company made silver-plated pins bearing women's names. These were popular birthday gifts in the nineteenth century for Emma, Fanny, Grace, or Belle. The company also made souvenir spoons, forks, and letter openers carrying the name of a town, state, school, or college.

The town of Taunton was a major center for silver and pewter ware. In 1824, Isaac Babbitt created a pewter alloy, which he called "Britannia metal." Babbitt established the Taunton Britannia Manufacturing Company and hired several skilled craftsmen, including Charles E. Barton, to fashion trays, kettles, and bowls using this metal. In time, Barton took over the company and formed a partnership with a local businessman, Henry G. Reed. Their company, known as Reed & Barton, set high standards with its pewter products. In the 1870s, Reed & Barton took advantage of the drop in silver prices and shifted from pewter into silver tableware. Reed & Barton was one of the leaders in electroplating technology and made the transition to silver plate when silver became expensive again.

Although Attleboro and Taunton were the major towns in Massachusetts manufacturing silver and silver plate jewelry and ornaments, Greenfield was home to Lunt Silversmiths, while the town of Gardner had the Arthur Stone Company and the Frank Smith Silver Company. These towns supported generations of skilled jewelry workers. The costume jewelry and silverware produced there were sold widely at home and abroad.

In Massachusetts, pottery developed from utility to decorative art in the hands of the Low family of Chelsea and their employees William H. Grueby and Arthur Osborne. The Lows had roots in Chelsea dating to the eighteenth century. John Gardner Low (1835–1907) studied art in Paris before returning to Chelsea to work for the Chelsea Keramic Art Company. In 1878 he joined with his father to found the J. & J. G. Low Art Tile Company, also in Chelsea. Father and son impressed leaves, grasses, and flowers onto clay to give their tiles a "natural" look.

In 1879 the English-born sculptor Arthur Osborne went to work for Low Art Tile as its principal designer. Osborne brought with him the glaze techniques developed in his family over generations. His elegant designs included animal figures, landscapes, biblical scenes, and mythological creatures, all done in his unique glazes. Many of the fireplaces and doorways in Chelsea and Boston homes were decorated with Osborne-designed ceramic tiles. Osborne returned to England in 1898 to start his own business. Meanwhile, Low Art Tile expanded its product line beyond tiles to jugs and vases. The company enjoyed success until 1907, when John Gardner Low died. Falling standards and competition from cheaper imported brands led to the collapse of Low Art Tile, one of the great tile companies in America.

William H. Grueby (1867–1925), a native of Chelsea, started work at age thirteen for the Low Art Tile Company. He became expert in glazing

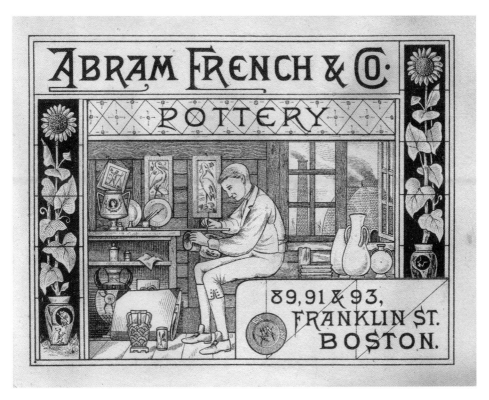

Abram French & Co. of 89–93 Franklin Street, Boston, sold American-made and imported pottery. This illustration dates from around 1880, although the image harks back to the age before mass production. J. & J. G. Low Art Tile and Grueby Faience were two of Boston's major ceramic companies of the time.

and the ceramic process, and at age twenty-six he formed his own company, Grueby & Atwood. The year 1893 proved to be the defining moment of his life when Grueby visited the World's Columbian Exposition in Chicago. He was inspired by the display of hand-thrown work by the great French potter Auguste Delaherche. On his return to Boston he established the Grueby Faience Company. Grueby departed from the traditional to express himself in avant-garde designs, using his own matte pottery glazes. His elegant lamps and vases, done in his distinctive matte green color, caused a sensation. At the 1900 Paris Exposition, Grueby won two gold medals and one silver medal for his pottery. His creativity and individuality contrasted with the mass-production methods of his

times. He became recognized as a leader in the Arts and Crafts movement and was associated with such masters as Gustav Stickley and Louis Comfort Tiffany. Grueby's delicate handcrafted vases and lamps with their luminous colors were soon copied by mass-marketers, who offered inferior but cheaper goods. Company sales fell, and Grueby was forced into bankruptcy. He emerged as the Grueby Pottery Company but finally closed his works in 1920.

The Chelsea Keramic Tile Company found it difficult to compete with its neighbor, Low Art Tile, and moved in 1892 to Dedham, Massachusetts. The company developed a blue and white crackle glaze decorated with crouching rabbits which emerged as the signature style of Dedham Pottery. The crackle effect was achieved by twice firing the pottery, painted with special glazes. The cracking of the glaze occurred when the still warm pieces of pottery came in contact with the cool air. Dedham Pottery produced a full range of tableware, expanding beyond its charming rabbits to include chicks, butterflies, dolphins, and polar bears among its motifs. The company closed its doors in 1943.

Massachusetts was also a major glass center. The New England Glass Company of East Cambridge opened its doors in 1818. Its wide range of objects included blown, pressed, colored, and engraved glass. By the middle of the nineteenth century, the firm employed over five hundred workers and was recognized as one of the largest glassworks in the world. New England Glass continued to grow until the 1870s, when it faced increasing competition from midwestern manufacturers who benefited from lower labor and fuel costs. In 1883 the company was taken over by Edward D. Libbey. Five years later he responded to a strike of the glass workers' union by closing the Cambridge plant and moving operations to Toledo, Ohio, where the Libbey Glass Company has remained to this day.

Deming Jarves worked in Cambridge for New England Glass but left in 1825 to start his own company on Cape Cod, known as the Boston & Sandwich Glass Company. The area had abundant sand for making the glass as well as plentiful trees to fuel his furnaces. In 1837, Jarves opened another glassworks, this time on First Street in South Boston. The company took the name Mount Washington Glass out of respect for the coun-

OPPOSITE: *Parker Brothers of 13–15 Winter Street, Boston, claimed to be New England's largest retail jeweler (ca. 1880).*

try's first president. In 1869 the company left Boston for the former whaling city of New Bedford. Over the years, Mount Washington Glass produced a wide range of decorated vases, flasks, and crockery in delicate colors.

The English-born silversmith Thomas J. Pairpoint was then working as a designer for the Gorham Manufacturing Company of Providence, Rhode Island. In 1880, Pairpoint was persuaded to move to New Bedford, where he established a pewter and silver company next door to Mount Washington Glass. The two companies combined their talents to produce glass and silver sets that proved popular. In 1894, Pairpoint merged his company with Mount Washington Glass to establish the Pairpoint Glass Company.

During the second half of the nineteenth century, over thirty glass companies were operating in Massachusetts. Nearly all of them were gone by the close of the century, victims of rising fuel costs, worker strikes, and fierce competition from midwestern manufacturers.

6

❧ THE PATENT MEDICINE INDUSTRY
OF LOWELL

Lowell was founded in 1822 as America's first planned industrial town. By the close of the nineteenth century, Lowell had become a great textile city of 95,000 people. The immigrants who built Lowell arrived with their large families. They had different habits and customs than the Yankee workers, mostly young women, who has come before them, and few, apart from the Irish, spoke English. Desperate for work and shelter, they accepted lower wages and poorer conditions. Unlike the factory girls, the new immigrants were not offered housing by the mills but had to find their own accommodations in the town. The Irish, French Canadians, Portuguese, Poles, Jews, Greeks, and other immigrants settled in their own sections of Lowell and developed ethnic enclaves. Relations between mill management and the workers grew steadily worse. There were frequent strikes, wage cuts, and mill closings. Working sixty hours a week with the constant clatter of the machines and the drudgery of daily life, the newcomers yearned for something better.

By 1874, Lowell had developed a fine downtown centered on Merrimack, Central, Suffolk, Middlesex, and Market streets. The city boasted thirteen banks and many grocery shops and clothing stores. Fifty lawyers and over one hundred physicians practiced in Lowell. The town had numerous boardinghouses, as well as dressmaking and hairdressing establishments. In the downtown area there were twenty-three apothecary shops. Most remained local businesses, offering the conventional remedies of the time. At least four of these shops, however, expanded into patent medicines, in the process bringing almost as much renown to the city of Lowell as its textile industries.

Wages in the Lowell cotton mills fluctuated with the booms and busts of the textile trade. The Boott Millyards were typical of conditions in Lowell's factories (Gross 1993). The supervisors were paid from $52 to

$72 a month (about 260 hours of work). Card grinders, who cleaned and repaired certain textile machines, earned 15.5 cents per hour for a monthly income of $43 to $46. The less skilled workers were paid at an hourly rate of 12 to 13 cents. Women were paid a third less than men. The women floor cleaners earned only 6 to 9 cents an hour, or a little over $20 for a month's work. Working with dangerous machinery and doing repetitive tasks, these laborers were willing customers for the offerings of the patent medicine businesses of Lowell, which were among the largest of their type in the nation.

In eighteenth-century England, the makers of medicines sought to protect their products by means of a royal patent. The term "patent medicine" gained wide currency in nineteenth-century America and came to cover an infinite number of concoctions claiming a wide array of benefits. Some called it snake oil medicine, others quackery. There were as yet no laws to prevent a medicine maker from putting anything he wished into his mix and claiming any benefit he liked without offering any proof. Many products contained heavy doses of alcohol, or even opiates or cocaine, which would account for much of their appeal. Usually presenting their products in liquid form, the manufacturers used distinctive bottles to separate their nostrums from the others'. The patent medicine men soon learned the power of advertising. Their newspaper advertisements excited public attention but also muzzled the press, which came to rely on the revenue.

In 1775 there were only four hundred physicians with university degrees in all of the North American colonies, most of them trained in Britain. During the first fifty years after the Declaration of Independence, locally trained physicians had little to offer, and sickness and pain were ever present. By 1842, only four states (New York, New Jersey, Louisiana, and Georgia) had any laws at all regulating the practice of medicine. Medical education was limited to attending lectures and serving an apprenticeship for a number of years under a practicing physician. No qualifications or examinations were required. The pharmaceutical industry had few effective drugs to offer. Epidemics of yellow fever, cholera, whooping cough, diphtheria, typhoid, measles, and smallpox swept the land, with little to help but isolation and folk medicines. In 1869, Harvard Medical School established a three-year hospital-based program with admission criteria and written examinations. Even then, bloodletting and cupping were the common medical treatments. Early death was common in the nineteenth century. As recently as 1900, men in America lived on average only forty-eight years and women fifty-two. In that year 18 percent of male children died before their first birthday.

By 1850 there were 1,500 different patent medicines offered for sale across the country, with some of the largest companies situated in Massachusetts. Advances began to be made in pharmaceuticals only toward the end of the nineteenth century with the development of antisepsis to control the spread of bacteria. The organism causing tuberculosis was discovered in 1882 and the cholera bacillus in 1883.

Overcrowding in smoke-filled industrial towns was a recipe for disease. The traditional folk medicines used by the various immigrant groups were not readily available in the New World. And the Yankees who moved off their farms to the cities left behind the vegetables and plants they traditionally used in healing. The need for money drove husbands and wives as well as their older children into the factories and changed the family structure. Women were burdened by the necessity to work as well as raise their families, shop, prepare meals, and care for the home. The ever-present anxieties over illness, physical appearance, and self-esteem made working people easy prey for quackery, with its promise of ready cures.

The medicine men of Lowell were not itinerant snake oil salesmen but were well-established pharmacists and physicians who claimed to have found the cure for life's ills. Their concoctions were bottled, heavily advertised, and sold to a vulnerable public eager to believe what they read. Patent medicine companies used trade cards extensively to advertise their goods. The extravagant claims written on the back of each card still make for interesting reading.

DR. JAMES COOK AYER

The Pure Food and Drug Acts of 1906 were not signed into law until many years after James Cook Ayer arrived in Lowell. He was born in Groton, Connecticut, in 1818 and educated in the local school. His father died in 1825, and at age thirteen James moved to Lowell to live with his uncle, for whom he was named. The uncle, James Cook, was a significant personage in the young town of Lowell, where he served as the agent for the Middlesex Company Woolen Mills. In 1859 he became mayor of Lowell. Having lost his own children to disease when they were small, he was pleased to take in his nephew. The young James Cook Ayer found work as a clerk in James C. Robbins's apothecary shop and studied medicine under the tutelage of two local physicians, Dr. Samuel Dana and Dr. John W. Graves. Assuming the title Doctor of Medicine, he borrowed money from his uncle and in 1841, twenty-three-year-old Dr. J. C. Ayer bought the apothecary shop for the sum of $2,486.61. Soon he began to make compound medicines. At first business was slow. In 1844 he introduced Ayer's Cherry Pectoral as a cure for "coughs, colds, asthma, croup, laryngitis, bronchitis, whooping cough and consumption." The ingredients included syrup of squills, spirits of nitre, and spirits of bitter almonds. This remedy was advertised as "a scientific combination of the medicinal principles and curative virtues of the finest drugs, so united chemically, as to insure the greatest possible efficiency and uniformity of results." Ayer's Cathartic Pills (introduced in 1854) were said to be "purely vegetable"; they were meant to be taken after dinner "to stimulate digestion in dyspeptic stomachs." Ayer's Ague Cure, a vegetable tonic, was introduced in 1857 as "a certain cure for all malarial disorders" as well as impurities of the blood, ague, and chill fever.

Ayer's Sarsaparilla (introduced in 1859) was the company's greatest success. Ayer touted his compound extract of sarsaparilla as " a real blessing" that "purifies the blood, stimulates the vital functions, restores and preserves health, and infuses new life and vigor throughout the whole system." It was a "skillfully prepared" mixture of sarsaparilla root, stillingia, yellow dock, and mandrake, mixed with iodides of potassium and iron. The list of illnesses for which this compound was "universally successful" is staggeringly long and diverse. Ayer's Sarsaparilla allegedly offered "rapid and complete cures" for at least twenty-five conditions, including scrofula, tetter, ringworm, sores, boils, pimples, ulcers, impurities of the blood, liver complaints, female weaknesses, jaundice, dyspepsia, and rheumatism, as well as promoting energy and strength and improving the intellect. It was particularly recommended to cure the "lassitude and debility peculiar to the Spring."

Some years after the introduction of his sarsaparilla compound, Ayer marketed his "Hair Vigor" ("Restoring gray hair to its original color and vitality") and his sugar-coated Ayer's Pills (to remedy constipation,

AYER'S
SARSAPARILLA

Purifies
the Blood,

Improves
the
Complexion.

Makes
the
Weak
Strong.

"How fair she grows from day to day."
SHE USES
Ayer's Sarsaparilla. over.

Ayer's Sarsaparilla and Hair Vigor were two of the products sold by James Cook Ayer. He trained as a pharmacist and as a physician but made his fortune selling patent medicines. Ayer owned stock in textiles mills, railroads, and newspapers. The town of Ayer, Massachusetts, is named for him. His money funded the American Woolen Company, once the nation's largest manufacturer of woolens.

AYER'S HAIR VIGOR,
FOR THE TOILET.

AYER'S HAIR VIGOR
RESTORES GRAY HAIR TO ITS ORIGINAL COLOR
AND VITALITY.
Prepared by Dr. J. C. Ayer & Co., Lowell, Mass.,
U.S.A.
COPYRIGHT, 1890, BY J.C. AYER & CO, LOWELL, MASS

Like James Cook Ayer, Charles I. Hood, a Lowell apothecary, also got into the patent medicine business. Hood's Sarsaparilla competed with Ayer's. This trade card (ca. 1890) advertises Hood's Liver Pills.

Eli Hoyt, another Lowell apothecary, manufactured his German Cologne to counteract the noxious odors of the times. His beautiful if oversweet advertisements showing young children are among the finest of the American trade cards (ca. 1890).

ABOVE: *Another Hoyt's German Cologne trade card. These calendar cards came perfumed.*

LEFT: *Augustin Thompson settled in Lowell after completing his medical training. He concocted Moxie as a tonic to cure nervousness and to restore vigor. The addition of cocaine had patients coming back for refills. In 1885, Dr. Thompson gave up his practice to concentrate on making and selling Moxie. Horse-drawn Moxiemobiles and later automobiles were regularly seen driving along the streets of New England towns advertising the drink.*

Allen's Root Beer Extract was sold as a concentrate for twenty-five cents a bottle, enough to make six gallons of root beer. Produced by Charles E. Carter, pharmacist, the third of Lowell's sarsaparilla kings. Carter copied James Cook Ayer's general formula. In addition to sarsaparilla, his extract contained dandelion, hops, sassafras, pipsissewa, ginger, and birch.

indigestion, dizziness, headaches, disorders of the liver, neuralgia, dropsy, kidney complaints, and colds, among a host of other conditions). Dr. J. C. Ayer knew the value of advertising. His advertising costs were $140,000 a year. The company's multicolored trade cards show pink-cheeked girls and beautiful young women restored to the fullest of health by one or another of the company's products. Promotional Ayer's Almanacs were distributed across the nation. The company business was conducted out of a five-story redbrick building at 90 Middle Street in Lowell. In 1871, Ayer's factory employed one hundred men and fifty women. In that one year the company processed 325,000 pounds of drugs, 220,000 gallons of spirits, and 400,000 pounds of sugar. The inventory of bottles alone was valued at $1.5 million. Sarsaparilla made Dr. Ayer a very rich man, and his products were sold all over the world. The bottles, almanacs, trade cards, and posters issued by Dr. J. C. Ayer & Co. of Lowell remain collectors' items to this day.

In 1860 the University of Pennsylvania conferred on Ayer the long-coveted degree of Doctor of Medicine, which he had previously only assumed. Ayer used his wealth to become the largest stockholder of the *New York Tribune* newspaper. He financed the water supply for Rochester, New York, and was the major shareholder in the railroad that ran from Lowell to Andover, Massachusetts. Ayer bought a stake in several of the mills in Lowell and became an active investor after 1857 in the Middlesex Mills there and the Bay State Mills of Lawrence. Much of his wealth was passed on to his brother Frederick, who, with William Madison Wood Jr., founded the American Woolen Company (in 1899), which became New England's largest employer and the world's premier woolen and worsted fabric maker.

CHARLES I. HOOD

James Cook Ayer & Co. was not the only sarsaparilla company in Lowell. Ayer's main competitor, Charles I. Hood (1845–1922), was born in Vermont. He came to Lowell at age fifteen and served as an apprentice at Samuel Kidder, Apothecary, at the corner of Central and Merrimack streets. Hood took over the business in 1870 when the previous owner died. He was undoubtedly impressed by Ayer's success with sarsaparilla. Using much the same rhetoric and advertising savvy, C. I. Hood & Co. marketed its Hood's Vegetable Pills and Hood's Sarsaparilla. Constipation and regulation of the bowels were the particular focus of Hood's products. Made with sarsaparilla, yellow dock, mandrake, dandelion, pipsissewa, juniper berries, and other vegetable materials, Hood's compounds provided one hundred doses for a dollar. Hood also made a tooth cleaning powder. These compounds were manufactured in the company's five-story plant in Lowell. Using trade cards, puzzles, and cookbooks, the company widely advertised its products across the nation. Hood hired Parisian artists to paint striking fin-de-siècle posters bearing the message "In the light of its record of cures take Hood's Sarsaparilla."

Before the modern pharmaceutical era, herbs, flowers, bark, and other natural substances were viewed as having healing powers. Sarsaparilla (smilax) is a woody vine and a member of the lily family which is found in the Caribbean islands and in South and Central America. For centuries the indigenous people used the roots of the sarsaparilla vine to cure their ills. Mexican and Honduran sarsaparilla was exported to Europe in the fifteenth century, where it was used in the treatment of syphilis and rheumatism. As late as 1850, the *U.S. Pharmacopoeia* recommends sarsaparilla as the treatment for syphilis. It became popular as an ingredient in beverages such as root beer, and was heavily touted (without any proof of efficacy) by various patent medicine companies as a blood purifier, a diuretic, a tonic to increase male potency, and a treatment for many other conditions. Today sarsaparilla has gone out of favor as a beverage but is still widely used in various herbal preparations.

Eli W. Hoyt and Hoyt's German Cologne

The Hoyts of Lowell could trace their lineage back to the early British settlement. Eli W. Hoyt (1838–1887) was born in Alexandria, New York, and arrived in Lowell when he was eight years old. He attended the local school before starting work as a clerk to a Mr. E. A. Staniels in his drugstore at the corner of Center and Middlesex streets. After the death of Mr. Staniels, the twenty-three-year-old Hoyt became the sole owner. In 1866, Hoyt's German Cologne became a great success. Eli Hoyt gave up his drugstore and built a factory on Church Street to manufacture his cologne, an antidote to the ubiquitous smells of late-nineteenth-century life. One could apply a few drops to a handkerchief, especially when going to the theater, the opera, or a dance. The cologne counteracted "any disagreeable odor about the clothes" and the odors of the sickroom. Hoyt later developed a foaming mouthwash called Rubifoam which allegedly sweetened the breath, whitened the teeth, and kept the gums healthy. The buyer was warned to "Beware of Worthless Imitations" and to "Refuse Substitutes." Hoyt's trade cards came perfumed with his German Cologne. Produced in the company's art department, they were particularly well drawn, using chromolithography, with colors still vibrant a hundred years later. This complex method of printing images, using a series of engravings on stone, became redundant early in the twentieth century, when cheaper photographic techniques came into use.

FATHER JOHN'S MEDICINE

George Carleton and Charles Hovey owned a small drugstore at 164 Merrimack Street in the center of Lowell. Around 1850, Carleton & Hovey came up with a cough medicine made from cod liver oil but with the taste of licorice. One of their good customers was Father John O'Brien, a local Catholic priest. Born in County Tipperary in Ireland, O'Brien came to America soon after his ordination and was sent to Lowell as pastor of St. Patrick's Church to minister to the town's growing Irish population. Concerned over the poor state of health of his parishioners, he helped raise the money to buy land on Livermore Street to set up a small hospital. This became known as St. John's Hospital.

Father O'Brien gained much relief from Carleton & Hovey's cough medicine and began recommending it to his parishioners. They would come to the drugstore and ask for a bottle of "Father John's Medicine." Thus was born one of the nation's best-known patent medicines. Carleton and Hovey were both dead by 1890. The little drugstore was closed and in its place came the Father John's Medicine Company, with the priest's name and likeness on every bottle. After 1900 the benefits claimed from the medicine extended well beyond cough suppression. It was now alleged to be a remedy for all sorts of lung and throat problems, a blood purifier, a body builder, and a nerve tonic as well. Sales were driven by an extensive advertising campaign. The fame of the product traveled well beyond Lowell to all parts of the country. The company remained in Lowell for nearly 150 years until it was sold in 1987 and moved to Wyoming.

Religion, then as now, was seen as the path from sickness to health.

Other patent medicine manufacturers copied the idea of combining religion with patent medicines. Father Kniepp's medicine was made in Germany, Father Mollinger's in Pennsylvania, Father Kroeger's in Ohio, and Father Bordas's in Michigan, among others. Some patent medicine makers used the names of saints on their labels. Father John's was the most successful of all these sanctified brand names.

"JUST MAKE IT MOXIE FOR MINE"

"Just Make it Moxie for Mine" ran the jingle heard at the 1904 St. Louis Exposition. Now eclipsed by the likes of Coca-Cola and Pepsi, Moxie was once America's favorite soft drink. This everyday thirst quencher had its start as a "Nerve Food," first introduced by Dr. Augustin Thompson and used in his medical practice in Lowell. Dr. Thompson was born in 1835 in Union, Maine. After the Civil War he attended the Hahnemann Homeopathic Medicine College in Philadelphia and then returned to New England to start his practice in Lowell. There are several versions of the story as to how Dr. Thompson became interested in Moxie. One holds that a Lieutenant Moxie returned from South America with the roots of the gentian plant and told Dr. Thompson that they produced a feeling of vigor. More likely the name was derived from Maine's Moxie Lake and Moxie Falls, lying a distance of some 120 miles from Union, the town of Thompson's birth.

Gentian, from which Moxie was made, is an herb with attractive flowers. The roots, despite their bitter taste, have long been used among indigenous peoples as an appetite stimulant. Dr. Thompson was soon busy in his laboratory discovering the medical uses of the plant. He concocted a mixture of gentian root extract mixed with wintergreen, sassafras, caramel, flavoring, and cocaine. He called his bitter-tasting mixture Moxie Nerve Food, claiming that a spoonful before each meal would improve the appetite, help sleep rhythms, prevent nervous troubles, relieve fatigue, and generally give a feeling of well-being and good health. He even claimed that his mixture prevented "softening of the brain" and imbecility and cured paralysis. Thompson bottled his mixture and sold it to his patients. The inclusion of cocaine in the mix kept them coming back for more.

In 1885, Thompson gave up his medical practice to concentrate on making and selling Moxie as a soft drink to the general public. The drink was sweetened with sugar and carbonated, to great public acclaim. The word "moxie" became synonymous with courage and strength. By 1886, Moxie beverages were sold throughout New England and farther afield. Thompson became an indefatigable promoter of his product. He died in 1903, but Moxie's greatest days were still ahead. The company's new owner, Frank Archer, introduced a brilliant marketing campaign. Newspapers everywhere carried the Moxie advertisements. Horse-drawn wagons (Moxie Horsemobiles), each carrying a huge bottle of Moxie Nerve Food, traveled from town to town. The company's new manufacturing plant opened near Fenway Park in Boston in 1928. Known as Moxieland, it became a major tourist attraction. There was a Moxie song and a Moxie radio program. The famous Boston Red Sox slugger Ted Williams promoted the drink. During the Great Depression, Moxie began to lose its lead and in time was relegated to a minor player in the soft drink industry, barely recognized even in Massachusetts.

OTHER MEDICINALS FROM LOWELL

For the sake of thoroughness it is worth mentioning some of the minor players in Lowell's vast patent medicine industry. A. W. Dow & Co. of Central Street (founded 1877) marketed a cough cure and a diarrhea syrup. Dr. George S. Mow sold his Cough Balsam, and George S. Hall of Middlesex Street marketed the Harvard Bronchial Syrup and Lyford's Magic Pain Cure. Dr. J. A. Masat sold his own Cough Balsam. Yet another nineteenth-century Lowell pharmacist caught the entrepreneurial bug: Charles E. Carter marketed Allen's Root Beer Extract. With the slogan "Health is Better than Wealth," Carter sold his concentrated extract for twenty-five cents a bottle. When mixed with water, it made six gallons of root beer. The choice of ingredients closely followed the formulas of some of his Lowell competitors. Carter's preparation contained dandelion, ginger, pipsissewa, hops, sassafras, spikenard, and black birch, among other herbs and roots. Both "pleasant and healthy," Carter claimed, the beverage "acts upon the kidneys and liver, gives an appetite and aids digestion." Carter also warned his customers against drinking iced water, "which undoubtedly causes Bright's Disease of the Kidneys."

7

THE MEDICINE MEN OF BOSTON ✎

Eben Norton Horsford (1818–1893) was a professor of chemistry at Harvard College who turned commercial with his obsessive faith in the rejuvenating properties of acid phosphate. Born in the village of Moscow, Livingston County, New York, he went on to graduate from the Rensselaer Polytechnic Institute as a civil engineer. In 1840 he was appointed professor of mathematics at the women's college in Albany.

In 1844, the twenty-six-year-old professor traveled to Germany to study advanced chemistry under Professor Justus von Liebig at the University of Giessen. Liebig was the most famous chemist of his era and attracted students from many countries. Liebig's interests shifted from pure science to the chemistry of living materials—both vegetable and animal. He was especially interested in health and sickness and extensively examined human blood, urine, bile, and mother's milk. During the years when Horsford was among his students, Liebig was engaged in studies of chemicals that could improve health. He discovered that phosphates of lime, derived from bone meal when treated with sulfuric acid, directly affected the growth of plants. He devised mineral fertilizers containing superphosphate of lime which vastly increased agricultural harvests. Liebig was the first to develop an infant food as an alternative to mother's milk. (Other Boston companies were influenced by the discoveries of Professor Liebig. Mellin's Baby Food was derived from Liebig's formula, and the Bradley Fertilizer Company shifted from the use of guano to superphosphates of lime.) Under the tutelage of Liebig, the American scientist began to study the health benefits of various chemicals, including acid phosphate. Horsford focused in particular on baking powder and food preservatives.

Soon after his return to the United States, Horsford was appointed to the Rumford Professorship of science at Harvard College. He met the tex-

Eben Norton Horsford studied in Germany under the famous Justus von Liebig. On his return to the United States, he was appointed professor of chemistry at the Lawrence Scientific School, Harvard University (funded by the textile tycoon Abbott Lawrence, for whom the city of Lawrence was named). Horsford's faith in the medicinal value of acid phosphate led him to give up academia for business, selling his drink as a cure for mental and physical exhaustion, dyspepsia, headache, and even cholera. Horsford later gave his scholar's endorsement to the theory that the ancient Norsemen settled along the Charles River near present-day Boston.

TOP: *Wistar's Balsam of Wild Cherry was prepared by Seth W. Fowle & Sons, Boston. It was used for the relief and cure of respiratory conditions such as coughs, sore throat, influenza, and consumption. The balsam was sold at fifty cents and one dollar a bottle.*

RIGHT: *Nichols' Bark and Iron was prepared by Billings, Clapp & Co., Boston. It was sold as "nerve tonic" especially adapted for "Clergymen, Counsellors, Journalists, and persons of sedentary habits." It contained Peruvian bark (Cinchona succirubra), a source of quinine, used then as now in the treatment of malaria.*

tile mill owner Abbott Lawrence, who had funded the Lawrence Scientific School at Harvard. Horsford submitted his plan to established America's first department of analytical and applied chemistry, based on what he had learned under Liebig at Giessen. Despite his tenured chair at Harvard, Horsford was still drawn toward the business side of chemistry. With George F. Wilson, he started the Rumford Chemical Works in East Providence, Rhode Island. The company's first product was a baking powder containing acid phosphates that was used to leaven bread. According to its advertising, Professor Horsford's baking powder formula "restores the phosphates lost with the bran, which is indispensable in the maintenance of health. A deficiency of the phosphates is a common cause of illness and of retarded growth." Horsford's advertisements carried the endorsement of his mentor, the great Professor von Liebig, as well as testimonials from many American physicians.

Next came Horsford's Acid Phosphate for the treatment of mental and physical exhaustion, dyspepsia, indigestion, headache, nervousness, hysteria, and other conditions. The preparation was a mixture of phosphates of lime, magnesia, potash, iron, and phosphoric acid. A powder, it was taken with water and sugar to make "a delicious and healthful drink." It was also recommended in the treatment of cholera. All of the health-providing compounds made by the Rumford Chemical Works were prepared "according to the directions of Prof. E. N. Horsford, of Cambridge, Massachusetts."

In 1887, Horsford became president of the Rumford Chemical Works, named for the professorship Horsford occupied at Harvard. Who was this Rumford? He began life as the humble Benjamin Thompson (1753–1814) of Woburn, Massachusetts. As a boy he moved with others from Massachusetts to settle in Rumford, New Hampshire (now the state capital, Concord). Being a loyalist to the Crown, he left his homeland in 1776 with the retreating British troops. In Europe he found employment with the Bavarian government and excelled in scientific observations into the nature of heat. He invented a more efficient fireplace and, for his achievements, he was given the title of "Count of the Holy Roman Empire." He called himself Count Rumford, taking the name of the town in New Hampshire where he had grown up. Next, Rumford moved to England to bask in the warmth of his famous fireplace design. At his death he left £5,000 to the Royal Society, but the bulk of his estate went to Harvard

College in his native Massachusetts. Some of this money was used to fund the Rumford Professorship.

Horsford's Acid Phosphate was sold across the nation to treat mental and physical exhaustion as well as cholera. The success of the Rumford Chemical Works required Horsford to spend a lot of time commuting between Cambridge and Providence. In 1863, the forty-five-year old Horsford resigned his position at Harvard to devote his full efforts to the chemical factory. He continued to live an intellectual's life in Cambridge in the shadow of Harvard, and to travel to his business in Rhode Island. It was a relatively short journey by horse car from Cambridge into Boston to the train terminal on Columbus Avenue, where he would board the Boston & Providence Railroad for the ninety-minute journey to his factory. Horsford took a special interest in Wellesley College, perhaps a reminder of his first teaching position at the women's college in Albany. He donated money for the college library and helped develop its chemistry laboratories.

Toward the close of his life, the wealthy Eben Horsford developed a rich man's passion. After meeting Ole Bull, a famed Norwegian violinist on a tour of America, Horsford became convinced that Norsemen had traveled across the ocean around AD 1000 and settled in various places along the Charles River. Horsford funded the exploration of these ancient Vinland settlements and claimed to have found evidence of Norse settlement in what is now Cambridge (conveniently only a short distance from his own house), as well as in Watertown, Waltham, and Newton. He estimated that ten thousand Norsemen had occupied these settlements. To commemorate them, Horsford built a stone tower on the shore of the Charles River at Norumbega. He also funded a statue of the Norse leader Leif Eriksson, created by the sculptress Anne Whitney and completed in 1886. The statue now stands on the mall of Commonwealth Avenue in Boston's Back Bay.

Horsford wrote extensively about the Norsemen of early Massachusetts. He claimed that Vinland was the lost Viking settlement in North America and hypothesized that it was part of a larger Norse settlement that extended from Rhode Island to the St. Lawrence River. Their economy, he believed, was based on wood, fish, furs, and farming. The last of the Norse ships, he said, returned to Iceland in 1347.

~

Medicines to purify the blood were among the favorites of the Boston-based medicinal entrepreneurs. H. R. Stevens made a small fortune with Vegetine, his extract made from bark, roots, and herbs. Available as a powder (at fifty cents a package) to be mixed with water, Vegetine was manufactured at 464 Broadway in Boston. It was billed as "Nature's Remedy" with "no equal as a blood purifier." The compound that could "invigorate the whole system" probably contained opiates. Vegetine provided Stevens with the life of a country gentleman. He and his family had a country estate replete with domestic staff in the bucolic village of Dover. Nichol's Bark and Iron, made with Peruvian bark and protoxide of iron, was made by Billings, Clapp & Co. of Boston. This "invaluable and never-failing elixir" was intended specifically for persons of sedentary habits, such as clergymen, counselors, and journalists suffering from "lassitude, lack of appetite, low spirits and a general feeling of weakness and exhaustion." This nineteenth-century mood stabilizer appealed to "those whose nerves are shattered and are subject to depression, melancholy or nervous excitement."

E. Hartshorn & Sons of 71 Blackstone Street, Boston, sold Dr. Hartshorn's No. 18 for the treatment of pain from sprains, bruises, stings, neuralgia, toothache, and sore throat. The medicine could be rubbed directly on the sore spot or taken by mouth. In addition to treating pain, the Hartshorn preparation could handle "numberless ills," including diphtheria. Hartshorn also sold a "cough balsam" under the slogan "It cures when nothing else will." Seth W. Fowle & Sons of Boston produced Wistar's Balsam of Wild Cherry. With a touch of exaggeration, this preparation claimed to have "the enviable reputation as the most reliable and effective remedy in the world for the cure of coughs, colds, hoarseness, sore throat, bronchitis, influenza, croup, whooping cough, asthma, consumption, and every affection of the throat, lungs and chest." Wistar's Balsam came in fifty-cent and one-dollar bottles.

Alexander B. Wilbor, Chemist, of Boston sold Wilbor's Compound, a mixture of cod liver oil with phosphates of lime, soda, and iron, added to reduce the "very nauseating character of cod liver oil." The compound was billed especially as a cure for consumption (tuberculosis), which was claimed to be "almost universally nothing more or less than a neglected cold." The answer was to treat it early with Dr. Wilbor's Compound. The Avery Lactate Company of Boston sold Lactart, a fermented milk product, as a cure for dyspepsia, nervous troubles, wakefulness, fevers, and headaches. When the powder was mixed with water and sugar, it made a refreshing drink that quieted "the over-worked nervous system." The Alaska Compound Company, in nearby Lynn, made Alaska Catarrh Compound for the cure of "colds in the head, nervous headache, dizziness, ringing noises in the ears and hay fever."

Dr. Bull's Baby Syrup, prepared by C. F. Wilson of 343 Main Street, Boston, assured its customers that it contained "No Opium" and "No Morphia." This vegetable compound promised to be effective in the treatment of colic, diarrhea, summer complaints, teething, and restlessness, among other ailments. Priced at twenty-five cents a bottle, it was available from all druggists. Kettredge's Remedy for Catarrh was sold from 763 Washington Street, Boston, at fifty cents a bottle, but was "worth one hundred dollars in gold" in relief from colds and coughs. There were many other druggists in Boston and the surrounding towns who made their own medicines and advertised widely. Without government oversight or requirements for evidence to back their extravagant claims, these patent medicine companies could and did say whatever they liked.

The shrewd businessmen who ran the patent medicine companies took care to list in their advertisements as many complaints and illnesses as could fit onto the page. One "skillfully blended" patent medicine compound claimed the power to cure a dizzying array of these conditions. The citizenry of Victorian Massachusetts were apparently much concerned about impure blood as well as kidney and liver ailments. Epidemic diseases such as cholera, whooping cough, measles, influenza, diphtheria, and other infections were very debilitating and frequently resulted in death. Tuberculosis was a slow killer that spread in the crowded tenements of the industrial towns. These illnesses were the bane of nineteenth-century life, and people were easily swayed by the unproven claims of the patent medicine companies.

The bulk of the complaints expressed in Victorian times are still familiar today. The trade cards suggest a great concern over common infections of the respiratory tract and the lungs—coughs, colds, influenza, laryngitis, and pneumonia—especially in cold weather. It is possible that the patent medicines (some containing alcohol or opiates) offered relief from coughing and pain, but it is most unlikely that they were effective against the virus or bacillus causing the disease.

Other groups of patent medicines clustered around abdominal complaints (excessive gas, constipation, diarrhea, pain) and the treatment of rheumatism (joint stiffness and pain). There were also many preparations for the treatment of emotional complaints (including nervousness, irritability, anxiety, depression, mania, listlessness, and poor memory). Expressing emotions as bodily ailments was probably as common then as now. In medical terms such complaints are called "psychosomatic" and are highly responsive to placebos. With or without treatment, these conditions generally improve. Many other products were aimed at enhancing one's appearance by bringing color to the face and the skin or restoring the luster of the hair. Then as now, the average citizen was troubled by somatic complaints, a fear of aging, and a wish to look youthful . Promises of rapid improvement after a dose or two of Dr. Ayer's Vegetable Pills or Lyford's Magic Pain Cure were too hard to resist.

These patent medicines were extensively advertised in the newspapers and were sold by druggists across the country. Most of the advertisements carried testimonials from grateful patients. Zealous salesmen and cheap postal rates help spread these nostrums to every corner of the nation. The medicines cost from fifty cents to a dollar a bottle—a significant amount of money at a time when a skilled worker earned one dollar for a twelve-hour day's work. It is little wonder that these patent medicines with their fantastic claims had such a great appeal in rapidly industrializing America. These cure-alls were by no means innocuous. The heavy doses of alcohol and narcotics fostered addiction, and other impurities could cause harm. The corrupting influence of the patent medicine industry was finally brought to heel through the efforts of muckraking journalists. The author Upton Sinclair, in his frightening book *The Jungle*, described the inhumane conditions in Chicago's meatpacking industry and aroused the concern of the nation. In 1906, Congress passed the Pure Food and Drug Act and the Meat Inspection Act, requiring more accurate labeling of products and controlling the movement of medicines, drugs, liquors, and foods across state lines.

Yours for Health

Lydia E. Pinkham

Lydia E. Pinkham's portrait appeared on the labels of her preparations, making her one of America's most recognized women, although she spent almost her entire life in Lynn. Her Vegetable Compound sold for one dollar a bottle, or five dollars for six bottles, and was packaged in her factory at 223–225 Western Avenue, Lynn. Her preparations found a ready market among the women of Lynn and elsewhere.

～LYDIA E. PINKHAM AND THE CITY OF LYNN

The village of Lynn, Massachusetts, was founded by settlers sent to Massachusetts Bay by the Dorchester Company of England.. Part of a group that landed on Cape Ann in 1626, they spread out along the coast to found Newburyport, Gloucester, and Salem. In 1627 some of these settlers bargained with the Sagamore Indians to buy a parcel of land called Saugust. A few years later the name was changed to Lynn, after King's Lynn in England, from whence several of them had come. These towns are older than Boston, founded in 1630.

Before the War of Independence the port towns of Newburyport, Gloucester, and Salem grew rich on trade with the British Caribbean, and after the war they prospered in the China trade. Lynn, however, remained a working community of farmers and fishermen. Some of the men had a winter trade as cordwainers (that is, workers in cordovan leather, an archaic term for shoemaker). They supported their families by growing crops or fishing for cod—and by making shoes, a product for which Lynn soon developed a reputation. By 1750, "Lynn took rank as the foremost place for the manufacture of ladies shoes in all of America" (Hurd 1888). By 1795 there were two hundred master shoemakers working in small shops known as "ten-footers." Working alongside the master shoemakers were six hundred apprentices and journeymen. By the close of the eighteenth century, Lynn was a town of some three thousand people, mostly locally born and residing there from one generation to the next. Shoemaking had become its major industry.

One such man of Lynn was William Estes. A forceful and able man, Estes supported his large family—remarrying after his first wife died, he fathered twelve children in all—by farming in the warmer weather and making shoes during the winter months. He also owned a salt works and made a tidy fortune during the embargo and the War of 1812. William

Estes was a Quaker. His second wife, Rebecca Chase, passed along to her children her strong spiritual beliefs, based on the revelations of Emanuel Swedenborg. This Swedish theologian claimed the ability to enter the spiritual world—between hell and heaven—where people went after they died; families and friends would meet again in the afterlife to live on forever in a spiritual kingdom of grace. In 1819, Rebecca was delivered of a daughter, named Lydia. She was dark-haired and remained slim throughout her life At five feet ten inches, Lydia was very tall by the standards of her time. She grew up near High Rock, with its view across the town to the Atlantic Ocean, and attended the local public school.

The rum trade was strong in Lynn, and many a workman could be seen staggering home drunk. Lydia saw the devil in alcohol and formed strong temperance views. By the 1830s the antislavery movement was gaining force in Massachusetts. Frederick Douglass, an escaped slave, spoke fervently about his life before meetings of the Anti-Slavery Society. When he came to speak in Lynn, some of the locals attempted to disrupt the meeting. Twelve Quaker girls, including Lydia Estes and her sister Gulielma, shielded Douglass from the hoodlums. The young Lydia met Douglass and became dedicated to the antislavery cause. In 1836, now seventeen years old, Lydia joined the Female Anti-Slavery Society of Lynn. Living at a time when there were few opportunities for a spirited young woman, Lydia put her feminist instincts on hold and chose teaching as a career.

In 1843 the twenty-four-year-old Lydia married Isaac Pinkham, a young widower with a five-year-old daughter. Like Lydia, he was of old New England stock, his forebears having arrived in 1640. Isaac was short and stout, a man of lofty dreams but little endurance. He flitted from one scheme to another. He tried shoemaking, selling produce and kerosene, and then land speculation. Lynn was entering a period of tremendous growth. Immigrants were coming to the town to work in the shoe business. Steam-powered factories, some employing hundreds of workers, were replacing the old "ten-footer" shoe shops. New methods of production were introduced. A worker no longer made a pair of shoes from start to finish. Instead, each worker would specialize in one component of shoe manufacture, performing the same task over and over again. Lynn's population grew with the market for women's shoes and reached fourteen thousand by 1850. These workers needed housing, and Isaac Pinkham saw his opportunity to make big money.

After Lydia's parents died, Isaac started to sell off their farmland and used the money to buy more land to develop the new suburb of Wyoma. He set himself up as a builder of homes. But this scheme ended in failure during the financial panic of 1873. Isaac retreated into permanent depression, leaving his family impoverished. Lydia was now fifty-four years old and the mother of four children. She named her first two sons Charles and Daniel after two of her Anti-Slavery heroes; they were followed by William and Aroline. (A fifth child died in 1847 of cholera.) Her children had to relinquish their hopes for a comfortable life. Charles found work as a conductor on the horse trolley that ran from Salem to Boston. Daniel became a letter carrier for the post office, and William gave up on his dream to attend Harvard College. The Pinkhams were forced to sell their house in Wyoma and move into a rented home on Western Avenue. Rather than give in to despair, however, Lydia rediscovered her determination and her feminism and found a way to support her family.

There are several stories told about the origin of Lydia E. Pinkham's Vegetable Compound. One credible version holds that a Lynn machinist by the name of George Clarkson Todd owed the Pinkhams the sum of $25. Being unable to pay the money, he offered in exchange a recipe for a home medicine. For years Lydia would follow this formula and hand out bottles of her medicine to friends and family for free. She was also much influenced by the home remedy suggestions found in John King's *American Dispensatory*. With the family fortunes now so low, Lydia decided to take the family finances into her own hands and sell bottles of her formula. At that time, vegetables were viewed as beneficial to health; thus Lydia chose the name Vegetable Compound to describe her product.

Lydia got down to work in her kitchen. She rolled up her sleeves and, using her regular pots and pans, she measured out the ingredients of her original Vegetable Compound, according to the following formula:

UNICORN ROOT (*Aletris farinosa*) 8 OZ

LIFE ROOT (*Senecio aureus*) 6 OZ.

BLACK COHOSH (*Cimicifuga racemosa*) 6 OZ.

PLEURISY ROOT (*Asclepias tuberosa*) 6 OZ.

FENUGREEK SEED (*Trigonella foenum-graceum*) 12 OZ.

SUSPENDED IN ALCOHOL (18 PERCENT)

The appealing face of one of Lydia Pinkham's granddaughters livens up this trade card (ca. 1880). Pinkham's Vegetable Compound was offered as a cure for numerous "women's complaints," including tumors of the uterus and kidney diseases. The original compound contained a significant dose of alcohol, despite Pinkham's strong temperance views.

Note that despite her lifelong temperance views, Lydia Pinkham used alcohol as a significant component of her Vegetable Compound. (Later, the formula was altered to include Jamaica dogwood, ferrous lactate, and ascorbic acid.) After allowing sufficient time for it to meld, she poured the liquid mixture into small bottles, crudely labeled and ready for sale.

Lydia and her children scraped up enough money to have one thousand handbills printed. The children, already adults, remained at home and pooled their earnings to support the family. After they returned home from work, they would go from house to house around Lynn, handing out the advertisements. Local druggists were asked to take a dozen bottles on consignment. At first sales were very slow, but every dollar helped to put food on the table. Because of the lack of money, only small amounts of the compound could be made at a time. William traveled regularly into Boston to buy the next batch of herbs. Sons Daniel and Charles walked as far as Salem to distribute the handbills. Later Daniel gave up his job to travel to Boston, Fall River, and Providence in an effort to drum up business. The firm of Weeks & Potter, Chemists and Druggists, at 360 Washington Street, Boston, took several dozen bottles. Weeks & Potter was an established druggist with its own line of remedies. One of these was Cuticura, which allegedly purified the blood, improved the skin, gave luster to the hair, and prevented "scrofurious humors" and "scald head" in children.

Sales in New England remained slow. The increasingly assertive and determined Lydia decided on a bold new strategy. Lydia E. Pinkham's Vegetable Compound was formally registered in 1876 with the patent office in Boston. Daniel was sent to live in New York, the great center of trade and opportunity. During his first months there he led a threadbare existence while trying to establish contacts with patent medicine druggists and wholesalers. Despite his impoverished state he persisted, making contacts and picking up new ideas. He wrote home that he was hearing a good deal about kidney and uterine complaints and that the Pinkham handbills should say something about curing these conditions. He suggested that the family print small, cheap trade cards for easy distribution. Soon the backs of these small cards were crammed full with details— written by Lydia herself— about the many illnesses that could be cured by regularly taking the Vegetable Compound. When Daniel recommended that they add a picture of a woman to the label, the family decided to use Lydia Pinkham's own likeness as the trademark on each bottle. Her reassuring portrait greatly increased sales, and Lydia E. Pinkham, the country's first great female entrepreneur, became one of the best-known women in the United States.

Daniel Pinkham got his big break when he met Charles Nelson Crittenton, one of the largest wholesale druggists in New York. (Crittenton was the founder of the Florence Crittenton homes, named for his daughter, who died at age four. The Crittenton homes were originally planned to help prostitutes escape the life of the streets. Later, they offered shelter to unwed mothers and their children.) Crittenton took a liking to Dan and paid cash for a large order of the Vegetable Compound.

At the same time, William met with success in Boston. He placed an expensive advertisement on the front page of the *Boston Herald*, a newspaper with a circulation of fifty thousand. Very soon, the orders started to pour in. Lydia and her family now realized the power of advertising. They hired an advertising company, and soon Lydia E. Pinkham's Vegetable Compound was being sold across the United States and abroad. Over the years, Lydia's company spent $35 million on advertising and shipping.

The family was becoming prosperous. Lydia made the important business decisions and wrote the copy for the advertisements. Her sons ran the business under her leadership. By 1879, Lydia had moved into an attractive wood-built Victorian house alongside the company's Lynn laboratory and packing rooms. (Some years later, a four-story brick building was erected on the site at 233–235 Western Avenue.) Now workers, both men and women, were employed to steep the herbs, mix the ingredients, and package the liquid in the distinctive bottles carrying Lydia's image on the label. The company expanded its line of products. In addition to her liquid Vegetable Compound, Lydia added her Liver Pills, a laxative, and her famous Blood Purifier.

The Pinkhams did not long enjoy their success. Hefty doses of her Vegetable Compound, marketed as a "positive cure" for numerous illnesses, did little to help Lydia or members of her own family. Her son Daniel became ill with tuberculosis. Lydia recommended her Liver Pills, pleurisy root, and marshmallow, taken four times a day. Despite this treatment, his health declined further, and Daniel died at thirty-three years of age. Son William also contracted tuberculosis and died at age twenty-eight, two months after his brother. Lydia herself was in failing health following a stroke, and she died in 1883 at the age of sixty-four. She had requested a spiritualist funeral, fully expecting to be reunited in the afterlife with her beloved sons. Her husband, Isaac, outlived her by six years, but remained ineffectual to his death. Her eldest son, Charles Hacker Pinkham, was left to run the business, with her daughter Aroline serving as company bookkeeper. Charles attempted to use his wife's likeness in place of Lydia's on the bottles. But Lydia's public would have none of this, and sales began to fall. Lydia's reassuring image was put back on the label, where it remained long after she was dead. By now Charles Pinkham was one of Lynn's leading citizens and was elected a director of the National

City Bank of Lynn. His own son Arthur became the bank's president before he reached his thirtieth birthday.

~

In 1819, the year Lydia was born, Lynn was still an agricultural town with a small population. By the time of her death, it had grown into a city of nearly forty thousand people. (The population of Lynn reached ninety thousand in the year 1910.) The town boasted an imposing Italian Renaissance–style city hall. Residents enjoyed walking on the town common or strolling through the vast Lynn Woods. Immigrants from Ireland, England, French-speaking Canada, Russia, Poland, and Italy continued coming to Lynn to seek work in the shoe factories: some 80 percent of the workers in Lynn were employed in the shoe trade. Lynn had indeed become the ladies' shoe capital of the world. The city built a special school—called the Shoemaker's School—to teach youngsters the trade that had made Lynn prosperous. By 1860, Lynn could claim 136 shoe and boot factories employing 2,862 women and 5,767 men. That year, 6 million pairs of shoes worth $6 million were made in Lynn's factories. By 1880, the value of shoes produced reached $20 million.

Working conditions were not easy. Newcomers lived in boardinghouses or cheap hotels until they were well enough established to rent a small house. Shoe workers earned between three and five dollars a week— well below subsistence wages. More than one member of a family had to work merely to put food on the table and pay for shelter. At the factories, the workers sat in long rows doing repetitive tasks, with the supervisor hovering behind their backs. The workday was up to twelve hours long, five or even six days a week, with only brief periods of rest. Efforts to unionize generally ended in failure. The owners could simply fire all the workers and hire the next group of desperate immigrants. The cutthroat competition between the Lynn shops and shoe shops elsewhere kept wages low and offered little job security. This was an era before health insurance, worker's rights, workman's compensation, or disability benefits. An illness or a work injury could very quickly drive the worker and his family into poverty.

Lynn was a divided city, with the Irish, French Canadians, Greeks, Jews, Poles, and other ethnic groups each gravitating to its own neighborhood. Here the migrants were comforted by their own churches and clubs,

"How Phyllis Grew Thin." The Lydia E. Pinkham advertisements were modernized to appeal to fashionable women of the 1920s. Long after her death, the Lydia E. Pinkham Medicine Company still claimed that "98 out of every 100 women benefited" from use of the Vegetable Compound. This booklet offers recipes for the weight-conscious woman.

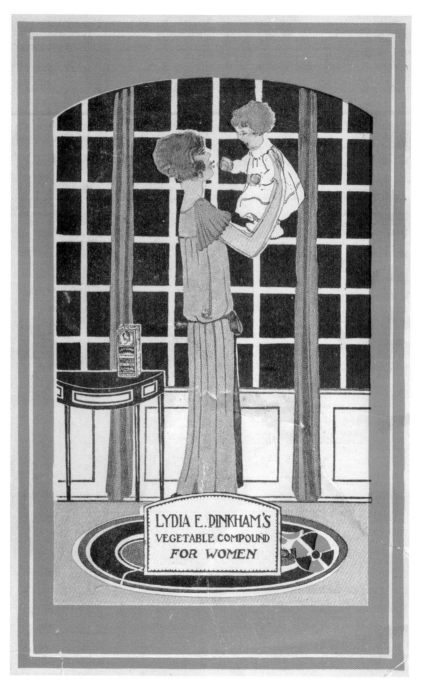

and by shops selling their familiar foods. The male workers drowned their frustrations with alcohol. The women, meanwhile, were burdened with large families, little money, and exhaustion from long hours of work. The repetitive jobs and mass production dampened their individuality and creativity. They felt oppressed and powerless. Little wonder that so many women responded enthusiastically to Lydia Pinkham's advice and to her medicine. Here, at last, was a true friend who understood them, and she had managed to become a successful businesswoman to boot.

The Lydia E. Pinkham Company published booklets filled with letters from grateful customers. Mrs. Peter Fritchel of Loveland, Colorado, wrote to say that she had suffered from "weakness, dizzy spells and headaches," which responded beautifully to regular use of the Vegetable Compound. Mrs. Joseph J. E. Gibson of 59 Paine Street, Dover, New Hampshire, wrote that for three years she used to "be so weak that I had to go to bed and stay there." Her lethargy prevented her from doing her work in the mill. Again, the Vegetable Compound was her salvation. The correspondents' most common complaints were chronic weakness, nervousness, feelings of being run down and depressed, often accompanied by joint and body pains.

Psychiatry is familiar with this ill-defined syndrome. Over the years it has been labeled hysteria, neurasthenia, dysthymia, reactive depression, and, in recent times, fibromyalgia. The condition is debilitating for the patient, even when no physical abnormality or abnormal test results are detected. The patient is relieved simply to find someone who takes the condition seriously and believes that she is suffering, not merely malingering. Lydia E. Pinkham was such a person. She was a staunch advocate for these ladies and their conditions. Above all, she was a passionate promoter of her Vegetable Compound, her Liver Pills, and her Blood Purifier. These concoctions could free women from their suffering. The medicine made them feel healthier, stronger, more independent. The docile housewife and mother of four had, in her mid-fifties, rediscovered her feminist voice. Determination led her—a woman of the Victorian era—to become the head of a prosperous worldwide company. With her Vegetable Compound, Lydia E. Pinkham was the savior of her sex.

The fantastic claims for Lydia E. Pinkham's Vegetable Compound can be read on the back of any of the various trade cards issued by the company. These messages were directed specifically to women. A typical message (ca. 1880) reads:

The Vegetable Compound will cure entirely the worst form of Female complaints, all Ovarian Complaints, all Ovarian troubles, Inflammation, Ulceration, Falling and Displacements of the Womb and the consequent Spinal Weakness, and is particularly adapted to the Change of Life.

It will dissolve and expel Tumors from the uterus in the early stage of development. The tendency to cancerous humors there is checked very speedily by its use. It removes faintness, flatulency, destroys all craving for stimulants, and relieves weakness of the stomach. It cures Bloating, Headaches, Nervous Prostration, General Debility, Sleeplessness, Depression and Indigestion.

That feeling of bearing down, causing pain, weight and headache is always permanently cured by its use.

It will at all times and under all circumstances act in harmony with the laws that govern the female system. For the cure of Kidney Complaints of either sex this Compound is unsurpassed.

The user of the Vegetable Compound was advised that the additional purchase of Lydia E. Pinkham's Liver Pills was highly recommended. These pills "cure constipation, biliousness, and turpidity of the liver." Lydia E. Pinkham's Blood Purifier had fantastic properties of its own: "This preparation will eradicate every vestige of Humors from the blood, and at the same time will give tone and strength to the system. It is superior to any other known remedy for the cure of all diseases arising from impurities of the blood, such as Scrofula, Rheumatism, Cancerous Humors, Erysipelas, Canker, Salt Rheum and Skin Diseases." The Vegetable Compound sold for a dollar a bottle or six bottles for five dollars, a week's wages for a Lynn shoe worker. The Liver Pills cost twenty-five cents per box. The medicines were available by mail from the company at 233–235 Western Avenue, Lynn, and were also sold by druggists across the nation.

The front of the trade card showed Lydia's kindly face or a picture of her grandchildren. There is even one card showing the Brooklyn Bridge with a sign for Lydia E. Pinkham's Vegetable Compound extending from one tower to the other.

The Lydia E. Pinkham Company continued to gross up to $1.5 million annually for a number of years after her death, but the clouds of decline were casting their shadow over the company. In 1905 the *Ladies' Home Journal* took on the patent medicine industry. The magazine let its readers know that Lydia had been dead for twenty-two years and that her faithful customers were being duped into continuing to write to her personally for advice. For years these letters had been answered by a pool of typists using form letters advocating continued use of the Vegetable Compound. The Food and Drug Act of 1906 now required patent medicines to state the alcohol content on the label, and Lydia E. Pinkham's loyal customers were shocked to learn that the Vegetable Compound contained a heavy dose of it. The increasingly powerful American Medical Association also did battle against the patent medicine industry. These pressures caused sales to fall, and the company went into decline. Nonetheless, the company continued in business for many years after Lydia's death. Friction among Lydia's descendents, attacks from the medical profession, and declining markets finally drove her company out of its home in Lynn. In 1968 the nearly one hundred–year-old company was sold, and manufacture of its products moved out of Massachusetts.

Lydia Pinkham lived her whole sixty-four years in Lynn. The town gave Lydia her identity and her beliefs. She did not trust doctors and believed categorically that her mixture of herbs and alcohol had vast curative properties. The tremendous reception from the women of Lynn and farther afield convinced Lydia of the curative powers of her compound and of the rightness of her role in making her medicine available to all who were willing to buy it. When she could no longer respond herself to the women all across the nation who wrote to her, telling her about their ills and seeking her advice, she hired an all-female staff to answer their letters. Even after she was long dead, this staff was hard at work writing in her name to the customers, advising them how best to use Lydia Pinkham's products.

≈

Close by Lydia Pinkham's home there lived another remarkable woman of Lynn who was offering her own cure at the same time Lydia was selling her Vegetable Compound. Mary Baker was born in Bow, New Hampshire, two years after Lydia's birth. At age twenty-two, Mary married George W. Glover. He soon died of yellow fever, leaving behind a pregnant widow. After nine years of widowhood, Mary married a dentist by the name of Daniel Patterson.

Mary suffered from bouts of weakness and depression. She tried various cures, including dieting, homeopathy, magnetism, and water cures. In 1864, Dr. Patterson opened a dental practice in Lynn. On February 3, 1866, Mary Patterson fell on the ice at the corner of Market and Oxford streets. She was reported to be seriously, even critically injured. She later claimed that she recovered through prayer and that the Word of God had healed her. She wrote down her thoughts, which later became the guiding principles of Christian Science. Soon afterwards, Dr. Patterson abandoned his wife. Mary faced poverty and moved from one cheap rooming house to another. She began teaching her new faith to the shoe workers of Lynn. In 1875 she completed her book *Science and Health.* Two years later she married Asa Eddy, a man in poor health who had come to her for treatment. Now Mary Baker Eddy, in 1882 she moved from Lynn to the larger arena of Boston, where she founded the First Church of Christ, Scientist.

Lydia Pinkham's home on Western Avenue and Mary Baker Eddy's on Broad Street in Lynn were a little over a mile apart. The two women experienced their great spiritual revelations during roughly the same period. They both had a profound effect on American life. One preached the power of vegetables, the other the power of faith. There is no record that Lydia Estes Pinkham and Mary Baker Eddy ever met.

~

Many of the roots, type of bark, and flowers used by Lydia Pinkham, James Cook Ayer, and the other nineteenth-century patent medicine manufacturers are still sold today as alternatives to prescription medicines. Some of these vegetable compounds do indeed contain active ingredients. For example, Peruvian bark contains quinine, effective in the treatment of malaria, and the beautiful foxglove contains digitalis, still used to strengthen the beating of the heart.

None of the nineteenth-century Massachusetts patent medicine companies made the transition from folk remedies into the science-based pharmaceutical industry of modern times. A few companies in other parts of the country achieved this transformation. John K. Smith was a country boy who opened an apothecary shop in 1830 on North Second Street in Philadelphia, where he made patent medicines and became a large wholesaler. In 1875 he joined with his bookkeeper Mahlon Kline to form Smith, Kline & Company. Many years later SmithKline joined an English drug company to form SmithKline Beecham. In the year 2000, it joined with Glaxo to form GlaxoSmithKline, one of the world's largest pharmaceutical companies. Charles Pfizer came to New York in 1848 and set up as a chemist. His first medical product was Santonin, a treatment for parasitic worms. Uriah Upjohn studied medicine in New York. In 1835 he and his family made their way west and settled in the Michigan territory. His ninth child, William Erastus (known as W. E.), also a physician practicing in Kalamazoo, developed his own patent medicines from various combinations of plants and chemicals. Upjohn's became a leading pharmaceutical company and the largest employer in Kalamazoo.

Infectious illnesses are now prevented by vaccination and improved public health services and are treated with antibiotics. The great advances in public health, clean water and air, and medical care achieved during the course of the twentieth century lengthened the lives of men and women in the developed countries by thirty years.

9

HOME AND GARDEN ✑

The first half of the nineteenth century saw the transformation of daily living from rural to urban and brought with it such innovations as heating and refrigeration, prepared foods, and water piped into the home. By the 1830s, main streets in the larger cities were illuminated by gaslight, with the gas flowing in underground pipes laid down by the local gas companies. Gas lighting inside the home allowed people to read and play music at night. Ducted heat from home furnaces replaced the wood-burning fireplace. Stoves and iceboxes became standard conveniences in the kitchen. After 1830, fresh water was piped into the house and wastewater was piped out. Indoor privies replaced the outdoor toilet. Canned foods were available and could be stored indefinitely.

The enormous flow of poor immigrants into the cities forced most into overcrowded tenements. They worked long hours in the factories, had little access to the countryside, and were dependent on food bought in stores. Many middle-class households in Boston and other cities could afford one or more servants, who lived in cramped quarters on the top floor and who were summoned by a series of chimes (Gordon 2004).

PREPARED FOODS

Since colonial times, Massachusetts had long experience in preserving fish by drying and salting. Early in the industrial age, the state was a pioneer in the preparation and preserving of foods for an ever-expanding market.

The demand for "prepared" foods first arose in connection with infant care. In the colonial era, a "wet nurse" was hired when a mother's milk supply was insufficient to feed her baby. When this method of infant feeding lost favor, whole cow's milk was substituted, but this led to problems because, although cow's milk has a higher concentration of proteins than in human milk, it has fewer carbohydrates and was more likely to pass along infections. With the beginning of the scientific age, the search for a good alternative to mother's milk gathered speed. The German scientist Justus von Liebig is credited with being the first, in 1867, to offer for sale an "ideal" infant food. His formula was a blend of cow's milk, wheat flour, and malt flour, mixed with bicarbonate of potash. Gustav Mellin in England modified Liebig's formula. Prepared infant food was a boon to working mothers who left their nursing children in the hands of grandparents during the day. Mellin's Food for the Infant became popular in the United States. It was marketed by Theodore Metcalf of Boston at the cost of sixty-five cents a container. Around 1880 the agency for Mellin's baby food was taken over by Thomas Doliber and Thomas T. Goodale, two of Metcalf's employees. Doliber-Goodale & Co. was located at 40–43 Central Wharf on Boston's waterfront. Its motto was "ora et labora" (pray and labor). The company advertised Mellin's Food as "the only perfect substitute for Mother's milk." Made from dried malt extract, Mellin's Food claimed to give the baby "strength and vitality" while preventing colic and constipation. Later, the market for Mellin's Food was expanded to include the elderly, invalids, and dyspeptics.

The food company best associated with Boston was Walter Baker & Company. The company got its start in Dorchester, well before that town became incorporated into Boston. The early colonists paid good money for chocolates made from West Indian cocoa beans. In 1764 a sawmill in Milton Lower Mills came into the possession of James Baker, a Harvard-trained physician, who decided to go into business instead. Dr. Baker had a chance meeting with John Hannon, an impoverished Irishman who had trained in the chocolate trade in London. The two struck up a partnership, and Hannon went to work converting bitter cocoa beans into sweet-tasting chocolate. The cocoa beans were ground in the mill, using the power of the Neponset River. One day Hannon went away, never to return, leaving Baker in 1780 the sole owner of America's first chocolate factory. His chocolates became the toast of the town, and additional mills were built along the banks of the Neponset to meet the growing demand. Baker retired in 1804 and handed the business over to his son Edmond. The War of 1812 curtailed European imports, boosting the fortunes of the company. In his turn, in 1824, Edmond passed the business on to his son Walter. Under Walter Baker's leadership the company grew into a six-mill complex on both banks of the river. The expanded factory was now renamed for Walter Baker. After Walter gave up control, the company came under the direction of a relative, Henry L. Pierce. The able Pierce served two terms in the U.S. House of Representatives and was twice elected mayor of Boston. On a business trip to Europe in 1881, Pierce visited the Dresden Art Gallery, where he saw the portrait *La Belle Chocolatière* by the Swiss painter Jean Étienne Liotard. Pierce received permission to use the painting as the official trademark of the Walter Baker Company. The subject of the painting was Anna Baltauf, the beautiful wife of an Austrian prince, who first saw her in a chocolate shop. Liotard painted her portrait in 1743.

At its peak, the Walter Baker Chocolate Company employed over 750 workers, who lived in nearby row houses. The head office moved to 45 Broad Street in Boston. The company produced sweet chocolates (called German chocolate), bonbons, and breakfast cocoa. Charming recipe books and trade cards highlighting the company's products were widely distributed. In 1896 the family gave up control, and Walter Baker & Co. became a public corporation.

Boston was a major center for the manufacture of candies. Walter M. Lowney began making bonbons and chocolates in 1883 in his shop at 89 South Street. The business grew rapidly with sales throughout the United States and Canada. In Boston the company opened a retail store at 416 Washington Street. William F. Schrafft started his candy business during the Civil War. His gumdrops were popular with the soldiers. Later, Schrafft branched out into chocolate-coated candies. His sons William and George joined the growing business. By the 1920s, Schrafft & Sons had moved into the huge building that still dominates the Charlestown skyline. The candy factory, with some 1,600 employees, occupied nearly 700,000 square feet of space. The plant was the largest producer of chocolate-covered candies in the nation. Another famed Boston candy company was started in 1847 by Oliver Chase. This grew into the New England Confectionery Company (Necco), which moved across the Charles River to occupy a large manufacturing plant in Cambridge.

In 1801 baker Josiah Bent of Milton, Massachusetts, sold a biscuit that made a crackling sound when chewed. These biscuits became known

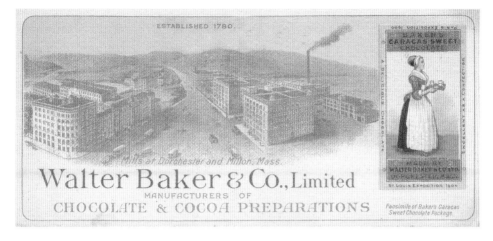

TOP: *A view of Walter Baker & Co., showing the mills in Dorchester and Milton, Massachusetts. This advertising card was given out at the company's booth at the 1904 St. Louis Exposition.*

RIGHT: *Mellin's Food for Infants was sold as an alternative to mother's milk. It allowed mothers to return early to their jobs in the mills while grandmothers cared for their children. Mellin's Food contained cow's milk, wheat, and malt flour mixed with bicarbonate of potash. The product was also marketed to invalids. Made by Doliber, Goodale & Co., 41–42 Central Wharf, Boston. Card (ca. 1890) designed by Armstrong & Co., Lithographers, Boston.*

LEFT: *Walter Baker & Co. of Dorchester, Massachusetts, is America's oldest chocolate maker. Started in colonial times (1764) by the Harvard-trained physician James Baker but named for his grandson, Walter, the company in 1881 adopted as its trademark "La Belle Chocolatière" from the original painting (1743–45) by Jean-Étienne Liotard, in the collection of the Dresden Art Gallery.*

TOP: *Kennedy's Biscuits were made in the Kennedy Steam Bakery, Cambridge. One of their best-known products was the Newton biscuit, named for the nearby city of Newton. With the addition of figs, it became the Fig Newton, still one of America's favorite cookies. The Kennedy bakery became part of the National Biscuit Company (Nabisco).*

LEFT: *The New England Confectionery Company (Necco) began in Boston in the late nineteenth century and then moved across the Charles River to Cambridge. Since 2004 the former confectionery factory has served as the world headquarters of the Novartis Institutes for BioMedical Research.*

RIGHT: *The United States Baking Company was yet another Cambridge-based cookie company that was absorbed into Nabisco. Illustration circa 1890.*

Henry Mayo & Co. was located on Arch Wharf, Boston. The company dealt in canned meat and fish products. These humorous trade cards (ca. 1880) were prepared by the National Color Products Company of Boston.

Rufus Stickney and J. R. Poor prepared mustards and spices out of a factory in Charlestown. The company headquarters were at 205–207 State Street, Boston. Stickney & Poor was one of several nineteenth-century Boston-based spice companies.

Standardized and packaged food products were widely available during the second half of the nineteenth century. T. M. Metcalf's vanilla, William Bell's poultry seasoning, and Preston & Merrill's yeast powder stressed the purity and reliability of their products.

These cards were from some of the
Massachusetts soap makers. The
Fisk Manufacturing Company of
Springfield exploited the late-
nineteenth-century fascination with
Japan. Its Japanese Soap suggested
cleanliness and health. Tucker &
Bryant of New Bedford made its
soaps from whale blubber. Several of
these soap makers were acquired by
the British company Lever Brothers,
later Unilever.

OPPOSITE: Morse Brothers of
Canton, Massachusetts, made
the Rising Sun brand of stove
polish. A shiny stove was a sign of
refinement and pride of home.
These humorous cards illustrate
the folly of buying the wrong polish
and the virtues of using the Rising
Sun brand.

Joshua S. Chase of Boston manufactured liquid glue. This advertisement displays the fad of collecting trade cards and pasting them in scrapbooks. Women and girls were the principal collectors of trade cards. Many of these scrapbooks have been discovered a century or more later with the cards still attached, probably with Chase's glue.

Le Page's liquid glue was made in Gloucester as a by-product of the fish-processing industry. The top card shows a young woman stuck by Le Page's glue to a park bench. The caption reads: "A Lady who keeps her place." The bottom card shows an idler stuck to the bench in the waiting room of a train station. Five policemen, with several more running to help, truncheons at the ready, are not able evict him. The man explains: "Hold on! It's no use pullin—I'm stuck with LE PAGE'S GLUE."

forever as "crackers." Another baker, Artemus Kennedy, founded the Kennedy Steam Bakery in 1839 in Cambridge. For many years the company occupied a five-story redbrick factory at 110–140 Green Street, off Central Square, close to where the Massachusetts Institute of Technology now stands. Kennedy Biscuits manufactured Champion brand as well as butterscotch and chocolate biscuits, ginger snaps, and tea biscuits. The company named some of its various products after nearby places. There was a Harvard and a Beacon Hill biscuit and, best known, a Newton biscuit, later renamed Fig Newton, created in 1891 from a recipe of Charles M. Roser's. At its peak, Kennedy's employed over 650 workers in its Cambridgeport plant. Kennedy grandly advertised its biscuits as "world-renowned and universally acknowledged superior to any other Biscuit ever produced."

C. F. Hathaway began baking bread in 1880 out of a small bakery in Waltham. Later his four sons joined the company. Hathaway and Sons moved to a larger plant in Cambridge, where the company produced a popular small loaf with a high percentage of added milk. During the first third of the twentieth century Hathaway expanded, with fifteen plants in New England and others in New York, Ohio, and Wisconsin. The company headquarters were at 10 High Street in Boston. The United States Baking Company at 465 Medford Street in Charlestown made a wide range of biscuits and chocolates, all packed in sealed boxes. The company had one of the first telephones in Boston. Its telephone number was 129.

Potter & Wrightington at 197 Atlantic Avenue in Boston were packers of canned fish, poultry, and soups. They marketed Ta-Ka-Kake, an easy-to-prepare cereal made of sugared corn flour. The firm declared its Boston Baked Beans mixed with pieces of pork to be the "the finest in the world," worthy of the highest prize awarded at a fair in Berlin in 1880. The Meriam Packing Company of 195 Devonshire Street, Boston, informed its customers (ca. 1890) that it fattened its beef cattle on the prairies "in a perfectly healthy condition" and that the beef was pure and tender, unlike the products of other herds where the cattle were crowded together and underfed. The beef used by the Meriam Company, allegedly free of bone and gristle, was roasted and then canned to preserve its freshness and taste for months to come. No longer was it necessary to shop every day or even to use refrigeration. The tin cans of Meriam beef were guaranteed airtight and rat-proof.

Gustavus Franklin Swift was born in the Cape Cod town of Saga-more in 1839. Not much of a scholar, he dropped out of school at age fourteen to work in his brother's butcher shop. Six years later he opened his own store in Eastham. Swift & Company grew to become a large wholesale meat business with branches throughout New England. In the 1870s, Swift moved to Chicago, where he brought order to the livestock trade. He bought his own animals and established the city's famous stock-yards. Swift used the conveyer belt system to cut up livestock carcasses on a massive scale and personally developed the systems used to package, ship, and market his products. With beef and pork raised in the Great Plains and the population still largely concentrated in the East, Swift was among the first to use the newly invented refrigerated railroad cars to carry his products to markets hundreds of miles away. Swift used the ani-mal by-products to establish allied businesses in glue, fertilizer, and soap. At the time of his death in 1903, Swift & Company was a huge enterprise that employed over 21,000 people and processed 4 million hogs, 2 million head of cattle, and 2 million sheep a year. Now centered in Greeley, Col-orado, the "Yankee butcher's" beef and pork company remains one of the largest in the world.

Spice making came early to Boston. In 1734 a dam and then a mill were built at Rumney Marsh (now part of the town of Chelsea). The mill, powered by the incoming and outgoing tides of the Atlantic Ocean, was first used to grind corn. Local farmers would gather at the mill to sell their products. In 1837, Henry Slade and his sons bought the mill with the idea of grinding and packaging spices. They started with cinnamon and found a ready market in Boston shops. From this humble beginning, the D. & L. Slade Company expanded to other spices and grocery products. The com-pany, which employed over sixty workers, prided itself on its "unadulter-ated" spices. Its products were sold worldwide.

In 1815, William Stickney of Charlestown began to sell mustard for the table. Stickney ground the mustard seeds by hand. Some thirty years later, his son Rufus Stickney opened his own mustard business in partner-ship with J. R. Poor. Stickney & Poor expanded its line to include spices and coffee. The company also marketed its own brand of paregoric (a mixture of alcohol and opiates) to soothe restless and colicky infants; paregoric became a major source of opiate addiction during the latter part of the nineteenth century. Stickney & Poor had its head office at 182–184

State Street in Boston. Davis, Sacker & Perkins of 5–11 Haverhill Street in Boston dealt in coffee, spices, mustard, and tartar. The company guaranteed its spices as "absolutely pure" and free of adulteration.

The United Fruit Company had its start in 1870 when Captain Lorenzo Baker brought a cargo of bananas from the island of Jamaica to Boston. Baker found backers to finance his scheme to import tropical fruits from the Caribbean through the port of Boston and from there to the rest of the United States. The United Fruit Company created a vast demand for tropical fruits throughout the United States and in Europe. Huge areas of Cuba, Costa Rica, Jamaica, and Santo Domingo were cleared of their trees to make room for bananas and other tropical fruits. Railroads were built to connect the plantations to the ports. Many hundreds of workers died in the fever-infested tropical forests.

After the War of Independence, Boston's leading men of commerce were in the habit of meeting at the Exchange Coffee House in Congress Square, near the Custom House and the wharves. Over cups of coffee, business was discussed and deals made. A number of the first banks in Boston were chartered by the men who regularly met at the Exchange Coffee House. In 1862, Caleb Chase and James Sanborn founded their coffee company. Chase & Sanborn claimed to import "the best coffees in the world," which were then ground and packaged in Boston. Later, the company expanded into tea and cocoa. Chase & Sanborn was the first ground coffee in America to be distributed coast to coast.

Keeping Clean and Tidy

The Victorian home was heated by wood or coal. With all the soot and dust in the air, it was hard work to keep the house clean and shiny. Housekeeping without electric-powered washing machines, dishwashers, and vacuum cleaners was a time-consuming activity. The well-off could afford servants to do the dusting, cleaning, washing, and cooking, but mostly it was the woman of the house who performed all these chores. Working in the factory with its own grime and smells created a market for cleaning materials.

Curtis Davis began making soaps as early as 1835. Eleven years later his son-in-law James Mellen became a partner. Curtis Davis & Co. found success with its Welcome brand glycerine soap. These soaps were extensively advertised. The company's Welcome trade cards, drawn by the lithographic firm J. H. Bufford's Sons of Boston, portray comical scenes of daily life. One card shows a delivery boy carrying a basket filled with vegetables. While he is busy playing a game with his pal, his horse is eating the vegetables. Another card shows two prosperous men being bowled over in the snow by young boys on their sleds. One surprised and chubby gentleman loses his gloves, his bowler hat, and his toupee in the process. Another card shows an old-timer fishing on the riverside as a young boy hidden behind him tickles the top of his bald head with a blade of grass. Yet another card depicts a young couple about to kiss and embrace while her father prepares to land a heavy blow on the young man's head. Curtis Davis grew into a large company with its own machine shop. The company patented and produced its own soap-making machinery. In 1898, Boston-based Curtis Davis & Co. was acquired by the British soap-making firm of Lever Brothers, which itself later became part of Unilever, the worldwide home products company. Other Boston-area soap companies such as Hale, Teele & Bisbee, and James C. Davis & Son were also absorbed into larger companies.

Toothpastes and powders also became widely available in Britain toward the end of the eighteenth century. Later borax powder was added to cause foaming. In 1866 the Florence Manufacturing Company near Northampton, Massachusetts, began experimenting with a substance made of resin, shellac, and wood fibers which was used to make buttons and daguerreotype cases. When the daguerreotype yielded to the photograph, the company looked for other uses for its new product—plastic— and began to make hairbrushes, lather brushes, and toothbrushes. In 1884 the Florence Manufacturing Company introduced the Pro-phy-lac-tic toothbrush to the mass market in the United States. In 1882, Codman & Shurtleft of Canton, Massachusetts, became the first company in the United States to sell dental floss. The Lowell firm of E. W. Hoyt, whose specialty was perfumes, also made a liquid tooth cleaner and mouthwash by the name of Rubifoam. Sold for twenty-five cents for a small bottle or a dollar for a large bottle, Rubifoam claimed to make the teeth shiny white, protect the gums, and sweeten the breath: "the perfect liquid dentifrice."

The Electric Lustre Starch Company of 54 Central Wharf, Boston, sold its products across the nation. It claimed to make the "Best Laundry

Starch in the World." Shirts, collars, and cuffs treated with Electric Lustre Starch were said to have an elegant gloss and to "look like new." The company trademark shows a young woman admiring her reflection in the shirt she has just ironed.

Local manufacturers made a variety of cleansers and polishers. Among these was the Excelsior Metal Polish made by the Walpole Emery Mills, with head offices at 114 Milk Street, Boston. Selling at twenty-five cents for a one-pound tin can, this metal polish could clean cutlery, brass, copper, and steel and objects from boilers to bicycles. A trade card shows a maid cleaning pots and pans in the kitchen, to the delight of the lady of the house, whose children smile at their reflections in the shiny utensils. Morse Bros. of Canton, Massachusetts, was another maker of household polish. The Rising Sun brand trade card shows a maid admonishing her man for bringing home the wrong polish. After he returns with Rising Sun stove polish, she is delighted and tells him he will get his supper after all.

Collecting trade cards to paste them into albums was a popular late-nineteenth-century pastime. The abundance of these cards down to the present day is testimony to the early interest in these cards. Chase's Liquid Glue, made by Joshua Chase Company of Boston, used a card showing a mother and daughters pasting cards into an album while the males of the household are busy with other matters. The Tenexine Company of Boston, according to its card, produced "The Most Powerful Adhesive Known." Its Egyptian Tenexine adhesive claimed to mend crockery, glassware, and household ornaments.

A competitor, Le Page's Liquid Glue allegedly mended "everything," including glass, china, ivory, leather, paper, and books. Even "fractured hearts and broken pledges may be made as good as new." The glue won gold medals in London in 1883 and New Orleans in 1885. Le Page's was advertised as the "Strongest Adhesive Known." William Le Page hailed from Prince Edward Island. Around the year 1857 he discovered a method of making fish glue. The Russian Cement Company in the Massachusetts fishing town of Gloucester manufactured Le Page's ready-to-use adhesive from 1876 to 1940. A comical Le Page's trade card shows five policemen trying to pull an idler out of a railroad waiting room. He has got himself stuck to the seat and yells back: "Hold on! It's no use pullin'—I'm stuck with LE PAGE'S GLUE." Another Le Page card shows a man in a park

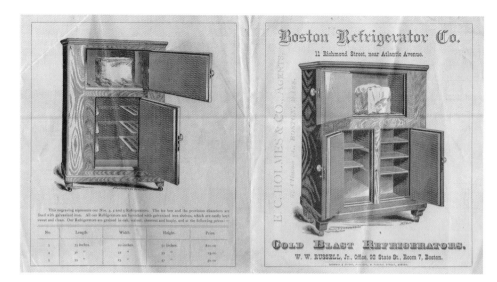

The Boston Refrigeration Company at 11 Richmond Street manufactured two- and three-door refrigerators, which were kept cold by the use of ice blocks. These refrigerators for the home, restaurants, and hotels cost from $20 to $30 and were in wide use by 1880. Drawings by the Photo-Electrotype Company, Boston.

walking off, leaving his beseeching girlfriend stuck to a park bench. The caption reads: "A Lady who keeps her place."

Mustaches, sideburns, and beards dominated the face of the well-groomed gentleman of the Victorian era. The clean-shaven appearance preferred by the twentieth-century man was in large measure due to the invention of a bottle-top salesman who grew tired of supporting his family on only $2,000 a year. King Camp Gillette (1855–1932) was descended from French Huguenots who escaped to England before sailing to Massachusetts in 1630. Gillette was born in Fond du Lac, Wisconsin, and raised in Chicago. He came to Boston as the sales representative of the Crown Cork & Seal Company. Here he pursued his obsession with the disposable safety razorblade. In 1901 he obtained a patent and established the American Safety Razor Company in an office above a fish shop at 424 Atlantic Avenue. In 1902 the name was changed to the Gillette Safety Razor Company. Gillette's beardless face (he kept his mustache) appeared on every one of his razorblade wrappers and in the advertisements, making him one of the most recognizable men in America (Adams 1978).

REFRIGERATION

The soil of Massachusetts yielded no gold, diamonds, or silver. Only small quantities of coal and iron were discovered. But the freezing winters provided an opportunity for a major business.

Frederic Tudor is credited with creating a vast nineteenth-century industry by exporting the ice cut during the months of January to March from the lakes of Massachusetts (Weightman 2003). Tudor's grandfather arrived in Boston from Devon, England, in 1715. The family prospered. By the close of the eighteenth century, Frederic's father owned a house in Boston and a country estate. Frederic, born in 1783, enjoyed spending his summers by the lake on the family estate. There he and his family would sip drinks cooled with ice cut from the lake in the winter and stored in the family icehouse. It occurred to Frederic that a fortune could be made shipping the abundant ice from Massachusetts to hotter climates. He reckoned that that there were many in the Caribbean, South America, India, and even temperate England who would enjoy a summer drink, cooled by Massachusetts ice. After many difficulties, the stubborn and determined Tudor set up a business cutting ice from Fresh Pond in Cambridge and other lakes around Boston. The large blocks of ice were packed in sawdust and hauled to Boston Harbor. Taking advantage of the cheap outward freight costs, Tudor shipped the ice to hot climates around the world. At foreign ports he had insulated icehouses built to store his frozen cargo until it was sold. Cafes in Havana, British clubs in Calcutta, and restaurants in New Orleans were offering ice creams and iced drinks, and Frederic Tudor was making a handsome profit. He became known as the Ice-King and built himself a grand retreat on the island of Nahant, near Lynn, where wealthy Bostonians gathered for the summers.

The great days for transported ice were yet to come. Chipped ice was carried on fishing vessels to preserve the catch. The use of refrigeration to keep food from spoiling became common during the second half of the nineteenth century. Ice wagons were a familiar sight along the streets of Boston, New York, and other cities. The icemen carried the two hundred–pound blocks of ice up the tenement stairs and placed them in the iceboxes. Other cold states such as Maine, Illinois, and Minnesota got into the ice business, and refrigeration became an accepted convenience in stores and homes across the land. Ice and coal delivery companies were established near the railroad stations of towns for convenient delivery to their customers.

The Boston Refrigeration Company at 11 Richmond Street, near Atlantic Avenue, took pride in its cabinet refrigerator, which it judged "perfect for family use" and "the best in the market." The airtight ice-boxes were lined in galvanized iron and held two hundred pounds of ice. The company's largest refrigerator stood sixty-one inches high, forty-six inches in length, and twenty-five inches in width. The large-size three-door refrigerator was intended for gentlemen's residences but was suitable also for boardinghouses, small hotels, and restaurants. The smaller two-door refrigerator was meant for the average home. The wood exteriors were grained in oak, walnut, chestnut, or maple. In 1880 these refrigerators cost from $20 to $45, depending on size and construction. The company's advertisements carried testimonials from satisfied customers. Austin M. Copp of Malden wrote in March 1879 that his Boston-made refrigerator "was put to a severe test during the summer and has given me perfect satisfaction." Samuel V. Lord of 19 Franklin Street, Boston, wrote on March 18, 1879, to say that the refrigerator he bought from the company "proved to be an economical one, and in every way satisfactory."

VENTILATION SYSTEMS

Benjamin Franklin Sturtevant (1833–1890), the son of a farmer from the village of Norridgewock in Maine, left home at age fifteen to become an apprentice shoemaker. Very soon his inventive mind devised new ways to make shoes. At age twenty-three he moved to Boston and opened the B. F. Sturtevant Company, using his wood pegging machine and his new wood lathe. But his workers complained about the wood dust floating about in the shoe shop. Putting his creative mind to work again, Sturtevant came up with a fan blower to ventilate the building. This invention had great appeal in the dust-filled factories dotting the American landscape. By the 1890s, the B. F. Sturtevant Company had been transformed into the world's largest producer of industrial exhaust fans, with manufacturing plants in Jamaica Plain and Hyde Park, Boston, and branches in New York, Philadelphia, Chicago, and London. Nearly three thousand workers were employed in the Boston-area plants alone.

In 1882, Sturtevant hired Eugene Noble Foss as general manager. Foss married Sturtevant's younger daughter, Lilla. After Benjamin Sturtevant died, Foss was elected president of the company. In the twentieth century,

Foss took the firm into new areas, including the manufacture of home vacuum cleaners, air conditioners, water cooling systems, even manufacture of the American Napier automobile. B. F. Sturtevant advertised the health benefits of good ventilation and heating. The 1906 company trade catalog stated that these benefits were no longer "regarded as a luxury rather than as an absolute necessity." According to the catalog, poorly ventilated rooms were associated with high rates of illness and death, while properly ventilated hospitals reported a dramatic fall in death rates. Even horses benefited from well-ventilated stables. With Sturtevant ventilation, people felt more comfortable, their vitality improved, and they were less susceptible to disease. Sturtevant expanded beyond exhaust fans into the scientific application of ventilating and heating equipment for large buildings, factories, and schools. The company's double duct system, which delivered cool air in the summer and warm air during the winter months, was made in Boston for installation in buildings across the land.

PARLOR STOVES AND KITCHEN RANGES

After 1865, coal- or wood-burning stoves, replacing open fireplaces, became a common amenity in the American home. Ironwork companies sprang up across the country to manufacture stoves. The early ones started small to meet local demand. In Massachusetts, cast iron stoves were produced in foundries in Plymouth, Florence, Chelsea, and Taunton. The stoves were sold by department stores or the company's own shops and through mail order catalogs and advertisements.

Union Street is the site of Boston's famed Union Oyster House, one of America's oldest restaurants. In the late nineteenth century, it was also the center for Boston's heating and kitchen equipment showrooms. The Smith & Anthony, J. P. Williams, Magee, Bay State, and Glenwood Range companies were all represented on Union Street. The Magee Furnace Company, founded in 1864 in Boston, grew to become one of the largest stove and furnace makers in the country. A huge Magee manufacturing plant was built on Marginal Street in Chelsea with the rear of the building facing the harbor. Ships came in to unload iron for the factory and took on board the completed ranges and furnaces. Magee Boston Heaters and Mystic brand cooking ranges found markets across the land. In the 1920s, Magee combined with the Edison Company to offer its all-in-one Electri-

The Magee Furnace Company teamed up with the Edison Company to use a combination of coal and electric power to heat a kitchen range. In the 1920s coal and wood were fast being replaced by electricity and gas. Magee, however, as well as Weir, Smith & Anthony, and other Massachusetts-based stove and range companies, did not successfully make this transition.

OPPOSITE: *Kitchen ranges and parlor stoves were introduced into the home by the middle third of the nineteenth century. New Hub wood- or coal-burning ranges, manufactured by the Smith & Anthony Stove Company, show the advances made since the days of the open hearth.*

MAGEE Combines Coal and Electricity by using
EDISON Electric Equipment with their Coal Ranges

THE MAGEE ElectriCoal Range is dual in its make-up, combining a complete coal range and a fully-equipped electric range. The electrical equipment (Edison) includes an oven, broiler, and three top cooking discs. The electric oven, insulated on all sides, is a perfect fireless cooker. The coal range is complete, from the large baking oven to the efficient brass coil for heating water.
The Magee ElectriCoal Range is made in gray Por-cel-a (washable enamel) or in ebony black, both nickel-trimmed, with polished tops.
These ranges are carefully crated, with complete instructions, so that they can be shipped and installed anywhere.

Sold through local dealers or direct. Send for illustrated booklet

MAGEE FURNACE COMPANY
(Dept. C)   Boston, Massachusetts

Coal ranges, which used electricity to heat the broiler and stovetop cooking discs, while coal was used to heat the large baking oven and the coil for hot water. The company helped transform the quiet waterside residential town of Chelsea into an industrial satellite of Boston.

South of Boston, in the town of Taunton, were several more parlor stove and kitchen range companies. John Eddy in 1843 is the first to be credited in Taunton as a manufacturer of stoves. The site of the stove companies was in the Weir's Village section of Taunton alongside the Taunton River, which flows into the Atlantic Ocean at Narragansett Bay. In that section of Taunton were the Phoenix Manufacturing Company, Oscar G. Thomas Foundry, Globe Stove Company, Union Stove Lining Company, Taunton Iron Works, Williams Stove Lining Company, Presbey Stove Lining Company, Taunton Stove Lining Company, and Weir Stove Company. The raw materials were carried by barge up the narrow Taunton River and the completed stoves were sent downriver. After 1840 the Old Colony Railway line ran near the foundries and the goods were sent by rail.

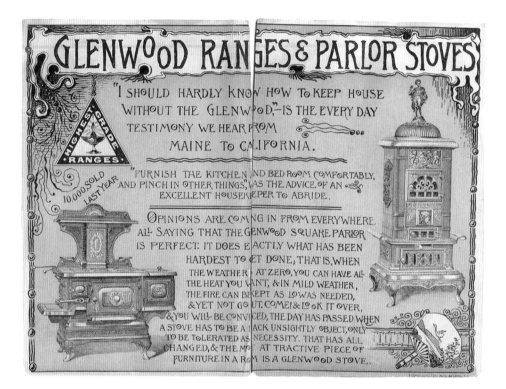

The Weir Company was one of several stove companies in Taunton, Massachusetts. During the cold New England winters the company's Glenwood brand ranges kept the kitchen warm while the stoves heated the bedrooms and the parlor. Advertisement circa 1890.

OPPOSITE: The Clark's Cove Guano Company was established in the 1860s, a time when whale oil was replaced by petroleum for lighting. Instead of carrying home whale blubber, the New Bedford whaling ships carried guano (bird droppings) from the isolated islands of the Pacific Ocean to be packaged as Bay State brand fertilizer. The vegetable and fruit "people" shown on these cards illustrate the benefits of guano fertilizer.

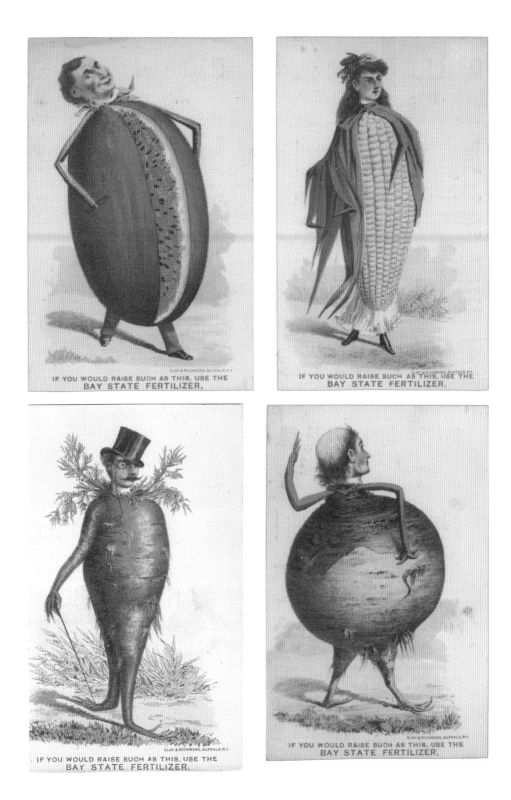

IF YOU WOULD RAISE SUCH AS THIS, USE THE
BAY STATE FERTILIZER,

IF YOU WOULD RAISE SUCH AS THIS, USE THE
BAY STATE FERTILIZER,

. IF YOU WOULD RAISE SUCH AS THIS, USE THE
BAY STATE FERTILIZER,

IF YOU WOULD RAISE SUCH AS THIS, USE THE
BAY STATE FERTILIZER,

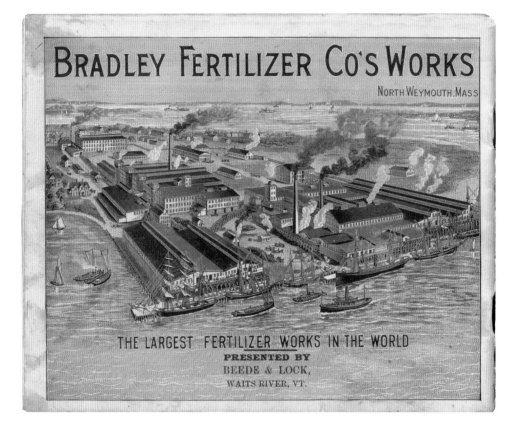

The Bradley Fertilizer Works began as a guano company. The former whaling ships carried their cargo of guano from the Pacific Ocean, around Cape Horn, and up the east coasts of South and North America, skirting Cape Cod to offload at the Bradley Fertilizer Company in North Weymouth, which billed itself as the largest fertilizer works in the world. After 1870, Bradley shifted from guano to superphosphate of lime, mined near Charleston, South Carolina. In 1899, Bradley Fertilizer was consolidated into the American Agricultural Chemical Company, and the Weymouth plant was closed.

The Weir Stove Company began in a Taunton barn in 1879. Charles Baker, William Walker, and George Wilbur, each with a capital investment of $100, combined their skills as designer, foundry worker, and metal mold maker to build a melting furnace to manufacture small stoves for the local market. They started with local bog iron, making four stoves each day. Soon the company grew and began importing large quantities of pig iron from Pittsburgh and the Great Lakes ports. By the start of the twentieth century, the company had expanded to a huge plant in Taunton and was one of America's leading stove producers, shipping out another Glenwood stove every two minutes. Over one thousand people worked in the plant, which was one of the largest of its kind in the world. The innovative Glenwood stove had a chute, which carried the ash through an opening in the kitchen floor down into a storage barrel in the basement. By sliding the damper once each day, the owner could ensure that the ashes dropped into the basement without leaving any soot in the kitchen. In addition to coal and gas ranges, the Weir Stove Company built parlor stoves, furnaces, and water heaters. Acknowledging the popularity of the product name, the Weir Stove Company changed its name to the Glenwood Stove Company.

Another range and stove company situated in Taunton was the White-Warner Company, established in 1882 by Charles White and George Warner. Their Household and Quaker ranges were popular. Around the year 1890, a cast iron kitchen stove cost from $17 to $30. At their peak, these Taunton stove companies were bringing in some fifteen thousand tons of pig iron a year from Pittsburgh to feed their production line.

FROM WHALING TO GUANO AND FERTILIZERS

The southern Massachusetts town of New Bedford was once the whaling capital of the world. Hundreds of sailing ships built in its shipyards carried its sailors to the ends of the oceans in search of whales. During the first half of the nineteenth century, the dock area of New Bedford was lined with factories turning whale blubber into lamp oil, lubricants, soap, and candles. Baleen—the bony ribs in the mouths of some whales needed to strain plankton—found uses as corset stays, skirt hoops, umbrella ribs, and buggy whips. New Bedford's golden age as a whaling port ended with the discovery in 1859 of petroleum in Pennsylvania. The price of whale oil fell dramatically. Even the use of baleen declined as it was replaced by spring steel.

The whaling ships brought another industry to New Bedford. In their hunt for whales, New Bedford men set foot on a number of small, isolated islands occupied only by millions upon millions of birds feeding off the rich sea life in the Pacific waters. Over the millennia, the bird dung had accumulated and dried to form a dense organic material rich in nitrates and phosphates. Because of the heavy rainfall over these islands, the organic components were largely leached out of the guano, leaving rock-hard deposits of concentrated phosphate of lime. The islands still reeked of ammonia, making it very difficult for the men to remain close by for longer than twenty minutes at a time. Known as guano, the hardened bird dung was exploited as a fertilizer and brought great wealth to the Peruvian government, which sold the guano to Britain and the United States.

Howland Island lies near the equator some 1,650 nautical miles southwest of Honolulu. On September 9, 1842, Captain George E. Netcher of New Bedford on board the whaling ship *Isabella* first sighted the island. Nearby Baker Island was discovered in 1832 by Michael Baker, also of New Bedford. Both islands, rich in guano, were later sold to the American Guano Company under the leadership of Alfred Benson, who attempted to form an American monopoly. At his urging, the Guano Islands Act of 1856 was passed by the U.S. Senate to encourage American occupation of similar islands. Atlases of the period used the name "American Polynesia" for the collection of small Pacific islands, rich in guano.

With whaling in decline, the New Bedford–based ships began to carry cargoes of the smelly guano from the Pacific Ocean islands back to their homeport to be processed at the Clark's Cove Guano Company, of which Edmund Grinnell was the president. The Grinnell family had holdings in whaling and textiles as well as in guano. The guano was turned into fertilizer by pulverizing the rock and mixing it with the organic matter of locally caught fish that had been treated with sulfuric acid. The acid in turn was obtained from sulfur imported by ship from Sicily. In its advertisements the Clark's Cove Company promised an early start and rapid growth for crops and flowers treated with its guano. The guano trade continued to add to New Bedford's wealth until the close of the nineteenth century, when chemical fertilizers became available.

New Bedford was not the only town in Massachusetts where a large fertilizer business developed out of the whaling industry. Across Buzzards Bay, the nearby port of Woods Hole on Cape Cod also turned to guano when whaling started its decline. In 1863 the Pacific Guano Works opened for business. The port was now full of vessels bringing guano from the Pacific Ocean islands as well as ships carrying sulfur from Italy, nitrates from Chile, and potash from Germany. Boston shipping merchants funded the guano company and arranged for a branch of the Old Colony Railroad to arrive at Woods Hole to carry the processed guano to Boston.

Provincetown at the northern tip of Cape Cod was yet another community that developed a guano industry. Up to two hundred men labored at Nickerson's Oil & Guano Company processing the Pacific Islands guano hauled by sailing ship into Provincetown Harbor. Another line of the Old Colony Railroad reached to the end of Cape Cod to carry out the processed guano from Provincetown. When the guano deposits of the Pacific Islands were finally exhausted, the ever-resourceful Boston merchants found fresh supplies on islands in the Caribbean Sea, some four hundred miles east of Key West, Florida. Guano brought both wealth and stench to Woods Hole and Provincetown until the advent of chemical fertilizers. The Pacific Guano and Nickerson's Oil & Guano companies ceased operation in 1889. The loss of the guano trade disrupted the economy of Cape Cod until tourists discovered its beauty and its beaches. Woods Hole emerged as a world center for oceanographic research and the mainland terminal for the ferry to the islands of Martha's Vineyard and Nantucket. Provincetown gained fame after 1916 when Eugene O'Neill settled there and opened a theater in a shack on Fisherman's Wharf. O'Neill's early plays were first staged in Provincetown and then taken to New York, where they opened a bold new era in American drama.

In 1861, the William L. Bradley Fertilizer Company opened on Weymouth Neck, a few miles south of Boston. The Bradley family manufactured fertilizers from the guano and whalebone brought back from the Pacific to Massachusetts on the whaling ships based at nearby New Bedford and Woods Hole. The company prospered on sales of its organic fertilizers to markets in the United States and abroad.

The perils of the business were displayed on January 10, 1884, after a cargo of guano sent from Weymouth to Savannah, Georgia, on the schooner *Edwin I. Morrison* was contaminated by seawater. The vessel, built in

1873, had three masts and was 155 feet in length. The Bradley Fertilizer Company sued the owners of the schooner, claiming that the ship "was not tight, stanch, strong and every way fitted for said voyage as agreed." The company claimed that when the schooner left Weymouth, the bilge-pump hole on the portside of the schooner was not properly covered. As a result, the ship was not seaworthy, and seawater entered the hold and ruined the cargo. The owners of the schooner argued that they were not negligent and that the ship was indeed seaworthy. They explained the leak and the damage to the cargo as an act of God, due to strong gales and the perils of the sea. The case worked its way up to the United States Supreme Court, where it was heard ten years after the event (*The Edwin I. Morrison*, 153 U.S. 199 [1894]). The justices found that the damage to the cargo of guano was not due to the "fault or negligence in the navigation of the vessel or care of the cargo [but] was caused by a danger of the seas" and dismissed the case with costs.

The family-owned Bradley Fertilizer Company showed spectacular growth late in the nineteenth century, when it billed itself as "The Largest Fertilizer Works in the World." Factory buildings were built on pylons extending into the bay to allow ships under sail and steamships to dock alongside the plant. The factory successfully turned from natural guano and whalebone to the use of chemicals, especially superphosphate of lime, as the key ingredient of its fertilizers. William Bradley learned about the large amounts of phosphate rock close by Charleston, South Carolina. In 1870 he formed a partnership with the Marine and River Phosphate Mining and Manufacturing Company, which held the monopoly to mine phosphates in South Carolina. The phosphate rock was sent for processing to Bradley-owned fertilizer factories in Cleveland, Baltimore, and Charleston as well as in Weymouth.

According to its advertising, the company's headquarters were at 92 State Street in Boston. Its main product was Bradley's superphosphate, a "complete fertilizer for general use on all farm and garden crops." The company continued to sell manure, seafowl guano, and fine bone fertilizers for crops, as well as meat meal used as poultry food. Its brochures were filled with examples of abundant crops of potatoes, corn, and other vegetables grown using Bradley fertilizers, together with gushing testimonials from satisfied customers.

After William Bradley died in 1894, his sons Peter and Robert ran the business. In 1899 the family-owned Bradley firm was consolidated with twenty-two other fertilizer companies across the nation to form the American Agricultural Chemical Company. Boston-based Bradley Fertilizer Company was now but a subsidiary of a much larger enterprise; it gradually lost its importance and was closed down. In the 1950s the site in Weymouth found a new use as a Nike antiaircraft missile base. Some thirty Nike Ajax and Nike Hercules missiles were stored there in underground facilities. These missiles were tracked by radar operating from the nearby Little Hog Island. The missile site was dismantled in 1974. Occupying prime land near Boston with panoramic views across Hingham Harbor, the site now had appeal for housing. A section of the property was sold to developers, who planned an upscale gated community. But the past came back to haunt the new venture. The residue of guano, phosphates, and other chemicals left behind by fertilizers and missiles had contaminated the soil. The site was cleaned up, and the hazards to the environment were removed. The Webb Memorial State Park, part of the Boston Harbor Islands National Park, sits atop the site of the former fertilizer plant and underground missile base.

10

WORCESTER COUNTY ~

Central Massachusetts comprises a number of towns, with Worcester, the second city of Massachusetts, at the center. The towns of Fitchburg, Gardner, and Winchendon stretch north to the border with New Hampshire; the towns of Uxbridge and Webster are close to the border with Rhode Island. The area was agricultural until the early nineteenth century. Town centers began to develop, usually close to a river or a stream. Here small gristmills and sawmills were set up to make use of waterpower. It took the railroads and steam power to give industrialization its great boost. After 1835, the railroads linked Worcester with Boston and New York. There was also an important rail link from Worcester to Woonsocket, Rhode Island, and on to Providence. This line followed the Blackstone River, which saw the development of light industry well before the Merrimack River to the north. The Boston & Albany Railroad ran through the county to the north of Worcester. By 1889, Worcester County had a total population of 244,000, with 68,000 in Worcester and 20,000 in Fitchburg. The other towns of Worcester County had much smaller populations, fewer than 5,000 each. Despite their small populations, most of them shared in the industrialization of nineteenth-century Massachusetts.

In addition to the grist, flour, and sawmills that served these communities as early as the middle of the eighteenth century, the small towns later developed cotton and woolen textile mills, shoe and boot factories, brick kilns, and sash and blind makers. The town of Clinton, already a minor center for textiles, benefited from the enterprise of Erastus and Horatio Bigelow. Using the power of the Nashua River, the Bigelow brothers invented a new loom to weave carpets which put their town on the national map. The Bigelow Carpet Company (incorporated in 1838) introduced broadloom carpet and became one of the world's leading carpet makers. As early as 1866, Bigelow Carpets established a presence in New York, with offices at 136 Madison Avenue.

Furniture making, and in particular chair making, became a specialty of several of the towns to the north of Worcester. The town of Templeton also had chair makers, but it was in Gardner that this industry flourished. James Comere, who moved from Lexington to Gardner in 1805, started the chair-making business. His specialty was hand-made rocking chairs with cane or rattan seats. Soon others in Gardner and the surrounding towns took up the trade. The factory system brought mass production and standardization. Gardner once had a host of other industries (including the manufacture of clocks, oil stoves, and nails, as well as tanneries), but chair making has stood the test of time. To this day, Gardner specializes in rocking chairs, to be given as gifts to graduates of many of the nation's leading universities and colleges. The Massachusetts skill in cabinetry can also be seen in the sewing machines and wind organs made in Worcester County.

The town of Shrewsbury remained largely agricultural. Its farmers developed a lively trade in butter, cheese, eggs, chicken, and beef for the Boston and Worcester markets. The daily traffic between the cities provided work for the town's stagecoach and transport wagon makers. Leather from the plentiful herds of cattle found its way into the tanneries and the shoe shops of Worcester County.

The town of Fitchburg had many home-grown entrepreneurs who developed a wide range of industries. The town was named for John Fitch, who with his family was carried off to Canada in 1748 by Indian bounty hunters working with the French. The family returned from captivity the following year. The town center of Fitchburg was located on the Nashua River, which was to play a major role in the town's industrialization. In 1765 the population was only 259; by 1850 it had risen to 5,000, and by 1888 the population had reached 20,000, supported mainly by the timber industry. Fitchburg produced paper, lumber, chairs, and furniture. The metal trades were also well represented. Using local iron ore, a large machinery industry developed, making railroad engines, power tools, saws, knives, and even nails. Machinery for woodcutting was a town specialty. Fitchburg was the original home of the Buckeye Mowing Machine Company before it moved to Worcester. In 1883 the Wachusett Electric Light Company began to produce streetlights for the growing town. Fitchburg was also the home of the Iver Johnson Company, which began as an arms manufacturer and later made bicycles. By 1900 the city's population exceeded 30,000. Starting early in the twentieth century, local owners sold out to national businesses, and, as in many other New England towns, industries began their exit from Fitchburg, leaving behind abandoned mills and a declining commercial center.

Hopedale and Whitinsville are two other towns in Worcester Country with great industrial histories. In 1841 the Reverend Adin Ballou and thirty of his followers settled in a section of the shoe town of Milford which became known as Hopedale. This sect called itself the Independent Restorationists. Its members believed in the fatherhood of God and the brotherhood of mankind. They hoped to set up a Christian Socialist community based on abstinence, pacifism, and "the co-equal rights of the sexes." The sect was fervently abolitionist and was against aggression of all sorts, even in protecting oneself. First called the Fraternal Community No. 1, and later the Hopedale Community, the members sought to work together and to share equally. Their idealism did not hold up long, and soon there was friction among the members. The brothers Ebenezer and George Draper believed that they could do better on their own. The Drapers were aware of the booming textile industry spreading across New England, and they began to manufacture textile looms at Hopedale. Within a few years they built a colossal plant with over five thousand men making the Northrop loom. The one-industry town of Hopedale prospered into the early twentieth century, until the decline of the local textile industry and competition from other manufacturers resulted in bankruptcy. The factory was abandoned, and the town of Hopedale went into decline.

Whitinsville, which lies a few miles to the west of Hopedale, shared in its fate. Paul Whitin moved to the area in 1809 and soon after founded a cotton mill alongside the Mumford River. It was his son John who designed a cotton-picker machine that initiated the great Whitin Machine Works, producing machinery for the cotton industry. At its peak the machine works gave employment to thousands who came to Whitinsville from Canada, Ireland, and England. The factory achieved peak capacity soon after World War II, with over 4,500 workers. In the 1970s the company left the town of its birth and relocated in the South.

THE RISE OF INDUSTRY IN WORCESTER

The first Europeans came to Worcester in 1679 and settled the area around Lake Quinsigamond. The city is located at the headwaters of the Black-

Main Street, Worcester, showing trolleys and automobiles, circa 1910. The city built the machines for the industries of America. The Crompton & Knowles Loom Works, the Norton Company, American Steel & Wire, and the Coes Wrench Company, among many others, were located in Worcester.

The Richardson Manufacturing Company of Worcester built the Buckeye mower. This trade card, circa 1882, shows Father Time proudly introducing one of the innovations in farm machinery.

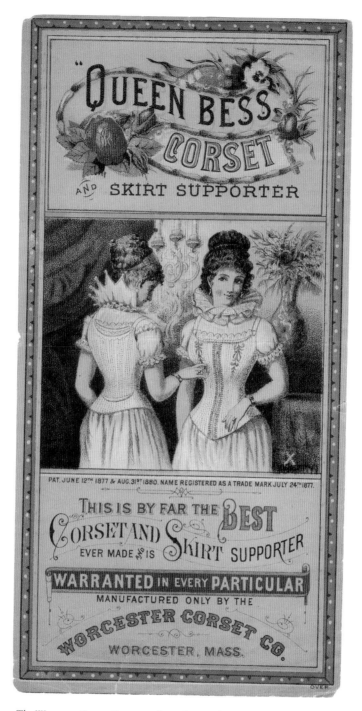

The Worcester Corset Company (later the Royal Worcester Corset Company) was established in the 1860s. At its peak, two thousand workers were kept busy making corsets in the large factory. Once the pinched waistline went out of style during World War I, the corset companies began to fail.

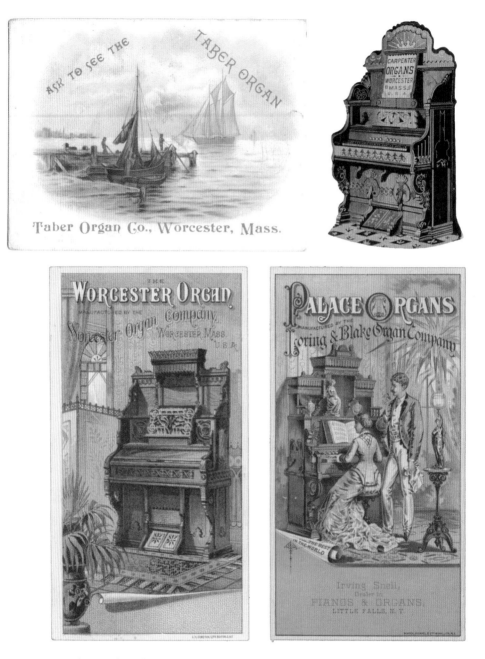

These are the trade cards of the major Worcester home organ factories. Production of these reed organs grew out of the craft of cabinetmaking. The home organ declined as the piano gained in popularity. Worcester was also a major supplier of piano wire.

stone River, which flows a mere forty-six miles before it enters Narragansett Bay at Providence. The river, which forms part of the boundary between Massachusetts and Rhode Island, was the source that provided power to the first industries in the United States. As with many eighteenth-century Massachusetts towns, Worcester had its corn and lumber mills. In the 1760s a local potash industry found ready markets in England and helped pay for the finished goods imported from the mother country. In 1793, Samuel Slater came to the river to build the first cotton mill in the United States, powered by a waterwheel such as he had seen in his native England. By 1800 there were dozens of textile mills, tanneries, paper mills, and other factories along the banks of the river, especially near the Pawtucket Falls. A canal alongside the river was dug from Worcester to Providence, causing fears that it would divert trade away from Boston. The canal was chartered by Rhode Island and Massachusetts in 1823 and opened for business in 1828, with the first barge from Providence arriving in Worcester. The canal closed down less than twenty years later because of competition from the Providence & Worcester Railroad. The chemical waste that was dumped into the water by the factories heavily polluted the Blackstone River.

In 1820 the population of Worcester reached 2,262. Over the nineteenth century, Worcester grew into a major industrial center. It is the home of Clark University (founded in 1887), the College of the Holy Cross (1843), and the Worcester Polytechnic Institute (1865). These schools supplied the technical and intellectual support for the development of the city.

The growth of industry in Worcester attracted thousands of machine workers. They came from the local farms as well as from the various countries of Europe. Worcester had its shoe factories and textile mills, but their expansion was limited by lack of sufficient waterpower. Instead, Worcester's workingmen specialized in making the precision tools for the mills and the many other industries of New England. The toolmakers, foundry men, carpenters, bricklayers, and masons—then known as mechanics—were the future of Worcester. Mechanics Hall, which opened in 1857 as the showplace for the Worcester County Mechanics Association, demonstrated their importance to the local economy. At the meetings of the association, the members called for better working conditions for themselves and better schools for their children. The concert hall at Mechanics

Hall is still hailed as the finest built in pre–Civil War America. Here Charles Dickens read from his works and Enrico Caruso sang his arias.

The coming of steam power after 1840 brought vast opportunities for the mechanics of Worcester. The city became the incubator for American industrialization. The Wheelock Engine Company and the Washburn Steam Works were among the first to produce the boilers to harness this new source of energy. The Cleveland Machine Works, Curtis & Marble, and the Gilbert Loom Company were among the major companies in Worcester making machinery for the textile mills.

Lucius James Knowles and his brother Francis Bangs Knowles were gifted machinists who saw their opportunity in building machinery for the fast-growing textile industry of New England. The Knowles Loom Works (founded in 1856) made looms for all types of textile fabric. In 1897, Knowles merged with another Worcester loom maker, owned by George Crompton. Crompton got his start in 1848 making tools for the textile industry. Ten years later he began to manufacture looms. The Crompton & Knowles Loom Works remained the world's leading producer of fancy looms until the 1940s. The company made specialized looms for the manufacture of silk, carpets, cotton, ribbon, tape, and other products. Crompton & Knowles employed inventors and engineers who speedily met the demand for more complex looms. This innovative ability was lost early in the twentieth century, and the company could no longer keep up with its competitors. The loom works sputtered along until 1980, when Crompton & Knowles closed its antiquated plant in Worcester and moved its base to the South. The remainder of the company, now known as CK, moved from Worcester to Connecticut, where it has emerged as one of the world's major chemical companies and the producer and marketer of polymers, specialty chemicals, and polymer-processing equipment. The company's products, including dyes, lubricants, rubber chemicals, and chemicals used in agriculture, are sold the world over. The grand home on Main Street, Worcester, once owned by Lucius J. Knowles became a funeral parlor.

Franklin B. Norton and his cousin Frederick Hancock started out as the makers of pottery, founding the Norton Company in 1885. Norton soon switched over to the mass production of the grinding tools needed to build and maintain the machinery used in American industry. Its equipment found extensive use during the expansion of the railroad and trolley networks, and Norton became one of Worcester's first-rank companies and the source of much wealth. The company offered good bene-fits and health care to its workers. Norton-owned farms provided small plots of land for workers to grow their own vegetables. The company eventually diversified into abrasives used for sanding furniture and finishing the blades of turbines. Over the years Norton has expanded its operations beyond its base in Worcester. In 1909 it built a plant in Europe and later expanded to dozens of countries. The company was acquired in 1990 by Saint-Gobain, the old-line French engineering firm, which further weakened its ties to the city of its birth.

The history of the Norton Company is closely linked with that of one of the best known of Worcester's families. In 1892, Milton P. Higgins, a native of Maine, became the president of Norton and turned it into Worcester's largest single employer. John Woodman Higgins worked for his father at the Plunger Elevator Company, and later at the Worcester Pressed Steel Company. In 1906, young John and his wife traveled to Europe, where his fascination with suits of armor had its beginnings. Over the years he built up one of the world's great collections of armor. In 1931, John W. Higgins launched a new building as the headquarters of the Worcester Pressed Steel Company with a Gothic-style great hall to house his collection.

The demand for iron and steel, especially the growth of the railroads, provided much work for Worcester's foundries. Sumner Smith and Luther Shaw built large companies to supply the tools, wheels, nails, and screws for the industries of America. Worcester became a center of America's wire industry. Wright Wire and Spencer Wire were two of the larger companies in Worcester producing wire. Charles F. Washburn, who opened his wire mill in 1820, joined with Philip Moen to use scrap iron to make barbed wire for farm fences, piano wire for the burgeoning piano factories, and corset wire to keep trim the figures of the local ladies. The Washburn & Moen Company later became the American Steel & Wire Company. It grew mightily with the demand for wiring for the railroads and for the electrification of the street trolley networks linking cities with their suburbia. At its peak, American Steel & Wire employed over three thousand workers in Worcester alone and was one of the world's great wire companies.

In 1836, Loring Coes (born 1812) and his brother Aury Gates Coes (born 1817) started in the wool machinery business. Four years later they began to make wrenches and knives after their own patents. The Coes wrench, used to loosen or tighten screws, was, according to company publicity, "the first screw wrench that could be adjusted by the hand which held it." The Coes Company built wrenches up to six feet tall "that will remove the valve bonnet without spoiling it." These large wrenches weighed in at over fifty pounds apiece. The Coes Screw Wrench Manufactory was located on Webster Square in Worcester. Coes wrenches were sold throughout the United States and abroad.

Osgood Bradley came to Worcester in 1822 to seek his fortune. He opened a shop off Main Street to build stagecoaches for travel between New England's towns. Horse-drawn furniture-moving vans and lunch wagons were also built in Worcester. With the coming of the railroads, Bradley was one of the first (in 1833) to build passenger cars. In the beginning these were simply modified stagecoaches. Bradley also built railroad sleeping cars for the Boston to New York run. Later, Bradley built the electric trolley cars that played so important a role in urban transit in the United States from 1890 until the coming of the automobile. In 1930 the Bradley Company was absorbed into Pullman Standard and continued building railroad cars in Worcester until 1960. The massive need for metal wheels for the rail transportation systems created yet another industry for Worcester. Nathan Washburn's Car Wheel Company employed over four hundred men to cope with the demand.

The firearms industry was another that was extensively developed in Worcester. The firm of Allen & Wheelock opened its firearm plant in 1860. One of its employees, Sullivan Forearm, married one of Ethan Allen's daughters. A second Allen daughter married Henry Wadsworth, an officer in the Union Army. With these family arrangements in place, the firm emerged as the Forearm & Wadsworth Firearm Manufacturing Company, making revolvers and shotguns of various sizes. The company was later taken over by Harrington & Richardson Manufacturing Company, and still later by New England Firearms Corporation. Gilbert H. Harrington and his partner William A. Richardson set up shop in Worcester in 1871. They made revolvers carried by the police. The Harrington & Richardson factory was extensively equipped with milling machines and cylinder turning and drilling machines. The H & R revolvers and shotguns were famous for their accuracy. After 1910, H & R expanded to make handcuffs and leg irons, as well as automatic pistols. After World War I, the company added teargas guns.

Steam power created a host of new industries in Worcester. The Hudson

Belting Company produced the long leather belts that allowed the central turbine of steam-powered factories to turn the looms, drills, and grinding wheels. Fitts, Rice & Company was among the early builders of hydraulic elevators.

Several Worcester companies built farm equipment to meet the conditions specific to New England. The Richardson Manufacturing Company was the largest of several Worcester companies making farm equipment. Richardson built the horse-drawn Worcester Buckeye mower and the hay tedder (a device that turns and loosens hay after mowing to hasten drying). Richardson claimed that its chain gear mowers had "the best cutting apparatus in the world" and would not clog.

The Worcester Corset Company was the largest of the seven corset makers in the city. It was founded by David Hale Fanning. Born in 1830 and orphaned seven years later, Fanning made his way to Worcester, where, at age thirty-one, he started to manufacture hoopskirts to meet the fashion needs of the times. Fanning, who had a good eye for fashion trends, decided to switch to corset manufacture. Worcester Corset occupied a whole block of Grand Street. Inside the great factory, two thousand workers fashioned corsets using baleen whalebone. The company produced three brands of corsets; the Royal Worcester, the Bon Ton, and the Adjusto ("for the fleshy woman"). David Fanning finally sold out at age ninety-five to a syndicate of men from Worcester, Boston, and New York. During World War I the corset succumbed to a call to patriotism issued by the War Industries Board asking the women of America to turn in their corsets with their steel-reinforced ribbings to aid the war effort. Twenty-eight tons of metal retrieved from these garments went to build the weapons used in the war. American women were at last freed from the constrictions of the corset and its emphasis on the pinched waistline (Evans 2004). Changing fashions led to the demise of the great Worcester Corset Company.

The tremendous burst of industrial creativity during the late nineteenth century brought wealth and pride to Worcester. Yankee machinists who came to Worcester to seek their fortunes built the factories. A lucky few became captains of industry and the great benefactors of this machinist city. By 1910 the population had grown to 146,000 (from fewer than 3,000 ninety years before), predominantly white. The city attracted many immigrants from Europe. At the start of the twentieth century, fewer than one resident in three had both parents born in America. Another third was foreign born, and the remainder had one American-born and one foreign-born parent. Ireland, the Scandinavian countries, French-speaking Canada, and England were the main sources of immigrants seeking work in the factories. Worcester's industries benefited mightily during the Civil War and World War I, but the Great Depression led to a precipitous loss of business and employment and brought hard times to the city.

Decline of Worcester Industry after World War II

Worcester, with its many skills, recovered thanks to military orders during the Second World War. The Harrington & Richardson firearms company was busy during the war making rapid-fire weapons and submachine guns for the U.S. Marine Corps. Armaments made by H & R were extensively used in the Korean conflict as well. In the 1980s, however, the buildings of the Harrington & Richardson Manufacturing Company of Worcester were torn down.

In 1950 the Royal Worcester Corset Company closed its doors. Shoe, textile, and carpet companies were soon to follow. In 1958 the once-great American Steel & Wire closed and was followed by Pullman Standard (1960), the Crompton & Knowles loom company (1980), Johnson Steel & Wire (1986), Coes Knife (1991), and Heald Machines (1992). The departure of these venerable companies caused the loss of thousands of local jobs, especially in the precision machinery industries. Worcester's experience since the 1950s is a microcosm of the story of America's de-industrialization. In 1940 the population of Worcester reached 193,694. Since then, the city has steadily lost jobs and population. Only 172,648 lived in the city by the year 2000. Medical industry–related companies in science parks built around the city perimeter have replaced Worcester's old industries near its center.

John Higgins died in 1961, and the Worcester Pressed Steel Company no longer exists. The Higgins Armory at 100 Barber Avenue in Worcester still houses his collection of three thousand pieces of armor and one thousand firearms and other weapons, paintings, and engravings. Most of the collection is European, though it also contains objects from Africa and Asia. It is said to be the only museum in the Western Hemisphere dedicated wholly to the display of arms and armor.

11

⌁ SPRINGFIELD AND THE CONNECTICUT RIVER VALLEY

In its early years of development Boston had the benefit of the Charles River and the ocean. The textile towns of Lowell and Lawrence were sited on the Merrimack River to take advantage of its waterpower. New Bedford and Fall River sent out their ships on great journeys to hunt the whale. For its part, the western Massachusetts city of Springfield benefited mightily from its setting along the Connecticut River. The early toll road ran west from Boston for a distance of ninety miles to Springfield, then turned south to follow the western bank of the river before continuing to New York City.

The Connecticut River begins at the Canadian border and flows south through forests and farmland, hamlets and cities, for a distance of 410 miles until it empties into Long Island Sound. The river became an important highway into the interior, making it possible for large boats to navigate up to Springfield. In 1795 a system of locks and canals was completed to circumvent the falls at South Hadley and Turner's Falls, thus permitting steamboats to penetrate farther upriver. From White River Junction in Vermont, through Massachusetts, and down to Hartford, the Connecticut River Valley attracted the metalworkers who fashioned the precision tools that ensured America's industrial dominance.

Western Massachusetts was the site of Shays's Rebellion during the early years of the American republic. The state, confronted with massive war debts, imposed heavy taxes on its citizens. The economy was disrupted as farmers found themselves deep in debt and faced with the foreclosure of their properties. In 1786, Captain Daniel Shays, a veteran of the Revolution, led an armed force of farmers who occupied the courthouse at Northampton before moving on to the Springfield courthouse. Governor James Bowdoin sent General Benjamin Lincoln from Boston with 4,400 militiamen to put down the rebellion.* Shay and his followers attacked the federal armory in Springfield but were repulsed by Lincoln's troops. The rebellious farmers scattered and returned to their homes, but their leaders were captured and sentenced to death for treason, though these sentences were later rescinded. Shays's Rebellion convinced George Washington and other like-minded founding fathers of the vital importance of a strong national government; Massachusetts became the sixth state to ratify the new federal Constitution. The unpopular Bowdoin was voted out of office, and John Hancock, signer of the Declaration of Independence, became governor of Massachusetts.

Greenfield and Millers Falls

Levi J. Gunn and Charles H. Amidon started their careers in the early 1860s in western Massachusetts as machinists with the Greenfield Tool Company, making hand planes. Later, the two went into the business of manufacturing cloth wringing machines and bit braces (a device for gripping and turning tools for boring or drilling). In need of more waterpower to expand their business, they moved ten miles east to the village of Millers Falls, which had developed around the junction of the Vermont & Massachusetts and the New London railroads. Gunn and Amidon built their factory at the point where the Miller's River takes a U-bend and drops seventy feet over a series of rapids. In 1868, Gunn, Amidon, and their partners established the Millers Falls Manufacturing Company to make precision tools. In time they built a larger factory with a huge waterwheel transmitting power to an overhead system of pulleys and belts. Secondary belts ran down to each workbench to turn the individual lathes, drill presses, grinders, and milling machines. Over the years, the Millers Falls Manufacturing Company developed an extensive line of tools, including saws, miter boxes, wrenches, and wood planes. The company exported its products to many countries, and by the close of the nineteenth century, it could claim that it was the largest maker of machinist's and carpenter's saws in the world.

---

*General Benjamin Lincoln was a descendant of Samuel Lincoln, born in England, who settled in Hingham, Massachusetts, around 1650. Another branch of the family led by Mordecai Lincoln Jr. left Massachusetts early in the eighteenth century. The sixteenth president of the United States, Abraham Lincoln, born in Kentucky in 1809, was descended from the Lincolns of Hingham

The Millers Falls Company continued to grow during the first part of the twentieth century through acquisitions and further expansion of its product line and through the introduction of electric-powered tools. At its peak this western Massachusetts company employed over six hundred workers. The Great Depression brought hard times, however, and in 1932 the Millers Falls Company merged with the nearby Goodell-Pratt machine company.

NORTHAMPTON AND FLORENCE

Some ten miles downriver from Greenfield lies the town of Northampton, the home of Smith College. In the year 1842, the Northampton Association of Education and Industry developed a utopian community west of the town with a plan to set up a silkworm industry, making use of the local mulberry trees. The community was called Florence, after the Italian town at the center of Italy's silk trade. Despite their noble intentions, friction soon split the members, and the community fell into debt. The town became home to the Florence Machine Company, maker of the Crown sewing machine (1875), with agencies across the nation as well as in London and in Havana, Cuba; Lima, Peru; and Santiago, Chile. Before long the Florence Sewing Machine Company was crushed by Singer and went out of business in 1888. In addition to sewing machines, the company also made kerosene stoves. These small countertop stoves generated less heat than their larger coal- and-wood fired floor-standing rivals, and thus offered more comfort for home and restaurant use. The manufacture of Florence oil stoves was later moved to Gardner, Massachusetts, where they continued to be built until the Great Depression.

SPRINGFIELD, HOLYOKE, AND CHICOPEE

In 1636, William Pynchon and his small party traveled west from Boston into the wilderness in search of animal furs. Pynchon was an original shareholder of the Massachusetts Bay Company and was one of those chosen by King Charles I to help govern the new territory. Pynchon and his party established their settlement along the banks of the Connecticut River. They called it Springfield, after the town in Essex, England, where Pynchon was born. The town came into its own during the War of Inde-

This picture of Springfield's Main Street circa 1910 shows the shops and various modes of travel in the thriving city. Springfield was then a center of innovation and enterprise, making precision tools, firearms, farm equipment, lawn mowers, bicycles, and motorcycles. Greater Springfield was home to the Stevens-Duryea, Knox, and Rolls-Royce automobile companies.

pendence, when George Washington passed through on his way to Boston. On General Washington's recommendation, a federal arsenal was established in Springfield in 1777 to store arms for the revolutionary cause. In 1794, Congress voted to establish a federal armory in the town to manufacture muskets. This decision drew skilled metalworkers and mechanics and established Springfield as a center of invention and enterprise. The mass production of tools and machinery with interchangeable parts became the hallmark of Springfield's success. If a part was broken, it could rapidly be replaced, rather than taking apart and rebuilding the whole machine. In 1805 the town's first bridge across the Connecticut River opened to traffic, stimulating development in the surrounding area. The western portion of Springfield known as Ireland Parish broke off in 1827 to form the town of Holyoke, and in 1848 the northern part split off to form the town of Chicopee. The town of Ludlow was founded northeast of Springfield.

With its location alongside the Chicopee River, the village of Chicopee was chosen by the Boston Associates as the next site, after Lowell on the Merrimack River, to be developed for textile production. James K. Mills, Edmund Dwight, Patrick Jackson, and William and Nathan Appleton invested money to construct a dam across the river and to build their mills. The Chicopee Manufacturing Company and other textile mills dominated the town but did not crowd out other industries. The Ames Manufacturing Company (founded in 1834 by Nathan P. Ames) and the Belcher & Taylor Agricultural Tool Company gave employment to hundreds of men. Chicopee was also a center for bicycle and automobile production.

The nearby town of Holyoke on the Connecticut River took its cue from Lowell to become the second planned industrial city in Massachusetts. The town's visionaries saw the great potential of the river, in particular the rapids at South Hadley, as a source of power for the mills. Hundreds of Irish laborers, earning seventy cents a day, were recruited to dig the canals and erect the vast dam across the river. Textiles proved a failure when the Hadley Falls Company went into receivership. Instead, Holyoke developed as "the Paper City." Using rags, linen, and wood pulp, a great paper industry grew up in the town. In 1853, J. C. Parsons opened the Parsons Paper Company, making fine writing paper and envelopes. Five years later William Whiting built a large mill, also to make writing paper and envelopes. The Holyoke Paper Company specialized in linen paper and the Crocker Manufacturing Company in ornamental paper. The Norton Paper Company made disposable paper collars and shirtfronts, the fashion in those days. With over twelve large paper mills, Holyoke was recognized as the world's largest center for papermaking. The town's overdependence on paper manufacture became the prime reason for its industrial decline. Wages rose steeply, and competition was coming from paper makers in Wisconsin. Holyoke remained a small industrial town, never reaching the degree of development seen in Lowell.

The nation's first college for women was founded nearby in South Hadley. The school was the inspiration of Mary Lyon, who believed that women should receive the same level of education offered to men. The Mount Holyoke Female Seminary opened in November 1837. The success of the seminary, with its rigorous educational standards, encouraged the establishment of other colleges for women, including Wellesley and Smith colleges. In 1893 the name of the school in South Hadley was changed to

Mount Holyoke College. It remains one of the nation's leading colleges for women.

Springfield experienced huge growth during the Civil War. After the capture of Harper's Ferry by Confederate troops, the Springfield Armory was the only government-owned gun manufactory in the north. The armory was flooded with orders. Twenty-six hundred men were employed in the time-consuming work of manufacturing muskets for the Union cause. An estimated 800,000 muskets were produced at the Springfield Armory during the Civil War. Craftsmen were busy on the assembly line making the many separate components, which were then assembled into muskets. This marked a profound shift away from the old method of production, in which each craftsman built a musket from start to finish.

At the end of the Civil War, most of the men were let go. They sought work in the privately owned machine shops and foundries in and around Springfield, bringing with them the skills of mass production. By 1900, greater Springfield had over five hundred private manufacturing companies making a wide range of goods from railroad cars to jewelry. Among the leading firms were the Watson Car Company, which built railroad passenger cars; the Warwick Bicycle Company; and Milton Bradley, lithographers and the maker of games. The *Merriam-Webster Dictionary* had its origins in Springfield, as did the Monarch Life Insurance and the Massachusetts Mutual Life Insurance companies.

Horace Smith, who learned about firearms while working for the Federal Armory in Springfield, joined with Daniel Wesson in 1852 to found the firearm company of Smith & Wesson. Their early customers included the United States Cavalry and the imperial Russian government.*

Oliver Ames & Sons of Springfield manufactured plows, wheelbarrows, and other types of farm machinery. The Blair Manufacturing

---

* New England is the home of some of America's largest gunmakers. Massachusetts had Smith & Wesson, Iver Johnson, the J. Stevens Arms and Tool Company, Forearm & Wadsworth, and Harrington & Richardson. Eli Whitney, born in Westborough, Massachusetts, in 1765 and a graduate of Yale, is best known as the inventor of the cotton gin, which greatly aided cotton harvesting. Later, however, he returned to New Haven, where he started a gun factory in a former gristmill. With "machinery moved by water" he developed a new method of production whereby unskilled workers undertook various steps of manufacture before final assembly. This was a departure from the old method, in which a skilled artisan built each gun from start to finish. Oliver Winchester, born in Boston in 1810, started as a shirt maker in New Haven before founding the Winchester Repeating Arms Company. Hiram Stevens Maxim, who worked in a machine shop in Fitchburg, Massachusetts, invented the Maxim machine gun, which was used by British forces, with devastating effect, in the Matabele War of 1893. The Colt and the Marlin firearms companies are based in Connecticut.

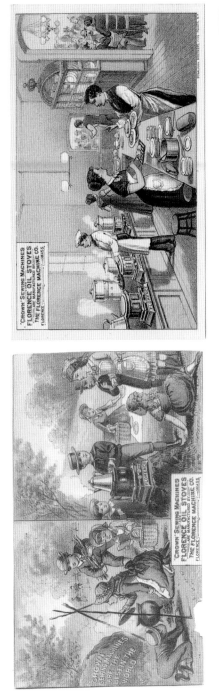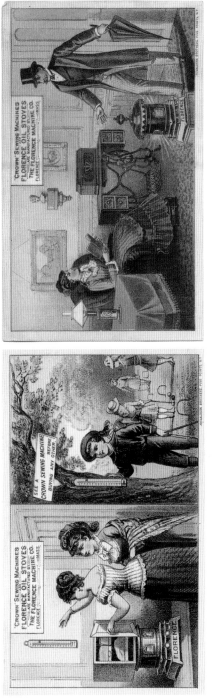

Florence, near Northampton, was founded as a silk-growing community. Later the Florence Machine Company came to the town, where it made Crown sewing machines and Florence oil stoves. The compact Florence oil stove could be used in the home kitchen or in restaurants, or could even be carried on picnics. The Florence sewing machine and parlor stove were among the prized possessions of the affluent home. These four trade cards from the Florence Machine Company depict scenes of American life around 1880.

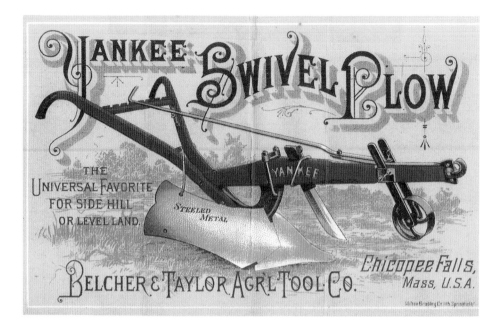

Belcher & Taylor Agricultural Tool Company of Chicopee made the Yankee swivel plow. The company (founded in 1786) started to make farming equipment after the railroad was extended to the town. Chicopee became a major industrial center, home to textile, bicycle, and firearms factories as well as the Stevens-Duryea Automobile Company. Milton Bradley Lithographers of Springfield designed this attractive trade card.

Hampden Park was the home of the Springfield Bicycle Club. This trade card advertises the Grand International Championship, held September 8–10, 1885. Amateur and professional cyclists competed on high-wheelers and safety bicycles for the speed championship of the world. This trade card was prepared by Milton Bradley, Springfield's most famous lithographer and inventor of games.

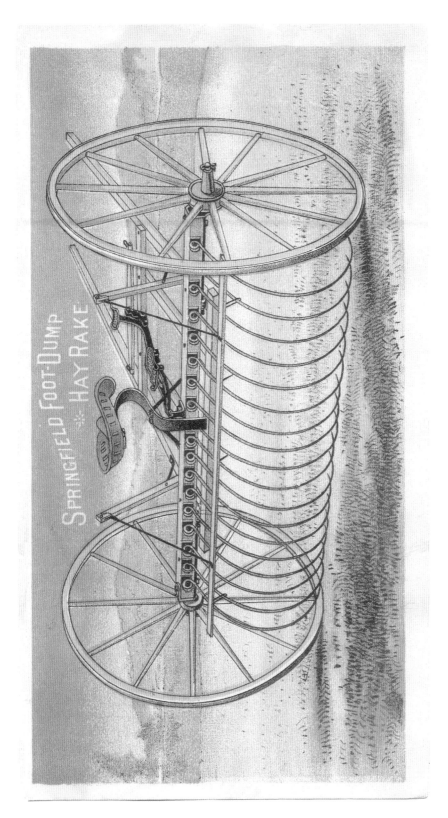

An advertisement for the Springfield Hay Rake for the 1884 growing season.

Blair & Fiske was a major manufacturer of lawn mowers, costing from $13 to $85 (1885 prices), depending on the width of the cut. The smooth-working Easy lawn mower could be pushed by children and adults alike, whereas competing brands were difficult to use and only led to frustration. The illustration shows the front and back of the company's trade card.

Company began building lawn mowers in Springfield in 1879. (The company was sold seventy years later and moved to Des Moines, Iowa.) The population of Springfield, which was under 4,000 in 1820, reached 62,442 in 1900; twenty years later it had more than doubled to 129,614.

Springfield, with its highly skilled workforce, did well during the first third of the twentieth century. It was the home of the Indian Motorcycle Company and of the American Rolls-Royce. The city suffered during the Great Depression but picked up again during World War II. The numerous metalwork companies and machine builders (such as Perkins Gear & Machine, Chapman Valve, and Van Norman Machine Tool Company) were kept humming with war orders.

SPRINGFIELD INDUSTRY AFTER WORLD WAR II

A new reality emerged at end of the Second World War. Springfield's workers enjoyed average hourly earnings that were much higher than comparable rates in the southern states and abroad. In 1952 the Bosch Company—a presence in Springfield since 1911—started to move its production to Mississippi and South Carolina. In 1958, Westinghouse, another large employer in Springfield, began to close down its plant, with a loss of some two thousand jobs. Between 1950 and 1987, over half of the manufacturing plants in greater Springfield closed their doors. A wave of mergers and acquisitions further weakened the bond between these companies and Springfield, leaving many abandoned buildings in the center of the city. The armory closed in 1968. Tool and machine making skills— a pillar of the New England economy—were fast leaving Springfield. In the short term the South benefited from Springfield's loss, but competition was fast increasing from Europe and Asia.

Milton Bradley was the founder of one of the few companies that kept its historic links with Springfield. He was born in Vienna, Maine, in 1836. At age twenty-four he set up his lithography shop in Springfield. He made money by selling copies of a portrait of the beardless Abraham Lincoln; but once Lincoln grew his famous beard, the picture did not sell anymore. Ever resourceful, Bradley produced a board game called "The Checkered Game of Life." The success of the game launched Milton Bradley & Co., the maker of games and children's books. In 1984, Hasbro of Rhode Island, the world's leader in games and puzzles, acquired Milton Bradley of Springfield.

In 1962 the Millers Falls precision tool company was bought by Ingersoll-Rand, which first cut the workforce, then reduced the Massachusetts manufacturing plant and moved most production to the South. The end came in 1982, when the remnants of the once proud Millers Falls Manufacturing Company left its home and moved to New Jersey.

12

❧ RECREATION

Farming before the age of machinery was physically demanding. There were fields for the farmer to work, using horses and a handheld plough. Planting, weeding, watering, and reaping were backbreaking tasks. Fishing likewise was demanding work. For their part, the women of the day were constantly cleaning, spinning yarn, making clothes, and cooking. After a long day's labor in the fields or on the seas, workers were dog tired and eager to go to bed early to rest up for the next day's labors. Machinery and factories transformed the nature of work. In the early days of industrialization, blue-collar workers lived near the factories. They stood or sat all day long and performed the same task over and over again. Waterpower, then steam power and electricity, lessened the physical burden of mechanical labor. The development of office jobs in banks and insurance companies created an army of white-collar workers tethered to their desks all day long. The horse car and, later, the electric trolley system allowed people to travel to work. By 1850, Boston was no longer a compact walking city. It was crowded with tenement houses, and the air was choked with smoke and grit. People had the understandable urge to get out of the city, to walk in the parks, and to get some exercise.

Boston's industrialists and men of business built their homes on Beacon Hill and in the Back Bay. Elegant townhouses were constructed along Beacon Street facing the Boston Common and along Commonwealth Avenue with its central mall. Many of the wealthy had weekend retreats and summer homes on the ponds of Newton and Jamaica Plain or near the ocean. One such Bostonian, Amos Lawrence, made his fortune importing fancy goods from Europe. He was able by the 1820s "to take his exercise on horseback: and almost daily he took long rides, sometimes alone, sometimes with a friend, about the environs of the city. The effect of exercise amidst the beautiful scenery of the environs of Boston was most beneficial to his health" (Lawrence 1856).

One of the popular Four-in-Hand Drags (ca. 1895). The Beaconsfield Stables arranged Sunday rides from June 1 until October 30. Passengers paid fifty cents a seat in an open carriage for the one-hour journey through the beautiful suburbs of Brookline and Newton west of Boston.

Touring in a horse carriage (ca. 1880). The North Shore Bridge Tourist Stable of Concord, Massachusetts, offered carriage tours of the sites of the Revolutionary War battle of April 19, 1775.

By 1850, Boston was filling up with impoverished newcomers. The South End, the North End, and the West End were overcrowded with poorly paid immigrants squeezed into tenements and boardinghouses. The well-to-do began their exodus to spacious homes outside Boston city limits. In 1864, Amos Adams Lawrence (son of Amos Lawrence) described his move to the country: "We moved to Nahant, to our new home on the rocks, and we are all well pleased with it. The addition, which I have made to it, has a good piazza all around on both stories and the sea view is excellent" (Lawrence 1888). For exercise, Lawrence walked around his property or rode his horse from Nahant to Lynn and back again. Among the wealthy with their country houses and among middle- and working-class city dwellers alike, the demand was growing for new methods and means of exercise and recreation.

BICYCLES

Albert Pope (1843–1909) could trace his American ancestors to the 1660s. He grew up in genteel poverty after his father lost his money on land speculation in Brookline, Massachusetts. Pope served in the Civil War and used the honorific title "Colonel" for the rest of his life. With the wages he saved from his war years, young Albert started his first business on Dock Square in Boston as the maker of tools for the shoe industry. He was very successful and took much pride in supporting his family, including two sisters who attended medical school and a brother at Brown University. In 1876 he visited the great Centennial Exposition in Philadelphia. Among the wonders to behold at the exposition was the velocipede—the early bicycle—brought over from Europe. The Boston tool manufacturer saw the great promise in cycling and soon sailed to England to visit the factories where the bicycles were made. Pope succeeded in getting a patent so he could manufacture bicycles in America. He began by importing bicycles from Europe and then making copies in his premises at 45 High Street in Boston. The first American bicycles cost $310, a fortune at the time, equal to one-half the annual income of a skilled worker. When his own factory proved too small, Pope sought a vendor to mass-produce the bicycles for him.

By 1877 the American sewing machine industry was already mature. Isaac Merritt Singer's sewing machines dominated the marketplace, leav-

Colonel Albert Pope founded his bicycle company in Boston in 1877. He introduced the high-wheeler for men and the tricycle for women. Pope advertised extensively and sponsored bicycle races. Later he moved production to a former sewing machine factory in Hartford, Connecticut. His Columbia bicycles dominated the American market until World War I.

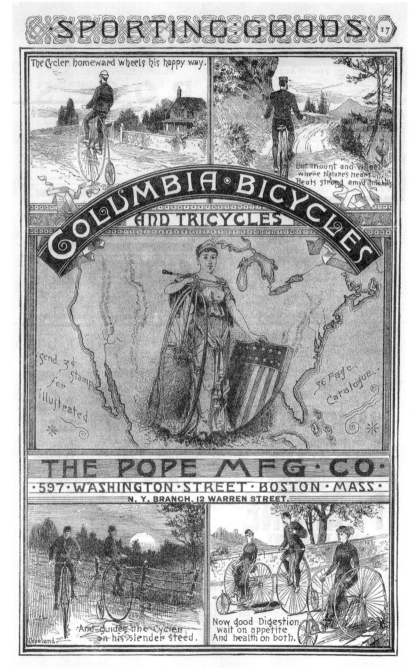

Columbia Bicycle

The Special Columbia is a light roadster, of close build, fine finish, and fitted with the most approved anti-friction ball-bearings, adjustable for wear. Having made several improvements in this machine since we first offered it to the public, we feel fully justified in pronouncing it the best and handsomest Bicycle in the market. We make the Special Columbia from 46 to 60 inches; price, for 46 in., $105.00 to 122.50 for 60 in., half bright. All bright, $10.00 extra; full nickel, $15.00 additional.

The Standard Columbia is a strong, durable roadster, built with a view to withstand the rough usage incidental to touring over ordinary American roads, and for hard work has no equal. It is of graceful model, built of the best materials and carefully finished in every particular. The thousands in daily use fully attest the merits of this favorite machine. The price of the Standard Columbia, half bright, is, for a 42 in., $80.00, up to $100.00 for 58 in. Full nickel, $22.50 extra. We will furnish the Standard with our most approved ball bearings for $10.00 extra.

Both of the above are confidently guaranteed as the best value for the money attained in a Bicycle.

The Mustang is a cheaper Bicycle, all painted, for those who cannot afford to buy a better one. We make them in smaller sizes, from 36 to 46 in.; price, for 36 in., $50.00, to $65.00 for 46 in.

Tricycles are rapidly coming into favor with Ladies and elderly Gentlemen; they can be seen on exhibition at our warerooms. Send 3c. stamp for 24-page catalogue with price lists and full information.

THE POPE M'F'G CO.,

No. 597 WASHINGTON STREET

BOSTON, MASS.

A troop of men on a night ride on the Columbia high-wheeler (ca. 1885). Note the bicycle headlights and the casual clothing of the riders. A fifty-eight-inch high-wheeler cost $100, equal to two months' salary for a skilled worker. Later mass production brought down the price and made the bicycle affordable to all.

ing other companies further behind. One such company was the Weed Sewing Machine firm, with its plant on Capital Avenue in Hartford, Connecticut. The directors of the company were more than happy to use their empty factory space to build bicycles for Albert Pope. Ever the showman, Pope took his prototype bicycle by train from Boston to Hartford. Upon reaching the Connecticut capital, he hopped onto the contraption and pedaled through the town, much to the delight of the local folk. Pope ordered fifty bicycles, to be ready in time for the Framingham Fair. The sewing machine company was able to retool and complete the initial order on time. The early bicycles had a sixty-inch-high front wheel and a small back wheel. In the United States they were known as "high-wheelers" and in Britain as "penny-farthings." The bicycles were a great success, and the Weed sewing machine factory received more orders. Pope opened a large salesroom and a bicycle riding school at 87 Summer Street in Boston. In 1881 he moved to a larger retail store at 597 Washington Street, Boston's premier retail district. By that point the production of bicycles at the Weed factory had outstripped the manufacture of sewing machines. Albert Pope gained control of the company in Hartford, which now became the Pope Manufacturing Company, but he kept his headquarters in Boston. He named his product the Columbia bicycle. With mass-production methods, the price of a Columbia bicycle fell to within reach of Everyman.

The bicycle was first seen as a hazard, and many towns fought against it. Nonetheless, cycling caught the fancy of the public. Retail shops selling Columbia bicycles opened in cities across the nation. Bicycle racing became a popular sport. Riding bicycles along Boston's streets and in the parks was a means of both transportation and recreation. Bicycling magazines and books, many bankrolled by Pope, became popular. Pope expanded his bicycle manufacturing in Connecticut, and in 1897 he built a large plant in Westfield, Massachusetts. Hundreds of thousands of Columbia bicycles were made in the Pope factories, which employed nearly ten thousand workers.

Pope made his fortune (late by Yankee standards) with the bicycle craze. He built an imposing three-story double-bow-fronted townhouse at 378 Commonwealth Avenue in Boston with the Harvard Club as his neighbor. Pope walked for exercise from his home to his headquarters on Washington Street. Later in life he bought a large estate facing the ocean on Jerusalem Road in the town of Cohasset, some fifteen miles southeast of Boston. The grand stone house, called Lindemere, contained dozens of rooms and sat on the hill above a park of fifty acres (Goddard 2000). By 1896, Pope had set his sights on a prize far larger than the bicycle: he was determined to manufacture automobiles. He put his faith in the electric car, but his new venture ended in failure as swifter automobile companies rushed ahead of him.

Following the fashion of the Italians and the French, Pope and other American bicycle companies issued colorful advertising posters to show-case their various makes. Pope advertised his Special Columbia as a light roadster, fitted with anti-friction ball bearings. The forty-six-inch-high bicy-

WARWICK
LEADS
THE WORLD.

WARWICK CYCLE
MFG. CO.,
SPRINGFIELD. MASS. U.S.A

COPYRIGHT 1890 BY THE WARWICK CYCLE CO. SPRINGFIELD MASS.

LITH BY DONALDSON BROTHERS NY

The Warwick Cycle made in Springfield "leads the world." This rare trade card was prepared by Donaldson Brothers, Lithographers, of New York and dates to around 1890.

The Northampton Cycle Company used the talents of Edward Penfield, another famed American poster artist. Wearing matching cap and trousers and argyle stockings, the cool, calm, and collected rider sets off on his Northampton bicycle.

The Orient bicycle was made by the Waltham Manufacturing Company. This Edward Penfield poster shows the Orient leading the pack. The unruffled rider glances back, assured of the superiority of his Orient cycle. Waltham Manufacturing later produced motorcycles and even automobiles.

The Iver Johnson bicycle was built by a firearms manufacturer in Fitchburg, Massachusetts. The company employed Marshall W. Taylor, the great African American bicycle champion, to ride its bicycles in competitions.

LIKE A FLASH

INDIAN MOTOCYCLE
HENDEE MFG. CO.
SPRINGFIELD, MASS.

TOP: *The Hendee Manufacturing Company of Springfield built the Indian brand motorcycle. George Hendee was a champion bicycle rider who ran a bicycle factory before he turned to building motorcycles. The Indian motorcycle and the Harley-Davidson were the two leading American brands. The Indian Motorcycle Company of Springfield closed its doors in 1953.*

BOTTOM: *The Indian Chief motorcycle (ca. 1930), made in Springfield.*

cle sold in the 1880s for $105 and the sixty-inch model for $122.50. The Standard Columbia bicycle was cheaper ($80 for the forty-two-inch and $100 for the fifty-eight-inch bicycle). Tricycles, too, were "rapidly coming into favor with Ladies and elderly Gentlemen." Pope also sold a cheaper bicycle, the Mustang, "for those who cannot afford to buy a better one." All the Pope bicycles were guaranteed to be strong and durable enough to "withstand the rough usage incidental to touring over ordinary American roads."

Columbia high-wheelers were heavy and clumsy to operate. Accidents and injuries were frequent. By 1885 they were being replaced by the Safety Bicycle, which had wheels of equal size and sat closer to the ground. The introduction of pneumatic tires made bicycle riding a pleasure even on the rutted roads of the period. The Safety Bicycle was especially popular with women and led to changes in women's wear, for some even a switch to pantaloons from skirts.

The American bicycling craze continued from 1880 until the beginning of the First World War. Other manufacturers entered the field. The Norwegian-born Iver Johnson (1841–1895) immigrated to Worcester, Massachusetts, and set up as a gunsmith. In 1892 he moved his company to a larger factory in Fitchburg. When Johnson died three years later, the business was taken over by his sons. Not content with their success in making revolvers and shotguns, they got caught up in the bicycle and motorcycle craze. The company was now called the Iver Johnson's Arms & Cycle Works.

To encourage sales, the company hired the famous cyclist Marshall Walter Taylor to race the Iver Johnson bicycle. Known as "The Major," Taylor was one of the great African American athletes of his era. He was born near Indianapolis into a poor family with eight children. At age thirteen he was given a bicycle and enjoyed speeding around town delivering newspapers. He found work in a bicycle shop doing repairs and teaching people how to ride. Taylor entered bicycle races in the Midwest before he moved east and settled in Worcester. Despite the racial prejudice of the time, he became the American sprint champion and went on to win the world championship in Montreal in 1899. With his contract from Iver Johnson, Taylor was the first black athlete with a commercial sponsor. He successfully raced Iver Johnson bicycles in countries around the world. The Major Taylor Velodrome in Indianapolis is named in his honor.

Over three thousand American bicycle brands have been identified. During the height of the craze from 1890 to 1900, tinkerers and mechan-

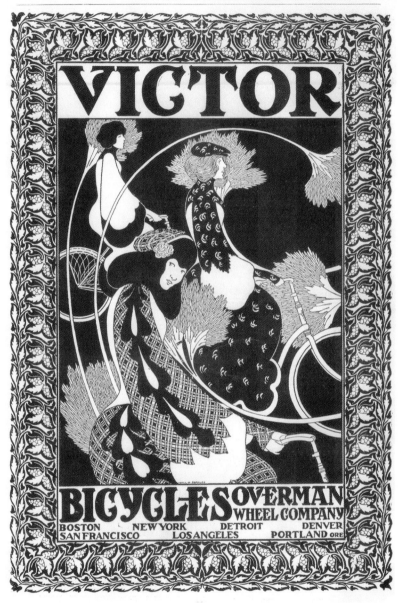

The Victor bicycle was produced from 1884 until 1900 by the Overman Wheel Company, Springfield. Boston-born William Henry Bradley, one of America's most famous graphic artists, painted stunning Art Nouveau posters to advertise the Victor bicycle. Bradley's bicycle

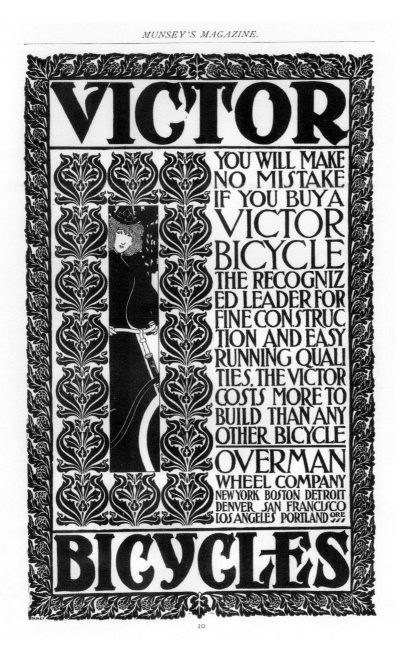

posters, printed from 1894 to 1896, initiated the poster craze in America. William Bradley
was strongly influenced by the work of the English graphic artist Aubrey Beardsley.

ics across the nation were busy building bicycles. Some of the companies began in toolsheds and others grew from failing sewing machine or firearm companies. Most of these businesses were small and lasted only a year or two before closing shop. Chicago and New York had the greatest concentration of bicycle makers.

One of Albert Pope's greatest competitors was in his own backyard. In 1884, Albert H. Overman gave up his profession as a papermaker to set up the Overman Wheel Company in a former sewing machine factory in Chicopee Falls. He built the Victor bicycle and boosted sales by advertising widely. Overman hired William H. Bradley, who designed the stunning Art Nouveau posters showing both men and women happily perched upon their Victor bicycles.* The Victor Safety Bicycle used a hollow steel frame and weighed only sixty pounds (still very heavy by modern standards). Albert Pope hired the leading patent attorneys to fight his crosstown competitor. Pope and Overman—both of whom went by the honorific title "Colonel"—wound up in court. The oversupply of bicycles and falling prices led to the collapse of many companies, including the Overman Wheel Company, which closed in 1900. The stronger Pope bought out seventy-five competitors to form the American Bicycle Company.

Albert Pope and Iver Johnson were the most successful of the Massachusetts bicycle makers. They built the largest factories and endured the longest. At one point Boston was home to some one hundred bicycle brands. The precision tool cities of Worcester and Greenfield boasted several bicycle companies, as did the carriage-making town of Amesbury. The Waltham Manufacturing Company and the Northampton Cycle Company were briefly in the race. The industrial city of Springfield, on the Connecticut River, became a major bicycle center. Here the Warwick Manufacturing Company and the Stebbins Manufacturing Company made some of America's best bicycles. Among the long-forgotten Massachusetts bicycle brands were the Puritan, Harvard, Tremont, Paul Revere,

---

*William Henry Bradley (1868–1962), one of America's most famous graphic artists, was born in Boston. At age eighteen he moved to Chicago, where he worked at Rand McNally as a wood engraver before starting out on his own as a graphic artist and designer. He returned to Massachusetts in his twenties and opened a studio in West Springfield. It was during his Springfield period that Bradley drew the posters for Victor Bicycles. His graphic designs were published on the covers of the leading magazines of the day. During his long career he served as the art editor for Collier's, Good Housekeeping, Metropolitan, and other magazines. Edward Penfield (1866–1925), another famed American graphic designer, made splendid bicycle posters for the Waltham Manufacturing Company and the Northampton Cycle Company.

the Hub King and the Hub Queen, as well as such exotic names as the Greyhound, Cleopatra, Eureka, and Tiger. Several of the Massachusetts bicycle makers also attempted to go into the business of making cars.

The Springfield Bicycle Club built a large bicycle track at Hampden Park where international tournaments took place. One-, three-, five-, and ten-mile races were held for both amateur and professional racers. Most of the races featured high-wheelers, but some featured the tandem tricycle. On September 9, 1885, the great one-mile professional bicycle race for the championship of the world was held in Springfield.

MOTORCYCLES

The American motorcycle was born in Waltham, Massachusetts, in 1895, when Charles H. Metz attached a motor to the rear of a tandem bicycle. The rear rider controlled the engine, while the front rider did the steering. Metz first used his motorized tandem to pace the riders of his Orient bicycles during their races. He then developed a commercial one-man motorcycle, which he introduced in July 1900 at the Charles River Race Track in Boston. The Orient motorcycle outpaced the mechanical bicycles and completed the five-mile run in a record seven minutes. The first American motorcycle race took place in Los Angeles in May 1901, and again the Orient won. By 1902 the one-person Orient motorcycle selling for $250 had a 2-horsepower engine and a five-quart gas tank, enough for a journey of one hundred miles. In 1902, Metz started his own company on Whitney Avenue, Waltham. Four years later he merged with the Marsh Company of Brockton. Known as the M-M, their motorcycle was built in Brockton from 1906 to 1914.

Hundreds of imitators sprang up all over the country. Eventually two motorcycle companies began to dominate. The battle between the Indian and Harley-Davidson motorcycle companies forced the closure of their smaller competitors, including Orient, M-M, and Iver Johnson, all of Massachusetts; Pope, of Connecticut; and Pierce, of Buffalo, New York.

The town of Springfield, Massachusetts, had barely fifteen thousand inhabitants in 1860, but it was fast becoming a major industrial center, and its population was growing apace. One of the sports heroes of the Springfield Bicycle Club was George M. Hendee. Born in Watertown, Connecticut, in 1866, Hendee took up bicycle racing at age sixteen. During the

The Waltham
Manufacturing
Company in 1895
added a motor to
its Orient bicycle
to create the
world's first motor-
cycle. Using a
3-horsepower
engine, the Orient
motor bicycle could
reach speeds of
over 40 mph. In
1896 the Orient
motor bicycle cost
$250.

course of his career he won nearly every race in which he took part, includ-ing the 1881 national championship held at Springfield's Hampden Park. Hendee capitalized on his fame by opening his own bicycle factory in Springfield. He sponsored other famous riders, and his bicycle business grew strong. After Hendee witnessed the excellent performance of a motorized pacing bicycle built by Carl Oscar Hedstrom, his ambitions turned from foot-powered bicycles to the mass production of motorized cycles.

At the start of the twentieth century, George Hendee invited Oscar Hedstrom to submit a design for a motorized bicycle. Hedstrom, born in Sweden in 1871, had arrived in the United States as a boy of nine. Young Oscar first worked at a watchmaker's shop and then in various machine shops. His passion was the bicycle. In his home workshop he built bicycles and fitted them with engines to serve as pacer bicycles at race meetings. These motorized bicycles were designed to block wind resistance in front of a bicycle racer attempting a speed record. Hedstrom was developing quite a reputation for the quality of his motorized pacer bicycles.

RECREATION

Charles Metz was the inventor of the motorcycle. After leaving the Waltham Manufacturing Company, Metz formed a partnership with the Marsh brothers of Brockton. The Marsh-Metz (M-M) motorcycle was in production from 1910 to 1914. The energetic Metz also opened a car company in Waltham. Here a motorcyclist in full uniform proudly displays his Marsh-Metz in a photographer's studio (ca. 1910).

Hendee was so taken with Hedstrom's design for a one-cylinder gasoline engine attached to a bicycle frame that he proposed a partnership. Hendee became president of the Hendee Manufacturing Company of Springfield, with Hedstrom as its chief engineer and designer. In 1903, Hedstrom showed off his motorcycle with a record speed of 56 mph. The company expanded rapidly with solid engineering and innovative designs and soon outgrew its small factory building. The name was changed to the Indian Motorcycle Company, and in 1912 the firm moved into a huge

193

five-story plant, called the Wigwam, with the production capacity of 60,000 motorcycles a year. Here the company built its famous Indian Chief motorcycle and seemed headed for glory. But its success was short-lived. Production peaked in 1913 at 32,000 motorcycles. The company was buffeted by competition from the Harley-Davidson Motorcycle Company as well as from the automobile, especially Henry Ford's Model T. Hedstrom left the company in 1913 and Hendee a few years later. Without their leadership, the firm went further into decline. In 1930, E. Paul DuPont, a racing enthusiast, bought the company and changed its focus to leisure and racing. DuPont gave up ownership in 1945. Weak leadership and poor engineering left the Indian Motorcycle Company of Springfield mortally wounded, and it closed in 1953.

❧ THE NEW ERA: MASSACHUSETTS BUILT AUTOMOBILES

13

The Massachusetts Bay Colony began as a commercial venture to bring wealth to Mother England. The forests were cut down to build the sailing ships that sailed regularly to England and its Caribbean sugar islands from Newburyport, Salem, Boston, and the other Massachusetts ports. The journey from England to Boston on board a sailing ship took up to twelve weeks. During the era of the China trade, sailing ships left Massachusetts ports for the long journey down the east coast of North and South America, around Cape Horn, and northwest to China. The trip to China and back took up to three years to complete. Other Massachusetts ships left New Bedford and searched the Pacific Ocean and the icy waters of the Artic Sea for whales.

New methods of transportation came to Massachusetts during the 1830s. Every town wanted to be linked by railroad, and soon goods and passengers could travel far and wide by rail. Boston had seven separate railroad terminals that linked the city with the other New England states, with New York, and with the new cities of the South and West. An extensive horse-drawn trolley system joined Boston with the surrounding towns. These trolleys ran on rails embedded in the roads. Deliveries to Faneuil Hall and to the shops along Washington Street were made by horse cart. After 1891 the trolley system was converted from horsepower to electricity. Harbor ferries connected Boston with the surrounding coastal towns, and larger steamships plied the waters between Boston and New York. By the close of the nineteenth century, Boston was the hub of an extensive transportation system comprising ferries, steamships, trains, and streetcars. The public transit system brought hundreds of thousands of people into the city each morning and took them home at night.

Horse carriage manufacturing was a major Massachusetts industry, especially in Amesbury, Cambridge, and Newburyport. Robert Henderson started his carriage business in North Cambridge in 1862; after his death

Many horse carriage manufacturers flourished in Massachusetts from the middle of the nineteenth century, especially in Boston, Cambridge, and Amesbury. This illustration shows the business cards of J. Andrew and J. Sawyer of Lynn (ca. 1855) and C. L. Walker of the United States Carriage Company of Newburyport.

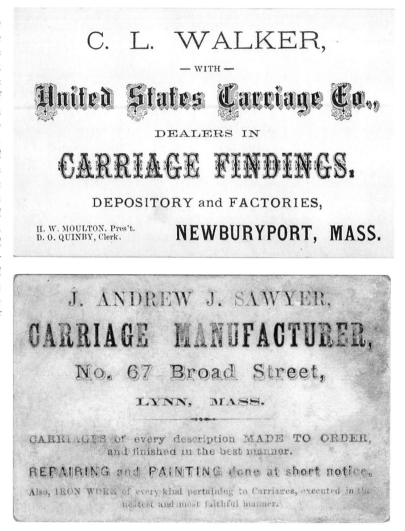

the business was taken over by his sons John and Robert Jr. The company made barges, wagons, and large carriages as well as two-passenger surreys. In 1892 the Henderson brothers moved their company into a large factory at 2067–2089 Massachusetts Avenue. Hugh Stewart founded his carriage factory in Cambridgeport, and Richard Tyner and his son had their carriage factory in East Cambridge. The Putnam Nail Company of Boston

The Boston Sociable (1881) was an elegant two-wheel carriage for family use. (Drawing by John A. Lowell & Co., Boston.)

claimed to make the "only hot-forged and hammer-pointed horse shoe nail in the world." A horse was only as good as the condition of his feet. Hence the company slogan, "No Foot, No Horse." The elite had their private means of transportation and could travel by carriage from their homes to the stores, the railroad station, and to visit with friends. In the wealthier suburbs, carriage houses were sited in back of the homes. Riding through the parks and along the Charles River Speedway became a popular recreation. Until the early twentieth century, horses were everywhere. The "Vehicle Department" in the 1908 edition of the Sears, Roebuck catalog devoted fifty pages to carts, carriages, and equipment for horses. The company offered a covered two-passenger buggy for $59.95 and a four-seater hansom for $104.95. Sears sold delivery wagons for the city and heavy wagons for use on the farm. The popular retailer also sold many types of saddles (from $5.95 up to $22.87), as well as bridles, harnesses, stirrups, and ropes.

One of the largest carriages makers in Massachusetts was the Keith & Ryder Wagon Company, located in Sagamore on Cape Cod. Founded in 1826, the company made horse-drawn stagecoaches, wagons, and buggies as well as ox carts. With the coming of the railroads, Keith & Ryder switched to producing more lucrative freight cars. The company, renamed the Keith Car Manufacturing Company, was a major supplier of freight cars for the New York, New Haven, and Hartford Railroad. In the early years of the twentieth century, it employed six hundred workers and was making a thousand freight cars a year.

All these carriage companies, together with the horse and most of the railroads and streetcars, were swept away by the automobile, which so changed the face of America starting early in the twentieth century. For some years it was unclear whether the automobile would be powered by steam, electricity, or gasoline before the abundant fossil fuel from Pennsylvania and other American oilfields emerged as the winner. A multitude of automobile repair shops, gas stations, battery stations, car dealerships, asphalt-paved roads, and highways heralded in this new era of transportation. The automobile was first seen as a toy for the wealthy, but it soon captured the imagination of America. Like "mill fever," the sewing machine, the bicycle, and the piano before it, the automobile was the latest craze. Countless mechanical whiz kids across the nation dreamed of making it big in the automobile business. Thousands of companies were started across the United States. Bankrupt bicycle and carriage factories were converted to making automobiles. Many of these early automobile companies were in Massachusetts, with its long tradition in precision tools and engineering.

THE STANLEY STEAMER

The Stanley family left Massachusetts in 1777 and became among the first to settle in Kingfield in Franklin County, Maine. Several generations of Stanleys earned their living as landowning farmers in this remote part of Maine, in the shadow of Sugarloaf Mountain. One branch of the family owned a house on Maple Street where they raised six boys and one girl, Chansonetta. The identical twin sons Freelan Oscar and Francis Edgar Stanley (born in 1849) were educated in the town's one-room schoolhouse before going on to the Western State Normal School. By the middle of the nineteenth century, innovation and invention were in the air, wafting over even the isolated communities of Maine. The twins, known as F. O. and F. E., became interested in photography and in 1883 perfected and patented the dry-plate coating process. They left Kingfield and estab-

The Putnam Nail Company of Neponset in Boston advertised "the only hot-forged and hammer-pointed horseshoe nail in the world." The company's trade cards portray the most famous sulky racers of the day, including Edwin Thorne, Robert Bonner, and John Jackson.

Boston Coach Axle Oil was a lubricant for carriages, cabs, and buggies. It was sold in one-pint to two-gallon containers and was guaranteed not to gum up or to corrode the parts. It was said to be superior to castor oil.

ABOVE: *The Crest Manufacturing Company of Cambridge began building cars in 1902 at 196 Broadway, close by Harvard College. The Crestmobile engine was air-cooled. In 1905 the car cost $750. The company moved to Boston but went out of business in 1906.*

RIGHT: *Stevens-Duryea was the most successful car company in Massachusetts. It began as a partnership between Frank Duryea and the J. Stevens Arms & Tool Company of Chicopee. Billing its vehicles as the finest example of New England engineering, the company built ever larger and more expensive cars, including its masterpiece, the 1922 Cabriolet, with a thirty-gallon gasoline tank, priced at $8,900.*

The Stanley Steamer is one of America's most beloved early automobiles. The picture shows the twins F. O. and F. E. Stanley, identical in appearance and in dress, driving their Steamer on its maiden journey along Maple Street, Watertown, in September 1897.

lished a business in the nearby town of Lewiston to manufacture their photographic plates. Soon the Stanley Dry Plate was outselling other brands. Eastman Kodak bought the patent, making Freelan and Francis Stanley men of wealth.

In 1890 the inventive and ambitious twins left Maine and moved to Newton, Massachusetts, to be near the excitement of the great city of Boston. Their sister Chansonetta also moved to Boston, where she gained fame as one of America's leading female photographers, specializing in New England scenes. The Yankee brothers were soon involved in their next great venture. In Newton they had become friendly with Sterling Elliott, who owned a bicycle factory on Hunt Street in neighboring Watertown, close to the Charles River. Elliott was the inventor of the quadricycle operated by foot power. He sold his bicycle company to the Stanley

The Waltham Manufacturing Company built bicycles and motorcycles before trying its hand at automobiles. Here is the 20-horsepower Waltham-Orient Model de Luxe, selling for $2,250 in 1905. Production ended in 1908.

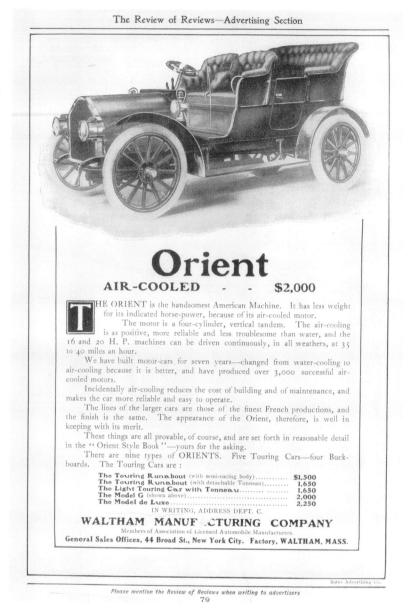

The Review of Reviews—Advertising Section

Orient

AIR-COOLED - - $2,000

THE ORIENT is the handsomest American Machine. It has less weight for its indicated horse-power, because of its air-cooled motor.

The motor is a four-cylinder, vertical tandem. The air-cooling is as positive, more reliable and less troublesome than water, and the 16 and 20 H. P. machines can be driven continuously, in all weathers, at 35 to 40 miles an hour.

We have built motor-cars for seven years—changed from water-cooling to air-cooling because it is better, and have produced over 3,000 successful air-cooled motors.

Incidentally air-cooling reduces the cost of building and of maintenance, and makes the car more reliable and easy to operate.

The lines of the larger cars are those of the finest French productions, and the finish is the same. The appearance of the Orient, therefore, is well in keeping with its merit.

These things are all provable, of course, and are set forth in reasonable detail in the " Orient Style Book "—yours for the asking.

There are nine types of ORIENTS. Five Touring Cars—four Buckboards. The Touring Cars are :

The Touring Runabout (with semi-racing body)............ $1,500
The Touring Runabout (with detachable Tonneau)......... 1,650
The Light Touring Car with Tonneau......... 1,650
The Model G (shown above)................................... 2,000
The Model de Luxe... 2,250

IN WRITING, ADDRESS DEPT. C.

WALTHAM MANUFACTURING COMPANY

Members of Association of Licensed Automobile Manufacturers.

General Sales Offices, 44 Broad St., New York City. Factory. WALTHAM, MASS.

Bates Advertising Co.

Please mention the Review of Reviews when writing to advertisers
79

twins, who modified the quadricycle and added a 4-horsepower steam engine. The driver had only to set the throttle and move the tiller for steering. This was the prototype of one of the earliest and best loved of the pioneer American automobiles, the Stanley Steamer.

The Stanley twins built their first steam car for their own amusement. On a fine day in September 1897, the sight of the bearded F. O. and his identical twin, F. E, dressed in matching top hats, sitting in their open horseless carriage and moving gracefully up the road, astonished the residents and alarmed the horses along Maple Street in Watertown. Word of this sensation spread, and soon orders for the Stanley Steamer came pouring in. The brothers gave up the bicycle business and formed the Stanley Motor Carriage Company, incorporated in Newton but located in Watertown. Their car proved to be a model of simplicity and efficiency. The early cars had only thirty-two moving parts and did not require a clutch, carburetor, timer, distributor, or sparkplugs. A four-inch movement of a single throttle up or down was all that was needed to move the car forward and to vary the speed. The water was stored in a twenty-two-gallon tank and pumped into a boiler, where it was heated by kerosene and converted to steam. The steam power was then transmitted through a series of cranks to the gearshift. The early Stanley Steamers needed ten minutes after the flame was lit to raise enough steam pressure to move the vehicle. These early steam cars required a water refill every twenty-five miles.

During August 1899, Freelan and his wife, Flora, took five days to drive their Model 93 Stanley Locomobile from Newton to the foot of Mount Washington in New Hampshire. On August 31 the couple drove their car up the 7.6-mile carriage road to the top of the mountain. The journey—the first by a horseless carriage—took two hours and ten minutes, with stops to add water to the engine, only a third as long as it took horse-drawn carriages to make the same journey. Modifications to the engine made the Stanley Steamer a very fast car. Later models had a separate fuel system to keep the water constantly at boiling point. The pilot light could burn for up to three days before the kerosene needed to be refilled, and the car was now ready to drive at a moment's notice. Added condensers conserved the water, and by 1902 the Stanley Steamer needed water refills only every two hundred to three hundred miles. That year Freelan Stanley drove his car up Mount Washington in only twenty-seven minutes. In January 1906 a car with a 20-horsepower Stanley engine established the world record for the mile with a speed of 127.6 mph. Later Stanley Steamers achieved speeds of nearly 200 mph.

The Stanley twins saw their car as recreational, a toy for the rich. They were not interested in mass production but wanted to maintain control over their business and to know personally all of their workers. The Model 725 Steamer, built in 1916, shows how far the company had advanced. This sophisticated five-passenger, 20-horsepower vehicle came with an aluminum body, leather upholstery, and electric-powered lights. It had a convertible top that could be raised or lowered by one person. The wheelbase measured 130 inches, and the wheels were 34 inches in diameter. The Model 725 cost $1,975 delivered in Watertown.

In 1917 the Stanley brothers sold their company. The following year Francis was killed in a car crash. The bereaved Freelan survived his beloved twin by twenty-two years. He lost interest in cars and spent his time whittling violin cases. Production of the famed Stanley Steamer ceased in 1924. In addition to patenting their dry photographic plates and their steam-powered cars, the Stanley twins were awarded many other patents, including one for an intercity railroad system powered by the Stanley steam engine.

The Stanley Steamer had many imitators. Between 1898 and 1905 there were some one hundred American steam cars available, of which forty originated in the New England states (Georgano & Wright 1992).

AUTO MANUFACTURE IN WALTHAM

Only a few miles up the Charles River from the Elliott bicycle works was another bicycle company. The town of Waltham was already famous as the home of Francis Cabot Lowell's textile mills (1814) and the Waltham Watch Company (1853). In 1893 the Waltham Manufacturing Company started building the Orient bicycle in that town. Two years later an employee, Charles Metz (1863–1937), hit upon the idea of adding a motor, and America's first motorcycle was born.

After its success with the bicycle and the motorcycle, in 1898 the Waltham Manufacturing Company decided to go into the automobile business. In 1901 the company discarded the water-cooled engine in favor of air-cooling. This innovation allowed the manufacturer to lighten the weight of the car by getting rid of the pumps and piping, as well as the water, which froze in the New England winters. The air-cooled engine was less prone to break down and used less gasoline than the water-cooled engine. By 1905 the company had built over three thousand air-cooled Waltham-Orient automobiles. Its Model de Luxe, with a 20-horsepower gasoline engine, sold for $2,250, while its 16-horsepower Model F sold for $1,500 and other models for $1,650 and $2,000. Despite its solid construction and reasonable price, the Waltham-Orient did not survive long, and production ended in 1908.

In 1902 the versatile Charles Metz started his own motorcycle company on Whitney Street, off Moody Street. A few years later he merged with the Marsh Company of Brockton, Massachusetts, to make two-cylinder, 4-horsepower motorcycles. Charles Metz had yet greater ambitions. In 1909 he bought a bankrupt wooden car manufacturer and established the Metz Car Company, offering car packages for home assembly. The customer bought the first box of parts and followed up with the purchase of thirteen more boxes, each costing $25, sold on the installment plan over a two-year period. Assembling his own car from a kit offered the buyer the opportunity to become fully conversant with its works. By 1911, Metz was offering fully assembled cars with 22-horsepower four-cylinder gasoline engines equipped with friction transmissions. Metz met with early success and by 1915 had sold 7,200 cars. His company became the largest automaker east of Detroit. To celebrate his success, Metz bought Gore Place, Waltham's largest estate, which he used as his home and corporate offices. The mansion on the 120-acre estate was originally built in 1806 as the home of Rebecca and Christopher Gore, who served as governor of Massachusetts in 1809 and was appointed to the U.S. Senate in 1813. Charles Metz did not long enjoy success with his automobiles. In 1916 he was faced with declining sales and in 1922 lost his company. He moved to Glendale, California, where he operated a cabinetry factory. Charles Metz died of cancer in 1937.

THE CAR COMPANIES OF CAMBRIDGE, MASSACHUSETTS

The Crest Automobile Company began making cars in 1902 at 196 Broadway in Cambridge, Massachusetts, a mile from Harvard Yard. The following year the expanding company moved to 165 First Street, then in 1905 it moved across the Charles River to 172 Freeport Street in the Dorchester section of Boston. A year later the Crest Automobile Company went out of business. During the few years of its existence, Crest Automobile built one thousand cars. The elegant 1904 Model D Crestmobile was an open two-seater with a 2-horsepower gasoline engine; the car weighed nine hundred pounds. The company claimed that gasoline was simpler to use than steam power and cheaper than electric power. The Model D cost $750 without the tonneau or the lamps. The larger Model F closed touring car came complete at a cost of $1,250. These cars sported an 8-horsepower engine, with double-action brakes and direct-shift drive. The car measured eight feet ten inches in length, with a seventy-six-inch wheelbase and twenty-eight-inch wheels. The Model F weighed one thousand pounds. The gasoline tank held five gallons, and the car could travel one hundred miles between fillings.

George Cannon of Cambridge built cars from 1901 to 1904; William Clark built steam cars from 1901 to 1905; and Berkshire Motors functioned from 1912 to 1913. Samuel W. Prussian operated the Guaranty Motors Corporation at 864-868 Main Street and then at 436 Massachusetts Avenue. Guaranty Motors remained in business for less than a year.

The Cambridge companies were soon swept aside by more robust rivals. Henry Ford built his first car in 1896. He saw the future in mass production. In short order, Ford owned his own iron and coal mines, steel plants, and sawmills and was buying up rubber plantations. Starting in 1913 he built thirty car assembly plants across the nation. The parts were manufactured in Detroit and sent by rail to the assembly plants, one of which was at 640 Memorial Drive in Cambridge. The Cambridge plant assembled the Model T as well as Ford trucks and tractors for sale in the New England states. By 1926 the Cambridge assembly plant was too small; a larger plant, now closed, was built in Assembly Square in the nearby town of Somerville.

The Auto Makers of Springfield

By the close of the nineteenth century, New England entrepreneurs were moving west to start new shoe, textile, and machinery companies. Charles Duryea and his brother Frank of Canton, Illinois, were among the few carrying their innovative genius to the Northeast. Trained as mechanics, the brothers entered the bicycle business. They moved to Chicopee, Massachusetts, where Frank worked as a toolmaker at the Ames Manufacturing Company. The brothers used their talents to attach a gasoline-powered motor to a modified horse carriage, which they bought used for $70. On September 22, 1893, Charles and Frank took the carriage with its

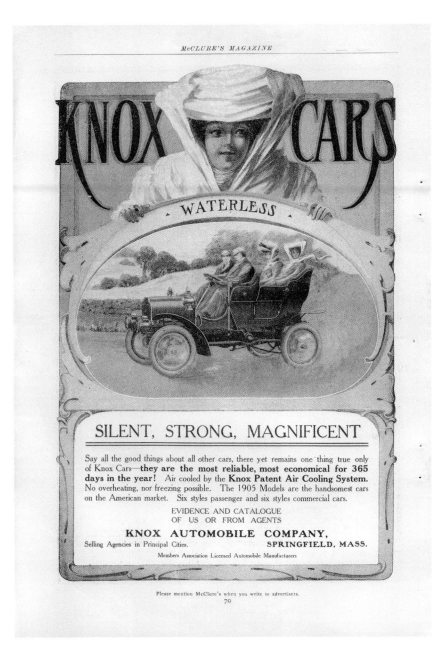

Harry A. Knox of Springfield built bicycles and motorcycles for the Overman Wheel Company. In 1901 he opened his own automobile company. Knox also built fire engines and delivery vans. By 1905, Knox was offering six styles of passenger car and six commercial vehicles, all with air-cooled engines to withstand freezing during the New England winters.

Springfield was the only place outside Britain where the Rolls-Royce was built. The picture shows the 1928 Rolls-Royce Phantom 1 Towncar from Brewster & Co. Coachbuilders. The Rolls-Royce was built in Springfield from 1919 to 1931 and cost up to $25,000. The Great Depression put an end to Rolls-Royce's American venture.

one-cylinder engine and three-speed transmission on a test run on the streets of Springfield. They cranked up the engine and set off at a top speed of 5 mph. Charles Duryea later said that the car "ran no faster than an old man could walk," but run it did. The Duryeas continued to work on the engine. On a snowy day in November 1895, the Duryea entry won the top prize in the fifty-four-mile race sponsored by the *Chicago Times-Herald*. The following year the Duryea Motor Wagon Company started the production of gasoline-powered horseless carriages using an 8-horse-power engine. Thirteen cars were built during 1896. The Duryeas' Springfield test drive marked the beginning of the American automobile industry. On a more somber note, in May 1896 a Duryea car struck a cyclist, and America's first automobile accident was duly recorded.

When the Duryea brothers arrived in Chicopee, the town was already well established as a center for the manufacture of machinist's tools. The famed New England gun makers Eli Whitney, Samuel Colt, and Edwin Wesson were close by. They all used interchangeable parts for the mass production of firearms. Among the local gun makers was Joshua Stevens (1814–1907), who established his own firm, J. Stevens Arms Company, in Chicopee Falls in 1845. The Stevens company later went into the precision tool business, making calipers, dividers, and machinist's tools. In 1886 the name was changed to J. Stevens Arms & Tool Company.

The Duryea brothers split up in 1898. Frank remained in Chicopee and in 1901 joined with J. Stevens Arms & Tool to build the Stevens-Duryea motorcar. The first car was the Model H, with a two-cylinder, 5-horsepower engine. Over the years the cars grew increasingly larger and more expensive. The 1906 Model U sported a six-cylinder, 35-horsepower engine, and the Model X was a four-cylinder convertible. The Stevens-Duryea masterpiece was its 1922 Cabriolet, with a thirty-gallon tank and two spare tires, and priced at $8,900. Some fourteen thousand Stevens-Duryea automobiles were built before the company ceased production in 1927.

Harry A. Knox caught the automobile bug from his neighbor Frank Duryea. Knox worked for an elevator company in Springfield before taking a job at the Overman Wheel Company of Chicopee Falls, which had plans to build cars. In 1900 he left Overman to set up the Knox Automobile Company in Springfield. The company started off by making air-cooled three-wheeler cars. In 1904, Knox built a snappy two-seater runabout with an 8-horsepower engine. The car sold for $1,350. Two years later the Knox Automobile Company produced America's first motorized fire engines. During the second decade of the twentieth century, Knox came out with a range of larger cars, including the Model M Limousine, priced at $6,000, and a seven-seater touring car with a 60-horsepower engine. The Knox Automobile Company went out of business in 1923.

Springfield's international reputation for loyal workers and exceptional craftsmanship attracted Rolls-Royce, England's preeminent luxury automobile company, to set up its American plant in the city. In 1919, Rolls-Royce recognized the United States as a major market. To avoid stiff import duties, Rolls-Royce built a plant on Hendee Street in Springfield. Merrimac and Biddle & Smart, two prestigious Massachusetts coach makers, built the bodies for the cars, which Rolls-Royce designed. In 1925 the venerable Brewster & Company of New York (which began in New Haven as a carriage maker) was bought by Rolls-Royce of America and moved to Springfield to become Rolls's primary car body builder. Rolls-Royce built some three thousand Silver Ghosts and Phantoms in Springfield over a ten-year period. The Springfield-built Silver Ghost Rolls, selling for $20,000, was the most expensive car in America and was favored by the Hollywood set and by high society. The Phantom I Rolls convertible built in 1931 had a six-cylinder engine. The car measured eighteen feet four inches in length with a wheelbase of 146.5 inches. The car carried two spare tires, one on each side of the hood. Despite its fine workmanship, there were too many who doubted that an American-made Rolls-Royce was as good as the "genuine" British-made car. Fourteen hundred men worked in the Springfield plant before it succumbed to the Great Depression. Springfield is the only place outside England where the Rolls-Royce has ever been built.

From the last years of the nineteenth century until the 1920s, 459 automobile companies were registered in Massachusetts (Maxwell 1988). Most of them were undercapitalized and had little staying power. Nearly two-thirds of these aspiring car companies did not even get beyond the planning phase of manufacture. Many others built only a prototype before closing their doors. Some of the Massachusetts automobile makers began as horse wagon or sleigh companies. Others began as sewing machine, bicycle, or motorcycle makers. Bramwell-Robinson of Hyde Park, Boston, grew out of a company that made machinery for manufacturing paper boxes. The Allen Company of Adams, Massachusetts, started in an ironworks. The Richard H. Long Motor Corporation of Framingham was the brainchild of a successful shoe manufacturer. Frank Mossberg of Attleboro became wealthy from the manufacture of bicycle bells, but was less successful building cars. Boston, Worcester, and Springfield were the major centers, but budding carmakers were found in many of the smaller towns throughout the state.

The Grout brothers, Karl, Fred, and Charles, of Orange, Massachusetts, manufactured the New Home sewing machine. Their sons used the family money to build steam-powered cars (1899–1912) until family strife drove their company into liquidation. The Crompton Motor Carriage Company of Worcester (1903–5) was established by the textile loom manufacturer. The Cameron Car Company was founded in Beverly and the Pope-Robinson Company in Hyde Park. The Springfield bicycle manufacturer Albert H. Overman failed in his efforts to build an internal combustion automobile. Charles A. Royce, who owned the Royce Laundry of the same city, funded the Springfield Motor Vehicle Company. Royce planned a fleet of vans to deliver the laundry, making his company the first to build automobiles for commercial use. Colonel Albert Pope of Columbia bicycle fame had only a brief success as an automobile manufacturer in Westfield, Massachusetts, and Hartford, Connecticut. Despite his success in selling millions of bicycles, Pope's production of automobiles never exceeded seven hundred a year. The Pope-Hartford automobile company shut down in 1914, a few years after the colonel's death.

During the feverish early days of the automobile industry, nearly eight hundred automobile companies were registered in New England. After Massachusetts, Connecticut and Maine had the largest number of licensed companies, but relatively few produced cars and very few were even briefly successful. The New England production ended with the Great Depression and became a mere footnote in the annals of the American automobile industry.

Conclusion ✒

The transformation of Massachusetts from an agrarian to an urban-industrial society began early in the nineteenth century and was well established by the start of the Civil War. During the period from 1860 to 1920, Massachusetts had its own banks and insurance companies, its own industries and department stores. Boston was a world-class port and center of the raw cotton, wool, and leather trade. Coal and iron were shipped into the port of Boston, which accepted these raw materials for the factories and exported the manufactured goods. Boston had twelve daily newspapers and several magazines. The city was a hub of ideas and culture. Worcester and Springfield also emerged as major industrial centers. The textile towns of Lowell, Lawrence, Fall River, and New Bedford and the shoe towns of Lynn, Haverhill, and Brockton were humming.

All this activity was the product of Yankee entrepreneurship and innovation beginning early in the nineteenth century. The machinists of Massachusetts designed and built the looms for the textile mills and the machinery for the shoe factories. The firearms, sewing machines, parlor stoves, bicycles, motorcycles, and automobiles that were manufactured in Massachusetts came out of the long tradition of skilled craftsmanship using locally made precision tools. The workers clustered close to the center of these cities and towns and walked or took the streetcar to their jobs. They shopped in the local stores and purchased locally made goods. Massachusetts-made products were sold across the nation and around the world. This period can well be described as the Gilded Age of Massachusetts industry.

These achievements of Massachusetts industry were proudly displayed at the World's Columbian Exposition held in Chicago from May 1st to October 31st, 1893. Massachusetts based companies supplied one-quarter of the all the exhibits dealing with cotton textiles and one-third

MASSACHUSETTS BUILDING AT THE COLUMBIAN EXPOSITION.
(After the old John Hancock House.)

The Massachusetts Building at the World's Columbian Exposition in Chicago (1893). The building was modeled after the home of John Hancock on Beacon Hill. The state pavilion displayed dioramas of the Boston Massacre and the Battle of Bunker Hill as well as portraits of famous Massachusetts personages and books by prominent writers. A grand piano donated by a Boston piano company stood in the front parlor. The pavilion of the Commonwealth of Massachusetts complemented the numerous exhibits of products displayed throughout the fair.

of those dealing with woolen textiles. Coffees and teas supplied by Chase & Sanborn were served at many of the State pavilions and restaurants throughout the fairgrounds. Massachusetts jewelry companies displayed their wares, as did the Pairpoint Glass Company of New Bedford. The Waltham Watch Co. had an exhibit of its timepieces. The Oliver Ames Co. of Worcester showed off its line of agricultural tools and Springfield's Smith & Wesson its guns and rifles. Worcester companies displayed steel, copper and iron wire. The Walter M. Lowney Company of Boston distributed bonbons and Walter Baker & Co sold chocolates from its own pavilion. The Doliber-Goodale Co. provided Mellin's Food to feed the infants left at the creche, while their parents enjoyed the exposition. The Royal Worcester Corset. Co., the Columbia Cycle Co. and other Massachusetts companies also had special exhibits at the Chicago Fair.

The Fate of the Redbrick Mills of Massachusetts

The paternalism of the early-nineteenth-century textile mills gave way to conflict between the owners living in Boston and the workforce fighting for higher wages and shorter hours. Worker strikes generally failed until the famed "Bread and Roses" confrontation in Lawrence in January 1912. The 27,000 immigrant workers stayed out for sixty-three days before winning meager concessions from their bosses. By then the cotton textile industry in the American South was already competing with the mills in New England. Not only was the South the source of the cotton, but also it had the advantages of lower taxes, cheaper power, and especially a cheaper and more compliant labor force. Bit by bit the Boston financiers moved their money from the old and outdated mills in the Northeast to the new factories in the South. In 1880 only 5 percent of the nation's textile spindles were located in the South. Thirty years later the figure was 40 percent, and by 1937 over 70 percent were in the South.

In Lowell in the 1920s, the Middlesex and the Bigelow mills closed their doors. The Hamilton mill went into receivership, and the Appleton mills moved to South Carolina. The Kilburn Cotton Mill of New Bedford closed and transferred operations to North Carolina. Between 1923 and 1927, over $100 million of mill capital left New England for the South (Gross 1993). The Great Depression was a heavy blow to what remained of the textile industry of Massachusetts. Left abandoned in Lowell, Lawrence, New Bedford, and Fall River were the huge and inefficient mills built a century earlier for waterpower. These old textile towns were devastated by the departure of their primary industries, leaving them close to bankruptcy. Services were cut, and the cities went into decline. The closing of the mills affected allied industries as well. The great Massachusetts loom machinery works in Whitinsville, Hopedale, and Worcester all closed down for lack of orders.

William Carter's knitwear company was established in Needham, Massachusetts, in 1865. Many years later Carter's moved to Atlanta and grew into one of the leaders in children's clothing, operating its own stores throughout the country as well as supplying the major national chain store companies. Carter's, Inc., bought its rival Oshkosh B'Gosh (established in 1895), the venerable Wisconsin children's clothing company. Instead of making their clothing in the United States, however, companies such as Carter's have evolved into marketers of goods manufactured and imported largely from Asia and South America.

John Peters Stevens was not content to sell only those woolen products made by his family-controlled company. He struck deals with other cotton and woolen textile mills to market their products. In time, J. P. Stevens & Co. came to represent many more cotton than wool companies. In the 1920s the company also began to deal in rayon. World War II was a boon to the Stevens family enterprises, which received huge military orders. The last of the Stevens dynasty was Robert Ten Broeck Stevens (1899–1983). He was born in Fanwood, New Jersey, but, following the family tradition, was educated at Phillips Andover Academy in Massachusetts before going on to Yale. At age thirty he succeeded his father as president of J. P. Stevens. Robert Stevens accelerated the company's move from the Northeast to the South. During the 1970s the directors of J. P. Stevens decided to merge the manufacturing and the selling arms and to become a public company. This decision brought to an end the family control of J. P. Stevens & Co. and its 150-year connection with the Stevens family of Andover.

In his review of the textile industry in North Carolina, Brent Glass (1992) has shown the early contribution made by Massachusetts. North Carolina textiles relied heavily on the technical knowledge of New England mill managers as well as New England machinery, and money. Many of the southern mills were designed by Boston architects, with heating and ventilation systems installed by B. F. Sturtevant and loom machinery made by Draper & Co., Crompton & Knowles, or the Whitin Machine Works, all of Massachusetts. The early southern mills were built to conform to the standards established by the Massachusetts machinery makers and by the New England insurance companies.

On December 11, 1995, a fire engulfed one of the last of the Massachusetts textile manufacturers, Malden Mills of Lawrence, Massachusetts, which burned to the ground, putting three thousand people out of work. The event attracted national attention when the mill owner, Aaron

John Hancock Mutual Life Insurance was the quintessential Massachusetts company. It was named for John Hancock, born in Braintree in 1737, a Harvard graduate, prominent Boston businessman, and first governor of the Commonwealth. His flowing signature graces the Declaration of Independence. The insurance company was chartered in 1862 and began in business at 41 State Street, Boston. In 2003, John Hancock became a wholly owned subsidiary of the Toronto-based Manulife Financial Corporation.

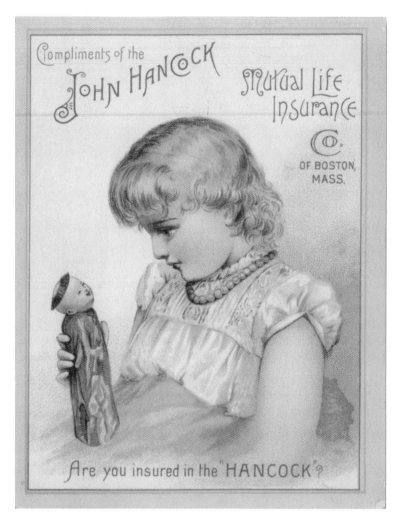

Feuerstein, spent millions of dollars to continue paying his workers their salaries with full benefits. He told his employees that he fully intended to rebuild the mill and get them back to work making the company's Polartec fabrics for outdoor activities. Feuerstein was the third generation of his family since 1906 to run Malden Mills. Rather than retire, the seventy-seven-year-old owner of the privately held company chose to use the insurance money to rebuild his textile factory in Lawrence. Malden Mills reopened but was burdened by heavy bank debt and a weak retail market. On November 29, 2001, Malden Mills Industries, Inc., filed for bankruptcy, and Aaron Feuerstein lost his mill. This event was the final chapter for the proud textile industry of Massachusetts, once the state's largest employer.

The decline of textiles in Massachusetts was followed by losses in other industries. The dominance of Lynn in women's shoes, Brockton in men's shoes, and Malden in rubber shoes was lost early in the twentieth century as competing factories opened in New York State, Illinois, and the South. The United States Shoe Machinery Corporation of Beverly, Massachusetts—once the world's largest shoe machinery company—closed in 1987. Chickering and Mason & Hamlin pianos became part of the American Piano Company, which moved to Rochester, New York, while the Aeolian Company absorbed Vose, Emerson and the George Steck piano companies. The National Piano Company absorbed the remaining Boston-based companies, including Briggs, Merrill and Hallet & Davis. Piano production in Boston and Worcester came to an end in the 1930s.

After the deaths of Erastus and Horatio Bigelow, their carpet company in Clinton, Massachusetts, merged with the Hartford Carpet Company to form one of the largest corporations in New England. In 1929, Bigelow-Hartford merged with the Sanford Carpet Company of New York. The enlarged company, called Bigelow-Sanford, later merged with southern carpet mills, left the Northeast, and moved its headquarters to Delaware. The consolidation of the American carpet manufacturers continued apace during the twentieth century. Bigelow merged with Karastan and in 1993 became one of the many acquisitions of the vast Mohawk Industries, based in Calhoun, Georgia.

The nineteenth-century Massachusetts patent medicine companies failed to evolve into modern, science-based pharmaceutical enterprises. The venerable Boston food companies were merged into larger concerns. In 1927 the Walter Baker chocolate company (founded in 1764) became a unit of the Postum Company, later known as General Foods. Then General Foods merged with Kraft. The Walter Baker factory on the banks of the Neponset River closed in 1966, ending its two hundred–year identification with Boston. Today, Kraft Foods, Inc., of Northfield, Illinois, still makes Baker's Chocolates under the slogan "Chocolate is chocolate, but Baker's is love."

The Kennedy Biscuit Company of Cambridge opened bakeries in Chicago, New York, and Philadelphia. In 1890, Kennedy was sold to the New York Biscuit Company, which in 1898 joined with other companies to form the National Biscuit Company (Nabisco). The Fig Newton, made by Nabisco for over one hundred years, still remains one of America's most popular cookies, but has long since left Massachusetts. The former Kennedy factory in Cambridge has been converted into luxury loft apartments. The Chase & Sanborn coffee company, sponsor of a 1930s radio show featuring Eddie Cantor, is now a division of the Sara Lee Company. The brand name survives, but the coffee is no longer ground or packaged in Boston.

With branches in the major American and European cities, the B. F. Sturtevant Company of Boston became an international concern. Its president Eugene Foss resigned in 1910 to serve as governor of the Commonwealth of Massachusetts. Sturtevant exhaust fans were used to ventilate New York's Holland Tunnel. During 1923, B. F. Sturtevant bought the bankrupt Brown-Corliss Engine Company of Corliss, Wisconsin. In gratitude, the town changed its name to Sturtevant. During World War II, hundreds of American fighting ships were equipped with Sturtevant steam turbines and Sturtevant heating and cooling systems. At the end of the war, the Westinghouse Corporation bought B. F. Sturtevant and moved most of its work to New Jersey. Westinghouse then sold Sturtevant to American-Davidson, but the company continued to decline. The Boston workforce dwindled to 125 machinists before the plant was finally closed in 1989, bringing to an end 130 years of business in the city of its birth.

During the first half of the twentieth century, the Indian Motorcycle Company of Springfield, Massachusetts, and the Harley-Davidson Motorcycle Company of Milwaukee eliminated all other domestic contenders and were locked together in a battle for supremacy. The demise of Indian Motorcycle in 1953 left Harley-Davidson as America's last motorcycle company. In the 1950s and 1960s, Harley-Davidson had the U.S. market to itself. The company paid union wages but let its standards for engineering and design slip. Well-engineered and cheaper Japanese motorcycles entered the U.S. market, and soon Honda, Yamaha, Kawasaki, and Suzuki motorbikes were eating into Harley-Davidson's lead. In 1972, Harley-Davidson still had a virtual monopoly over the market for motorcycles with engines of 1,000 cc or more. A decade later, its share had dropped to

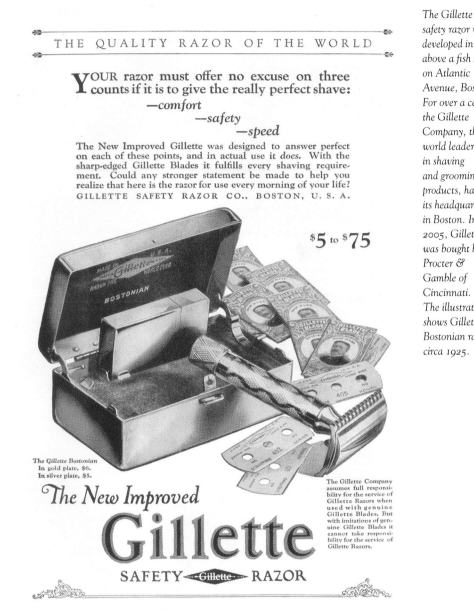

THE QUALITY RAZOR OF THE WORLD

YOUR razor must offer no excuse on three counts if it is to give the really perfect shave:

—*comfort*

—*safety*

—*speed*

The New Improved Gillette was designed to answer perfect on each of these points, and in actual use it *does*. With the sharp-edged Gillette Blades it fulfills every shaving requirement. Could any stronger statement be made to help you realize that here is the razor for use every morning of your life? GILLETTE SAFETY RAZOR CO., BOSTON, U. S. A.

$5 to $75

The Gillette Bostonian
In gold plate, $6.
In silver plate, $5.

The New Improved

Gillette

SAFETY · Gillette · RAZOR

The Gillette Company assumes full responsibility for the service of Gillette Razors when used with genuine Gillette Blades. But with imitations of genuine Gillette Blades it cannot take responsibility for the service of Gillette Razors.

The Gillette safety razor was developed in 1901 above a fish shop on Atlantic Avenue, Boston. For over a century the Gillette Company, the world leader in shaving and grooming products, had its headquarters in Boston. In 2005, Gillette was bought by Procter & Gamble of Cincinnati. The illustration shows Gillette's Bostonian razor, circa 1925.

less than 15 percent, as Japanese imports dominated the market with annual sales of 160,000 heavy motorcycles. Harley-Davidson Motorcycle Company, with its three thousand workers, was losing money and teetered on the brink of bankruptcy. In September 1982 the company petitioned the U.S. International Trade Commission (ITC) for protection. The ITC recommended that tariffs on imported heavy motorcycles (over 700 cc) be increased from 4.4 percent to a whopping 49.4 percent for the first year, with decreasing tariffs over the next four years.

On April 1, 1983, President Ronald Reagan accepted the recommendations of the ITC. The tariff wall against Japanese motorcycle manufacturers gave Harley-Davidson time to recover. After only four years of tariff protections, the company asked the ITC to rescind these barriers to free trade. With its good products, Harley-Davidson was able to regain some of its market share but continues to face stiff competition from Japanese and German brands, now built in the United States.

Automobile manufacturing in Massachusetts got off to a hopeful start during the last years of the nineteenth century and the early years of the twentieth. Over 450 companies registered their intention to build automobiles in the state. Two-thirds of these companies did not get beyond the planning stage of production. Many other companies built only a few cars before closing down. Only a handful of Massachusetts automobile companies entered into significant mass production. At a time when automobile ownership was still small, the Waltham-Orient, Stanley Steamer, Knox, Stevens-Duryea, and Springfield Rolls-Royce companies together built no more than forty thousand cars before competition from Detroit and then the Great Depression caused the local industry to fizzle out.

Nearly all of the nineteenth-century industries described in this book have disappeared from Massachusetts. Most simply closed their doors. The surviving Massachusetts manufacturers were bought out, and production moved to other states.

WHY MASSACHUSETTS INDUSTRY WENT INTO DECLINE

Various explanations have been offered for the industrial decline of Massachusetts. Some writers blame the lack of local entrepreneurship as well as increasing competition from other states. Others implicate the inefficiencies of the huge mills originally built for waterpower, as well as labor strife, changing fashions, technological advances, and the boom-and-bust cycles that have historically afflicted so many industries. The Great Depression led to the closure of many of the mills in Massachusetts. Some would argue, however, that Massachusetts has kept ahead of the curve by giving up its declining smokestack economy to embrace the new technologies of the information age.

The descendants of the British who came to Massachusetts between 1620 and 1640 were determined folk who built ships and developed an extensive trade with the Caribbean sugar islands, Europe, and the Far East. In the nineteenth century, they channeled their enterprise homeward in building their textile mills. The Yankees applied similar innovation to the mass production of shoes, sewing machines, prepared foods, patent medicines, pianos, and bicycles. Massachusetts native son Eli Whitney built the first cotton gin, Francis Cabot Lowell established the first textile mills, Elias Howe made the first sewing machine, and Samuel Finley Breese Morse of Charlestown invented Morse code. These Massachusetts Yankees were self-made men with the intelligence and the burning desire to succeed. They combined their proven mercantile skills with a passion to build an industry. But they used their wealth to become genteel and failed to pass on their entrepreneurial zeal to the next generation.

The Erie Canal in New York State, which was completed in 1825, joined Albany to Buffalo and the Great Lakes, opening up the Appalachians and the Midwest to settlement. Thousands upon thousands of New Englanders left their small, rocky farms to try their luck in the vast and fertile farmlands of the Midwest. Timber, flour, wheat, and other farm products were floated along the waterways and through the locks and aqueducts of the Erie Canal to the Hudson River and south to New York City. This route down the Hudson, running parallel to the western borders of Vermont, Massachusetts, and Connecticut, diverted traffic and goods away from New England. The Erie Canal also attracted commerce from Ohio, Michigan, Illinois, and Wisconsin which had previously flowed south down the Mississippi River to New Orleans. All this trade was sent now to New York City.

Cunard and the other European steamship lines no longer came to Boston but sailed to New York instead. These ships carried the elite above deck and the impoverished immigrants in steerage. New York eclipsed

Boston to become the nation's premier port and its greatest city. Chicago, as the center of the grain and meatpacking industries, experienced an explosive growth after 1870. The discovery of coal in Kentucky and West Virginia, petroleum in Pennsylvania, and gold in California drew additional people and industry away from New England. This shift was encouraged by the vast westward expansion of the railroads and later by the automobile and the airplane.

Massachusetts saw the beginning of the American Industrial Revolution. The technological innovations spread to other parts of the nation, leading to a fierce scramble for survival. During the latter part of the nineteenth century, the United States had over 250 startup sewing machine companies, hundreds of organ and piano companies, many parlor stove companies, and over three thousand bicycle companies, and, at the beginning of the twentieth century, thousands of aspiring automobile companies. Massachusetts alone was home to over 200 textile mills, several hundred shoe factories, forty sewing machine enterprises, and over 450 startup car companies.

Failing industries tried to adapt. Many of the sewing machine factories converted to making bicycles. Horse wagon companies shifted to turning out freight cars for the railroads. The early motorcycles were bicycles with a motor, and the early automobiles were horse carriages with an attached engine. Very few companies in Massachusetts, or for that matter nationwide, survived to maturity. Some industries declined because of fundamental changes in technology and in lifestyle. The organ yielded to the piano, and then the phonograph and the radio replaced the piano. The bicycle craze ended with the automobile. Sewing machine sales declined with the availability of cheap ready-to-wear clothing. Whaling ended with the discovery of petroleum. Some nineteenth-century industries disappeared entirely when fossil fuel replaced horsepower and when kerosene was replaced by electricity for light.

Rising labor and fuel costs accelerated the decline in Massachusetts of the fundamental industries of clothing, footwear, and prepared foods. The high costs of transporting cotton, wool, leather, foods, iron, and coal to its factories put Massachusetts at a disadvantage. The cycle of boom, bust, and consolidation was taking place with ever more rapidity. It took the Massachusetts textile and shoe industries some one hundred years to reach their peak and another half-century before they were gone. The

Massachusetts piano and organ factories and the state's successful sewing machine company were shut down after seventy-five years. The bicycle and motorcycle companies were closed after half a century, and Stevens-Duryea, the most successful of the Massachusetts car companies, lasted only a quarter of a century.

This business cycle is by no means unique to Massachusetts. The boom, bust, and consolidation cycle was also seen in the nineteenth-century railroad and telegraph industries. In our time this process has continued in the telephone, television, radio, tools, and computer industries. The Digital Equipment Corporation (DEC) had its start at the Massachusetts Institute of Technology in 1957 and built its first commercial computer in 1961. By the 1980s, DEC was the second-largest computer company in the world, with 100,000 employees, many working in the cavernous former textile factories. By the 1990s, DEC was losing money and sold off its remaining assets to Compaq, which in turn was absorbed by Hewlett Packard. An Wang was the founder of another Massachusetts computer company, Wang Laboratories, which began selling computers in 1965. Twenty years later, the company had spread worldwide and employed 30,000 people, many working in the old textile mills of Lowell. But in the early 1990s, Wang experienced difficulties and was replaced by swifter competitors.

Writing in the January 1954 issue of the *Atlantic Monthly*, the junior senator from Massachusetts, John Fitzgerald Kennedy, discussed the continuing decline of New England industry and the migration to the Southeast. Textiles, shoes, machinery, chemicals, hosiery, carpets, and precision tools were among the industries leaving New England. In Massachusetts alone, Kennedy wrote, over thirty thousand textile jobs had been lost since 1945. Latin America and Asia were rapidly industrializing and offered a willing and cheap workforce. It was only a matter of time, Kennedy warned, before "the South will suffer the same pangs of aging now suffered by New England" (Kennedy 1954).

America should heed Kennedy's prediction. The "old economy" that abandoned Massachusetts many years ago is rapidly leaving the rest of the United States. The textile and furniture industries, the manufacture of shoes, radios, and watches, and many other industries are closing down and moving offshore to low-wage countries in Asia and Central America. By 1990 the American shoe industry was already in a steep decline. In that year, 216,000 people in the United States were employed making leather products and footwear. By 2004 the number had decreased to 65,000—a 70 percent drop, despite a sizable increase of the general population. In 1990 the U.S. textile, fiber, yarn, and thread mills employed over 1.5 million workers. By 2004 only 733,000 remained—a decline of over 50 percent (U.S. Department of Labor). The technological cycle of boom and bust has now entered its global phase. With free trade agreements and the abolition of tariffs, most of the shoes and clothing, tools, cameras, television sets, and many other consumer goods that are offered for sale in the United States are now manufactured abroad. The increasing dependence on imported goods is causing a loss of production skills and a widening of the trade deficit between the United States and its trading partners.

Since the end of the Second World War, the American economy—and indeed the economies of western Europe, Australia, and Japan—has shifted steadily away from manufacturing and toward services. Massachusetts has emerged from its postindustrial depression to establish a vibrant service economy centered on money management, health care, biochemical research, high technology, and higher education. At the start of the twenty-first century, the service sector accounts for nearly four out of every five jobs in the overall economy. The cost to Massachusetts of entering the global market is the loss of much of its unique identity. The mills and factories that built the machinery and made the goods have closed. National chains have replaced the local banks, insurance companies, hotels, restaurants, and department stores.

How different it was a century ago, when the goods for sale were locally made. This illustrated book is my nostalgic tribute to Massachusetts during its industrial Gilded Age.

References

Adams, R. *King C. Gillette: The Man and His Wonderful Shaving Device*. Boston: Little, Brown and Company, 1978.

Anderson, V. D. *New England's Generation: The Great Migration and the Formation of Society and Culture in the Seventeenth Century*. New York: Cambridge University Press, 1991.

Bacon, E. M. *The Connecticut River and the Valley of the Connecticut*. New York: G. P. Putnam's Sons, Knickerbocker Press, 1906.

Chernow, R. *Alexander Hamilton*. New York: Penguin Books, 2004.

Cooper G. R. *The Sewing Machine: Its Invention and Development*. 2nd ed. Washington, D.C.: Smithsonian Books, 1977.

Dawley, A. *Class and Community: The Industrial Revolution in Lynn*. Cambridge, Mass.: Harvard University Press, 1976.

Dolge, A. *Pianos and Their Makers*. New York: Dover Publishing Company, 1972; first published by the Covina Publishing Company, Covina, Calif., 1911.

Domosh, M. *Invented Cities: The Creation of Landscape in Nineteenth-Century New York and Boston*. New Haven: Yale University Press, 1996.

Ensko, S. G. C. *American Silversmiths and Their Marks*. Mineola, N.Y.: Dover, 1983.

Evans, H. *They Made America. From the Steam Engine to the Search Engine: Two Centuries of Innovators*. New York: Little, Brown and Company, 2004.

Ferguson, L. C. *From Family Firm to Corporate Giant: J. P. Stevens and Company, Inc., 1813–1963*. N.p.: D. H. Mark Publishing Co., 1970; reprinted in 1974 by the Federal Reserve Bank of Boston.

"Fertilizer Companies Combine." *Boston Daily Globe*, May 23, 1899.

Fischer, D. H. *Albion's Seed: Four British Folkways in America*. New York: Oxford University Press, 1989.

Frisch, M. H. *Springfield, Massachusetts, and the Meaning of Community, 1840–1880*. Cambridge, Mass.: Harvard University Press, 1972.

Georgano, N., and N. Wright. *The American Automobile: A Centenary, 1893–1993*. New York: Smithmark, 1992.

Girdler, A. *Harley-Davidson and Indian Wars.* Osceola, Wisc.: Motorbooks International, 2002.

Glass, B. D. *The Textile Industry in North Carolina: A History.* Raleigh: Division of Archives and History, North Carolina Department of Cultural Resources, 1992.

Goddard, S. B. *Colonel Albert Pope and His American Dream Machines: The Time and Life of a Bicycle Tycoon Turned Automotive Pioneer.* Jefferson, N.C.: McFarland & Co., 2000.

Gordon, J. S. *An Empire of Wealth: The Epic History of American Economic Power.* New York: Harper-Collins Publishers, 2004.

Green, C. M. *Holyoke, Massachusetts: A Case Study of the Industrial Revolution in America.* New Haven: Yale University Press, 1939.

Gregory, F. W. *Nathan Appleton: Merchant and Entrepreneur, 1779–1861.* Charlottesville: University Press of Virginia, 1975.

Gross, L. F. *The Course of Industrial Decline: The Boott Cotton Mills of Lowell, Massachusetts, 1835–1955.* Baltimore: Johns Hopkins University Press, 1993.

Handlin O. *Boston's Immigrants: A Study of Acculturation.* New York: Atheneum, 1972.

History of Middlesex County, Massachusetts. Philadelphia: J. W. Lewis & Co., 1890.

Hogg, T. "1931 Phantom 1 Springfield Rolls Royce." *Road & Track Magazine* (April 1962): 61–65.

Holden, D. J. *The Life and Work of Ernest M. Skinner.* Richmond, Va.: Organ Historical Society, 1985.

Hoover, C. A., P. Rucker, and E. M. Good. *Piano 300: Celebrating Three Centuries of People and Pianos.* Washington, D.C.: National Museum of American History, 2001.

Hurd, D. H. *History of Essex County.* Vol. 1. Philadelphia: J. W. Lewis & Co., 1888.

———. *History of Worcester County, Massachusetts.* Philadelphia: J. W. Lewis & Co., 1889.

Josephson, H. G. *The Golden Threads: New England's Mill Girls and Magnates.* New York: Duell, Sloan & Pearce, 1949.

Kennedy, J. F. "New England and the South." *Atlantic Monthly* 193 (January 1954): 32–37.

Lawrence, W. *The Life of Amos A. Lawrence: With Extracts from His Diary and Correspondence.* Boston: Houghton, Mifflin, 1888.

Lawrence, W. R., M.D., ed. *Extracts from the Diary and Correspondence of the Late Amos Lawrence.* Boston: Gould and Lincoln, 1856.

Maxwell, R. H. *Cars of New England.* Brookline, Mass.: Compiled for the Larz Anderson Auto Museum, 1988.

McDermott, C. H., ed. *A History of the Shoe and Leather Industries of the United States.* Boston: J. W. Denehy & Co., 1918.

Minchin, T. J. *Don't Sleep with Stevens! The J. P. Stevens Campaign and the Struggle to Organize the South, 1963–80.* Gainesville: University Press of Florida, 2005.

Morison, S. E. *The Maritime History of Massachusetts, 1783–1860.* Boston: Houghton Mifflin, 1961.

Norris, J. D. *Advertising and the Transformation of American Society, 1865–1920.* New York: Greenwood Press, 1990.

Pierce, S., and C. Slautterback. *Boston Lithography, 1825–1880.* Boston: The Boston Athenaeum Collection, Boston Athenaeum, 1991.

Prude, J. *The Coming of Industrial Order: Town and Factory Life in Rural Massachusetts, 1810–1860.* Amherst: University of Massachusetts Press, 1999.

Quinn, T. C., ed. *Massachusetts of Today.* Boston: Columbia Publishing Company, 1892.

Roddy, E. G. *Mills, Mansions, and Mergers: The Life of William M. Wood.* North Andover, Mass.: Merrimack Valley Textile Museum, 1982.

Stage, S. *Female Complaints: Lydia Pinkham and the Business of Women's Medicine.* New York: W. W. Norton & Co., 1979.

Steward, S. C. *The Sarsaparilla Kings: A Biography of Dr. James Cook Ayer and Frederick Ayer.* Cambridge, Mass.: S. C. Steward 1993.

Stone, O. J. *The History of Massachusetts Industries: Their Inception, Growth, and Success.* Boston: S. J. Charles Publishing, 1930.

Tocco, V., Jr. History of the B. F. Sturtevant and Westinghouse-Sturtevant Companies. Available online at www.sturtevantfan.com.

U.S. Department of Labor, Bureau of Labor Statistics. Available online at www.bls.gov.

Washburn, C. G. *Industrial Worcester.* Worcester: Davis Press, 1917.

Washburn, R. C. *The Life and Times of Lydia E. Pinkham.* New York: G. P. Putnam's Sons, 1976.

Weightman, G. *The Frozen-Water Trade.* New York: Hyperion, 2003.

Whitney, C. R. *All the Stops: The Glorious Pipe Organ and Its American Masters.* New York: Public Affairs, 2003.

Wilson, K. M. *Mt. Washington and Pairpoint Glass.* Vol. 1. Woodbridge, Suffolk, Eng.: Antique Collectors' Club, 2005.

Index